KIDS
& CASH

KIDS & CASH

SOLVING A PARENT'S DILEMMA

BY KEN DAVIS AND TOM TAYLOR

OAK TREE PUBLICATIONS, INC.
PUBLISHERS, LA JOLLA, CALIFORNIA

To Trisha, Julie, Janie, Dana, and Mark

Kids & Cash: Solving A Parent's Dilemma text copyright © 1979 by Kenneth F. Davis and J. Thomas Taylor. Illustrations copyright © 1979 by Oak Tree Publications, Inc.

First Edition
Manufactured in the United States of America
For information write to: Oak Tree Publications, P.O. Box 1012, La Jolla, CA 92038

Library of Congress Cataloging in Publication Data

Davis, Ken, 1932-
    Kids & Cash.

    Includes index.
    SUMMARY: Advice to parents on how to teach their children to handle money and understand its value and suggestions to children on ways of earning money.
    1. Children's allowances. 2. Saving and thrift. 3. Finance, Personal. I. Taylor, Tom, 1930- joint author. II. Title.
HQ784.S4D38   332'.024   79-13092

ISBN 0-916392-26-0

CONTENTS

PREFACE

This book is our attempt to provide parents with a guidebook to handling the subject of money as it relates to children.

Few aspects of family life seem to offer as much potential for trouble as does money. In the search for techniques that can be used to solve problems, as well as head off future difficulties, ideas were drawn from the experience of hundreds of parents who have struggled with these problems with varying degrees of success. Our effort has been to reduce what appear to be the most workable techniques into a coherent and orderly system that can be applied and used by families of all descriptions.

This book is quite different from the book we set out to write in 1970. Then, our intent was to address the apparent lack of understanding of our economic system on the part of young people. We later concluded that explanations of how the world works are not enough; that certain basic skills and values relating to money must be developed as well, and that parents can and should play an important role in this process. As we developed this new emphasis, it became apparent that many, perhaps most, parents were unsure about many aspects of handling money with their children. As a result, our subject was again broadened in scope to its present form.

We are indebted to the many parents who shared with us their stories of both success and frustration. Also appreciated were the thoughts of several hundred school children on a number of subjects relating to money. The assistance of their teachers in gathering this data is especially appreciated.

Our interviews and correspondence with a wide variety of business, sports, and entertainment leaders enabled us to include many fascinating stories of how well-known Americans made money when they were kids, and their thoughts on how they feel about working and responsibility. We thank them for taking the time to share their thoughts with us.

Special thanks must go to Kathy Davis, Joanne Disibio, and Peggy Rothwell (who, along the way, became Peggy Taylor). Each made valuable contributions to the book, and their suggestions and comments resulted in a final product much better than we would have managed on our own. For the time they took from their own work to assist with reading, typing, and putting up with us, they have our gratitude.

For her careful attention to detail and sense of organization, this book owes much to our editor, Arlyne Lazerson, who not only kept us from straying too far afield, but contributed some valuable thoughts of her own.

Our publishers, Cindy and Charles Tillinghast of Oak Tree Publications in San Diego, provided both encouragement and support throughout. Their valuable assistance in helping us determine how best to approach the subject was an essential part of making this book possible.

CHAPTER 1

KIDS AND CASH— A PARENT'S DILEMMA

"My daughter has to have every new fashion that comes along," Barbara was complaining, "and I can't afford it anymore, now that she's 15. Our latest fight was over a $65 pair of boots. I finally told her, 'That's it! If you want $65 boots, go get a job.' I can't seem to make her understand that there are limits to how much money we have to spend. But even if I had it, I still think she should earn at least part of her own money for things like that."

"My ex-wife complains about money, too," observed Frank. "But she claims I spend too much money on the kids. I don't agree. It doesn't seem to me that she and her new husband give the kids enough to get by on."

Barbara interrupted, "You know how I feel about that. She's at least trying to teach your kids something about the value of money. I wish I had tried the same thing when my daughter was younger. Your kids will never learn if you come along and buy them whatever they want, especially if it's something your ex-wife doesn't think they should get. Remember the $25 watch you gave your son? It wasn't three weeks before it was lost. The thing

1

that frustrates me — and your former wife — is that you'll buy him another watch and you'll do it just because you feel guilty about the divorce. As long as you keep doing that, those kids will never learn to be responsible for anything."

"You obviously don't have to be divorced to feel guilty. Just ask Jane," said Jim, as he joined the conversation. He nodded in the direction of his wife, who was hoping they could get back to the card game. Money and the kids was a very touchy subject at their house right now, and Jane certainly didn't expect to be discussing it with two of their divorced friends. It had never occurred to her that either Barbara or Frank would have problems with their own kids over money.

Jim went on, "The cruise we took a month ago was something we'd saved for, for a long time. We owed ourselves a real vacation, now that the kids are older. But we hadn't been back a week when our 17-year-old son Matt announces that he's found a great car for only $750, and can we help him out with some cash. Jane said we'd try, and I said no way. Since then, all I hear from Matt is how we can afford to go on a cruise but can't help him out with a measly few hundred dollars. And Jane keeps telling me how we should try harder to be helpful. She thinks I'm being unfair, and I say she's feeling guilty just because we finally spent a couple of bucks on ourselves."

"That's not it at all," Jane responded quickly. "The car was a good buy, and why shouldn't we help our kids out when we can, even if we don't have a lot extra right now? If I do feel guilty, it's because we've always tried to give the kids money whenever they needed it before. How can we just change things now?"

The dilemmas these parents face are typical of the problems faced by many parents today, including stepfamilies and families headed by single parents. Particularly affected are parents who have enough money to live comfortably but who are unsure about how to approach a number of issues where the kids and money are concerned. These dilemmas generally revolve around two central issues:

1. How can I handle day-to-day money matters that involve the kids in a way that everyone in the family, kids and parents alike, feels is reasonable and fair?

At the same time,

2. What steps can I take to make sure my kids acquire the basic money skills and attitudes they need in order to be responsible and productive adults?

These are not easy questions to answer; sometimes the means we choose to make the day-to-day interactions smoother seem to contradict the goal of teaching the kids responsibility for their future.

2

Parenthood was once much simpler. Parents raised their kids the same way they had been raised themselves. Their children would go on to do the same. Society and the world moved more slowly. Changes happened over generations.

In earlier times, kids worked and helped out in many ways. They milked cows, fed chickens, and collected the eggs. Older kids plowed and harvested. There generally was little excess income. If all the family's efforts brought in enough to feed, clothe, and shelter its members, that was success. Anything extra was cause for congratulations. Spending decisions in this environment were easy.

At first, even with the change to an industrial economy, kids continued to work. They marched off, often to the same factories as their dads, and brought home their pay. Parents, however, got more in the bargain than help with the milking or a paycheck from a factory. They also benefited from a system that taught kids responsibility at an early age. It happened naturally, based on the necessity of the times. Kids learned the relationship between money and working. They were able to understand money's value because they had to work to earn it. What money they did have, they learned to respect and handle with care. A kid lucky enough to own a bike took care of it.

Some of today's parents may remember their own childhood as being simpler. Their parents had few conflicts about how much to give the kids, when to give it, when to say no—because there wasn't much extra to give out. And because every kid worked at some kind of a job or other, parents knew that their kids would learn the value of money and how to handle it.

Parents today who want their children to acquire a set of values and capabilities that can make money a useful and satisfying part of their lives must take deliberate steps to see that these goals are met. Where necessity once taught many of these values and realities to kids, the gap left by changes in the world of our children requires that specific efforts be made on their behalf. Setting forth ways for parents to accomplish these objectives is the purpose of this book.

Solving the Dilemmas

Family money dilemmas can be solved—the questions can be answered. The perfect solution might vary from one family to the next, but certain fundamental ground rules will apply in almost every situation. Those ground rules are presented here, along with specific techniques for handling everyday problems and procedures for teaching values and attitudes.

This book addresses the overall problem in four sections. An unusual feature of the book is that it contains material to be used both by parents and by kids in getting the family's financial interactions on a fair and forward-looking basis.

For Parents: Solutions to Dilemmas and Techniques for Avoiding Them

Section I offers parents clear and consistent policies in giving money to their children. It also offers guidelines that can help give the kids a sense of responsibility. This section looks at some common misuses of money, and points out that certain well-intentioned family money policies are almost sure to have negative results. It describes specific ways parents can teach their children basic money skills, like saving and sensible spending. It sets out, in detail, an allowance system that should enable any family to live together in peace while teaching the basics of responsibility. It explains why parents should bring their kids into the family partnership by sharing with them a reasonable understanding of the family's budget.

This section also looks at some of the special financial problems faced by single parents and by stepfamilies. Even parents of teenagers who feel that their family money situation is hopeless will find encouragement in a chapter that offers techniques to change the direction of things and to get relationships between parents and kids back on the right track.

Helping Kids Understand Economic Reality

Section II, Inflation, Taxes, and Other Mysteries, answers questions about basic economic subjects in simple language, using concrete examples that kids can understand: Where do jobs come from? Why is it important to save? Why are profits necessary? Why do we have to pay taxes? What causes inflation?

An important part of the problem parents have with their kids on money matters is that most children do not receive adequate information about how the real world works, either inside or outside the family environment. For example, how can they understand that the family has less money because of taxes until they understand how much of your income goes for that purpose (and how much they will pay some day)? They must be told that your family helps pay for the school crossing guard, for their teachers and their books, and for the local firemen. Until they know something about inflation, it will be difficult for them to appreciate the impact it has on your budget.

4

Many kids will be able to read and understand these chapters themselves. In other cases, parents who have had trouble answering these questions on a level their kids can understand can read the chapters and use the book's examples to get their ideas across.

Far too few parents have ever had a real discussion with their kids about important money matters that affect the family, even when those kids are getting old enough to go out on their own as young adults. One objective of these chapters is to give kids enough information so they can understand what their parents are talking about when such matters are discussed.

Every Kid Should Have a Job—and Why

The lost skill of making money should be reinstated for kids. Section III tells why. It's not just to give kids a feeling of accomplishment and personal value but also to teach them the relationship between money and their own efforts. It is doubtful if a kid can ever really understand the value of money until he has worked to earn it, until he has had the experience of doing "something real."

Bobby Hardwicke, age 17, expresses the frustrations of many of today's young people. Bobby attends an expensive private school in the East. His parents are professionals; the family, well-to-do. Bobby's views are related in *Psychology Today* (February, 1979) by Thomas J. Cottle, who has done a great deal of research with young people and their families.

"I'll go to college," Bobby says, "although I think the best thing for me would be to take a year out to work somewhere. I've never really worked—at something real, I mean. Something that would make the slightest difference to someone."

Bobby gets good grades, due, he says, to small classes and the fact that he "talks good." How does he feel about his success at school?

"So with all the studying and talking good, you know what I'd really like to do? I'd like to build a house, or fix someone's stairs or porch, something real."

Bobby will probably go on to be very successful, and his success will probably be due, in no small part, to the fact that he will have gone to college, even though he refers to school as "the great time-passer" and observes, "it's all a big invention to keep kids from becoming anything." His frustration focuses on the fact that kids want and need experiences and challenges that are "real," not just problems on exams. They want to feel the satisfaction of being useful, of doing something that makes a "difference to somebody."

5

It is unfortunate that in the name of doing something of value for our children, providing them with an education through college, we can end up taking away from our kids the very things that many parents consider were of greatest value to them as kids—the learning experiences they had outside the classroom, earning their own money, when they were young.

Section III explains why parents should help their kids get started earning some money of their own. It also suggests some practical ways parents can help their kids, and, very important, tells when *not* to help. It shows how parents can encourage the development and use of children's imaginations to help them uncover money-making opportunities.

Of all the possible approaches to teaching the value and meaning of money, encouraging a kid to earn some money on his own is probably the single most effective step a parent can take. The other steps are important, but without this one, the task is simply far more difficult.

The final section will help make this step easy for both kids and parents.

Jobs for Kids

Section IV, is for kids who want to make some money. However, it is also for parents who want to help encourage their kids to have the experience and benefits working can provide. Jobs for kids are not a substitute for school. They are a supplement. Working and going to school at the same time will make both more meaningful. A mistake on a math test is one thing. Giving a customer too much change may mean that the money is gone forever. That's a lesson that has impact.

But where should a kid start? Who will hire a 12-year-old? Chapters 21 through 28 give kids more than 125 ways to earn money. The jobs described in this section are not ordinary jobs. They are really small businesses where a kid is an independent business person. The list includes jobs that can be done by kids of all ages, even as young as 8. Here kids will also find tips on how to sell their services or products, how to put competition to use for their own benefit, how much to charge, how to get customers, and how to make more money in less time.

The challenge for a parent is to help a kid see that making money can be an adventure, that it can be fun. Once a kid is successful, it might even ease the strain he puts on the family budget. One longer-term benefit to a kid will be that he gets an education in economics. For example, any kid who understands the meaning of competition and how it affects profits has a better chance at success than the kid who does not. That knowledge will be even more important to him as an adult and may make a sizable difference in his income.

An Approach for Parents

In general, parents have two central objectives in raising their kids. One is simply having a family whose members enjoy living together. Living together in harmony requires the establishment of some system regarding the family's money that everyone can live with. The system should be one that solves existing difficulties and heads off future conflicts as well. The other objective is to prepare the kids for a productive future. Because children learn best by experiencing, the system parents adopt should consciously provide those experiences that will help kids learn the money skills they will need in later life.

Many money-related dilemmas arise out of the lack of a workable system, and others come about because kids no longer *naturally* learn about the relationship between work and money—and the accompanying lessons about the value of money and how to handle it. This means that if kids are to learn about the real world *at all*, they must be consciously taught many of those lessons by their parents and must be given an opportunity to experience the real world.

This book is, in a sense, a lesson plan for teaching our children to understand and appreciate the value of money; for helping them learn the money skills they need—the things they must know in order to make money a useful and positive part of their lives; and for getting them to understand the concept of responsibility—toward money and the things money buys, toward other people, and toward themselves.

CHAPTER 2

MONEY—HOW IT'S MISUSED

By all popular standards, Jim Rock was a success. Even better, he was a self-made success, a fact in which he took great pride. He had arrived in this country when he was in his early twenties with no money, but he brought with him an excellent education and a strong desire to succeed.

At the age of 25, Jim went to work for a large electronics company. By the time he was 30 he was married and had three children. The early years were a struggle, but having a family only increased his desire to achieve financial success. He vowed that his kids would never have to struggle as he did when he was growing up. For Jim, his dedication to business meant long hours at work and limited time with his children. His response when his wife urged him to pay more attention to the kids was that he could do more for their future by becoming a business success.

During the ten years he worked for the electronics company,

Jim developed several new concepts that he felt had great promise. The company, however, was reluctant to develop any of Jim's ideas, considering them to be too speculative. As a result, at the age of 35 Jim left his employer and started a company of his own. Initially, Jim decided to manufacture a standard line of electronics parts, and he used the profits from his sales to finance development of his own ideas. Those ideas proved to be even more profitable than Jim had expected, and by the time he was 47 his company was worth several million dollars.

But success came at a price as far as Jim's family was concerned. Once he was running his own business, he saw even less of his family than before. Extensive travel was necessary to call on his company's clients. When he was not on a trip, he never seemed to have any available time. As a result, his children saw very little of their father as they grew up. Jim recognized this, to some extent, and he prided himself on sparing no expense to see that the kids had the best of everything. Their family vacations were the envy of the neighborhood, even when Jim couldn't find the time to go along. So were the new cars each of the kids received upon graduation from high school as they headed off for the carefully selected colleges they would attend. Jim loved his kids, but he had always had difficulty demonstrating his affection for them. For him, paying for riding and tennis lessons, clothes, trips, and the other things his income allowed him to afford was a more comfortable way for him to express how he felt. Jim's feelings about taking care of his family also meant that no one else had a job, including the kids. "No one works in this family but me," was the way he put it. "I earn more than enough money to take care of what everyone needs." Jim was furious when his oldest son got a part-time job during his second year of college, and he could not understand why the boy felt he needed to earn some money of his own.

For Jim, money and what it could buy had become a substitute for the love he had difficulty expressing directly. The end result, however, was not what Jim had expected. The good life his success enabled him to provide for his family came to be expected rather than appreciated. The gratitude he felt he deserved for the years of long hours and hard work was not forthcoming, and he came to feel that his children were less interested in him as a father than in what he could do for them. Now he feels frustrated and wonders if all those years of struggle were worth it.

Even with the best of intentions, parents sometimes adopt policies and attitudes relating to money that are doomed to turn out badly. Money can be misused in a number of ways that affect children. Several of the misuses most commonly encountered are worth examining.

Money as a Substitute for Love

Many people are inhibited to some degree in their ability to show emotions and affection toward others. For some, like Jim Rock, these inhibitions even affect how they relate to their own children, and they attempt to express their feelings by giving gifts instead of love and care. Children need attention—to themselves as individuals and to the things that are important to them. Presents are nice, but they are no substitute for interest and caring.

Finding time to spend with the kids is a problem faced by many of today's busy parents. Because they feel guilty, many attempt to offer material things as a substitute for the attention they feel they cannot adequately provide. But, like most things in life, quality means much more than quantity. It is not necessary to spend a certain minimum number of hours per week with youngsters, and there are ways for busy parents to relate to their kids without having to feel guilty.

One obvious approach is to make the time spent with the kids count. One insurance executive took his guilt feelings about not spending enough time with his kids to the company psychologist. The psychologist's response was that, rather than talking to him, the executive should be spending his time talking to his kids—making sure they know how he feels about them, the reasons he is unable to spend as much time with them as he would like to, and that he will always be available when needed. Kids can understand and accept that the time their parents spend with them often has limits. If the time together is "quality" time, there is no need for guilt feelings and for excessive gifts as compensation. What kids want is for their parents to give some attention to the things that are important to them: to their activities, their friends, their interests. They want praise for their accomplishments and encouragement when things don't go so well. And sometimes they just need to talk to their parents. Showing interest in the things they're involved in doesn't have to take a lot of time, if little is available. What's important is that the interest be real.

The actual time you spend with your kids, then, is not what is most important. Many parents are "with" their kids a great deal without ever becoming involved in their lives. If any parent deserves to feel guilty, it's the one who arrives home at 6:00 P.M., nods in the direction of the kids, sits down in front of the television set with a martini or a beer, and doesn't speak to them again for the rest of the evening. It's possible to be an "absent" parent without even leaving the house.

One company psychologist advises executives of the importance of letting kids know that you are always available to them when you are needed. Here's what Mary Kay Ash, founder and Chairman of the Board of Mary Kay Cosmetics, says about her childhood relationship with her mother: "As a child, I can never remember my mother being at home. My father was an invalid, and as a result, my mother worked to support our little family. She arose each morning at 5:00 A.M. in order to reach her job as a restaurant manager at 6:00. The restaurant did not close until 8:00 P.M., so she seldom reached home until after I was asleep. However, the one great tie that I had with my mother that proved to be the most priceless gift she could possibly have given me was the fact that I could call her at any time during the day, and because she could not do for her child what the normal mother would have done, she simply constantly encouraged me by saying, 'Honey, you can do it! You can do anything in this world you want to if you want to do it badly enough—and you are willing to pay the price!!' Those words became the inspiration of my childhood and the theme of my entire life. That 'you can do it' attitude caused me to always be the one who sold the most tickets for the school play as a child. Once I competed in an extemporaneous speaking contest and wound up second in the entire state, all because my mother said, 'you can do it!'"

Years later, after retirement, Mary Kay Ash started Mary Kay Cosmetics "to give women the opportunity to do anything in this world they were smart enough to do." Now, fourteen years later, sales of her company have reached $100 million, with 40,000 consultants in the United States alone.

Material support of the kind that Jim was able to provide for his children can never substitute for the kind of love and support Mary Kay Ash received from her mother. In fact, gifts in excess of what is reasonable can have the negative effect of denying children the opportunity to develop self-reliance.

You don't have to be wealthy to be a super parent. Love and support count for more than dollars.

Bribery

When adults use money to influence the behavior of other adults, it is called bribery. Parents often use money to influence the behavior of their children, and this use of bribery can result in your kids doing things for the wrong reasons. Would you rather have a child work to get A's in school for $10 or for the sense of personal accomplishment? Bribery comes in many forms. Withholding a child's allowance until he has completed his chores is one example. It clearly involves using money for the purpose of influencing your kid's behavior.

A far more dangerous form of bribery is paying children to be good. "If you'll stop crying, I'll buy you an ice cream cone." Or, "If you'll go outside and play for an hour while Mommy finishes what she's doing, I'll take you to the store and buy you something nice."

Taken individually, none of these examples is critical. But when a parent establishes a *pattern* of bribery to control behavior, things get serious. The message to a child is clear—desired performance equals a reward. And it follows that the child may come to the further conclusion, "If I'm not going to get anything for doing it, why should I do it?" At its extreme, the policy of using bribery to control behavior produces a child who does not behave properly just because children are supposed to behave, does nothing out of a sense of responsibility, but only does what his parents want him to do when there's a payoff.

Bribery can clearly be a convenience for parents, one that often works very well—at first. But the longer it is used, the less effective it becomes. Its use only sets the stage for serious conflict later on.

Letting Outsiders Make Family Financial Decisions

There may have been a day when within their own homes parents were relatively secure from outside interference in raising their children. No more! Today there are a multitude of influences from outside the family that can impinge on family financial decisions—if they are allowed to. Television commercials, for example, are always urging children, as well as their parents, to buy something. Television is a pretty direct and blatant influence.

Often influences are less direct. When your child tells you that "All the other kids are doing it, or wearing them, or going there," that is an indirect influence on your decision-making—but often a very potent one. Parents who succumb to these various pressures from the outside are inviting problems. For example, getting the kids everything they see on television can be expensive. Much more expensive is trying to keep up with all their friends. But bowing to outside influences can affect a lot more than your pocketbook. It can interfere with such basic things as discipline and the set of values your kids learn. It's your own values that are important, not someone else's.

Actually, it's pretty much up to you, isn't it? If you let yourself be influenced against your better judgment, let's see where you end up. Consider just one area of money relations with your children—the allowance. If you have a 10-year-old daughter who has been badgering you to pay her an allowance for some time now, your first decision is whether to pay one at all. Your next is how much. Who is involved in making this decision? At first glance, it's you and your daughter. She obviously favors the idea and might have a pretty good idea of how much she wants. But how about her friends? They only participate indirectly in the decision, but you may very well be influenced by how much they are receiving from their parents when you decide how much your daughter is to get. A subtle but nevertheless present fourth party consists of the parents of your daughter's friends. What might they think of you, based on your decision? If your daughter's allowance seems low by comparison, will they think you're stingy? If it seems high, will they think you're extravagant? And that's only the allowance. Multiply all those opinions by the number of individual decisions you have to make relative to your children, then throw in the influence of television and maybe the grandparents, and the whole thing is out of hand. No matter what decision you make on any of these subjects, you can't please them all. If you and your daughter reach a mutually satisfactory decision on the allowance, what else matters?

Trying to keep up with your neighbors' level of spending is a foolish misuse of money. And basing decisions that concern only your own family on what you think the neighbors might say seems equally unacceptable. The multitude of conflicting outside influences that bear on the family today make it necessary to answer this question: Who is going to make the financial decisions in your family—the neighbors, your kids' friends, grandma, the TV set, or you? If it's you, you can settle on one simple and basic policy: Raise your kids in a way that makes sense to you, is reasonable and fair to them, and fits comfortably within your budget.

Lack of Consistency

Children need rules to live by. They not only need them, they expect them and are entitled to have them. The family without them is in a state of disorganization, forced to operate on a day-to-day, week-to-week basis. Without a set of rules—a system—the parents' response to one crisis may be different from their response to the same type of crisis the week before, and different from what it will be to the same crisis next week. Where money is concerned, this approach virtually guarantees a never-ending sequence of conflicts for as long as the children are dependent upon their parents—and that's a long time. The children are placed in the uncomfortable position of having to ask or beg for whatever they get. Parents put themselves in the position of having to decide the merits of each new request. The logical result is irritation on the part of the parents and resentment on the part of the child.

Beyond the confusion caused by an inconsistent approach, the child from a family without rules is deprived of any opportunity to learn essential money skills. With no dependable source of income, like an allowance, the youngster cannot take those important first steps in learning how to plan ahead or budget. These children cannot form intelligent spending patterns if it's always a question of getting whatever they can talk their parents into giving them each time they want or need some money.

There are a number of steps parents can take that will enable a family to reduce, or eliminate, the constant hassles over money. These steps are explained in several of the following chapters, primarily in the discussion of allowances.

Secrecy

It's very common for children to be kept totally ignorant of their family's finances. They have no idea how much money comes in, how much goes out, or what things cost. The reasons for this policy on the parents' part range from "they wouldn't understand" to "we don't want them to have to worry about money." Whatever the reason, the result is basically the same. Children who have little or no information about the family's income and expenses and play no part in any form of family planning tend to end up with a distorted view of reality. The demands that they make on the family's resources will probably be unrealistic in terms of the actual money available.

Another unfortunate result of secrecy about the family's money affairs is that the children grow up and form families of their own with little or no advance warning of the potential financial problems they will face. The child who has some understanding of his parents' family finances is far better prepared to cope with his own finances later on.

Openness on this subject can benefit both parents and children, yet it seems to be one of the most difficult subjects for parents to deal with. There are many "modern" parents who freely discuss sex and aggression in front of their kids but make sure the kids are asleep and the door is closed before discussing any aspect of the family's finances.

Techniques for including the kids in a meaningful way are discussed in the chapters dealing with the family budget.

Attitudes Toward Money

What parents produce in their kids as a result of how the family operates financially is a set of attitudes toward money.

Misuses of money can produce the negative attitudes described in this chapter. But what is a positive attitude? What do we want our kids to know about the value of money and how it should be used?

Money must be recognized as a useful tool, not an object to be sought for its own sake. Recognition by a child that money has no value except in exchange for other things they want or need is important to getting the proper perspective on how money should fit into their lives.

As with all tools, it is necessary to know how to use money skillfully. The ability to manage money correctly enables a person to get the most out of what is available. An important part of that skill for a kid is to be able to budget his money and allocate between spending now and saving to spend later. Here is a sixth-grader's description of how he manages his money. It illustrates a mature and positive attitude about the ways in which money can be useful:

> The money I earn goes to the bank, or I keep a little of it for a bike or something if I need it. I'm saving the money in the bank for a good college, or when I grow up to put it into a good use.

In contrast, an eighth-grader reflects a negative view:

> The only thing I like about money is the things you can get with it. Money is annoying. I'm always losing it or spending it as soon as I get it.

Almost everyone has to earn a living, and the attitudes kids acquire about making money can vary from feelings of grim determination to feelings of excitement. Making money can be a challenging adventure, and it should be presented that way to kids. Here's the view of one sixth-grader:

> I think it's funner to find out ways to make money, like selling lemonade, than to see what you have gotten at the end.

This kid could turn out to be a millionaire, not for the sake of accumulating a million dollars but just because he enjoys the game of making money.

Taking reasonable risks with money is another skill that demonstrates a positive attitude. Both gambling — taking excessive or unreasonable risks — and the fear of taking any risk at all are negative attitudes. A kid who invests in a floor polisher with his own money is taking an intelligent risk in expectation of making a good return on his investment by providing a service that people will pay for. A kid who is afraid to take any risk with his money is likely to lose out on money-making opportunities as an adult, too.

Saying that children should have a positive view of money is not the same as saying that all children should want to become rich. Many will choose careers that will not make them much money at all but where their contribution to society might be very significant. Being comfortable with money might, in fact, be the thing that enables them to take that path while others are struggling in their search for security through accumulating wealth.

Here is a 10-year-old who seems to have things in perspective:

I would rather be poor with a good friend than to be rich with no friend.

It is unfortunate to encounter youngsters who have views toward money that would seem to assure future problems. Here are comments from a couple of eighth-graders that reflect negative attitudes:

I think money is bad. It causes so much trouble. A person will commit a crime to get money. When a person doesn't have money they steal.

My personal feeling about money is that it causes a lot of problems like stealing, murders, and kidnapping. I think we should be very careful how it is dealt with. But it all gets down to, we need it.

These eighth-graders are old enough to have acquired more realistic attitudes about money; just like 5-year-olds, they are attributing some magic and evil characteristics to an inanimate object, probably because they've been told that "Money is the root of all evil." If they had been carefully taught, they would know that money itself is never intrinsically good or bad. It is people's attitudes toward money that can "cause so much trouble." After all, the correct saying is: "The love of money is the root of all evil." In teaching kids proper money attitudes, parents should examine their own practices. If you spend every dime before it is earned, it will be more difficult to teach your kids to save. If you save every dime except what is needed for the bare essentials, your kids may learn to save but might never learn how to enjoy what they accumulate.

Being miserly, an often useful trait in the acquisition of a fortune, at the same time makes it virtually impossible to enjoy whatever is accumulated. Money, rather than what money can do, becomes the end purpose. From time to time the newspaper tells us of yet another person who lived and died in poverty, yet had tens of thousands of dollars in a closet or safe-deposit box. In his book *The Money Makers*, Kenneth Lamott tells how S. S. Kresge, founder of one of the most successful retail organizations in America, "regularly salvaged worn-out shoes by lining them with paper, discouraged his valet from pressing his clothes for fear of wearing them threadbare before their time, and was divorced by two wives for a variety of complaints, among which was simple stinginess. In middle age he was persuaded to take up golf, but he lasted only three rounds, most of which he spent hunting balls he had driven into the rough. Then he quit, explaining that, considering the number of balls he had used up, the game of golf was too expensive for him."

Cornelius Vanderbilt was another infamous miser. According to Lamott, he "practiced at home such a fierce parsimony that his unfortunate wife was at length committed to the Bloomingdale Asylum." It is said that Vanderbilt's doctor, when the old man was on his death bed, recommended a daily bottle of champagne to make him more comfortable. Vanderbilt groaned that he was unable to afford a bottle of champagne each day, and instructed that he be supplied with a bottle of soda water instead.

The literature contains just as many tales about famous spendthrifts—people who made a million dollars and spent two million. There is, of course, a wide and happy middle ground between being a tightwad and being a wild spender, and most parents want their kids to tread that ground.

Parents can assure that their kids have positive money attitudes by setting a good example; by avoiding the misuses of money described here; and by consciously setting up situations that give their children experience in handling money. The following chapters—in particular, Chapters 4, 5, and 6—suggest good ways to structure that experience. One of the best ways kids can learn the value of money and how to deal with it is for them to earn their own. This experience is worth a million words of advice. The last section of this book is devoted to exactly this objective. Many jobs that have been successfully done by kids are described, and Chapters 18, 19, and 20 tell how parents can help improve their kids' chances of success.

These, then, are some of the ingredients of a positive attitude toward money. It is possible, however, that the attitude that will have the greatest impact on a kid's financial future is the expectation of future successes.

Expectations create much of what happens to us in our lives. The expectation of financial success is often a self-fulfilling prophecy. A kid with positive expectations will enter a contest believing that there is a chance of winning, go looking for a job expecting to find one, find a way to go to college on his own because he assumed he would do it. Each success along the way can reinforce the expectation of the next success, and parents can help kids achieve some of those early successes.

The child who grows up expecting to be successful has a far better chance. "Wanting" and "expecting," however, are two different things. In a national survey people were asked: "Would you like to be wealthy?" Fifty-six percent said yes. But to the question: "Do you ever expect to be wealthy," only 12 percent said they expected to accomplish that goal.

Children programmed early in life *not* to expect financial success will have difficulty achieving it. They will tend to think of themselves as "poor." If, as adults, such people should suddenly come into an unexpected and substantial amount of wealth, they are often unable to handle it. Their perception of themselves as poor is in conflict with the reality of the money they have acquired. The story of what happened to one man illustrates this point very clearly.

Joe had been a clerk employed by a coal company for many years when, in 1937, he inherited $16 million. It happened that the company was for sale shortly after Joe received his inheritance. With his $16 million Joe bought the coal company. His first act as the new owner was to fire all the employees who had previously been his superiors. For all the key spots in the company, Joe then hired people with whom he was comfortable — his kind of people. By 1938, Joe had become somewhat renowned for buying cars for ladies to whom he took a liking. In 1939 one of Joe's friends ran his yacht aground and sank it.

Meanwhile, under its new management the mine did not prosper. By 1942 the company, and Joe, were broke. Joe's perception of himself as a clerk could not encompass the wealth that had come his way. It took him five years, but he got back to where he was comfortable. He was broke.

CHAPTER 3

KIDS—HOW THEY LEARN ABOUT MONEY

The psychologist is sitting on one side of the table, the 4-year-old on the other. On the table are two evenly spaced rows of checkers, and each row contains eight checkers.

"Are the rows the same," asks the psychologist, "or does one row have more checkers than the other?"

"They're the same," the child responds.

"Now close your eyes," directs the psychologist, mixing up the checkers. Once again he arranges the checkers into two rows of eight each, but this time one of the rows is longer, with more space between checkers. "Now tell me if one row has more than the other."

"This one has more," says the child, pointing to the longer row.

The majority of children under 5 will make the same choice. And for somewhat the same reasons, they may think that fifty pennies are more money than ten nickels, and ten nickels are more than five dimes.

Because small children cannot reason very well, they rely strongly on what they perceive. A row of spaced-out checkers appears longer and therefore must be "more"; a pile of fifty copper coins looks like more than five thin silver ones. As a parent, you have an *intuitive* understanding of your children's limitations in thinking. You would never attempt to teach your 5-year-old about taxes, for example, and you know that children are able to understand more and more about their world as they grow up. But few parents realize that as children mature, *the way they think changes qualitatively.* That is, the mind of a 3- or 4-year-old is different from the mind of a 9- or 10-year-old. The way their thinking process changes is illustrated by the following.

A 7-year-old is shown two tall, thin jars containing exactly the same amount of water. After the child has agreed that both jars contain the same amount, he watches the experimenter pour the water from one jar into a shorter, wider jar. The majority of children under 8 will say how the taller jar contains more water, even though they have just watched the pouring.

Just a year or two later, of course, this same child will say that the experimenter's question about "which jar has more" is silly because the amount has to be the same. The difference in the two responses comes about because of a natural development in the child's thinking abilities.

This progression in the understanding ability of children can be seen in their answers to questions about religion and birth, as well as about money.

On Religion

Answers to the question, "What is a prayer?"

A 5-year-old: A prayer is about God, rabbits, dogs, and fairies and deer, and Santa Claus and turkeys and pheasants, and Jesus and Mary and Mary's little baby.

A 7-year-old: That we should have water, food, rain, and snow. It's something you ask God for—water, food, rain, and snow.

A 10-year-old: Prayer is a way to communicate with God. To ask him forgiveness, to ask him if something would go right when it's going wrong.

(From *The Child's Reality*, by David Elkind.)

On Birth

Answers to the question, "How do people get babies?"

A 4-year-old: You go to the store and buy one.

A 6-year-old: Well, the father puts the shell. I forget what it's called, but he puts something in for the egg. I think he gives the shell part, and the shell part, I think, is the skin.

An 8-year-old: The sperm reaches the eggs. It looses them and brings them down to the forming place. I think that's right, and it grows until it's ready to take out.

A 12-year-old: The sperm encounters one ovum and one sperm breaks into the ovum, which produces like a cell, and the cell separates and divides.

(From "How Children Learn About Sex and Birth," by Anne C. Bernstein, *Psychology Today*, January 1976, pp. 31-36.)

On Money

Answers to the question, "Where does money come from?"

A 5-year-old: The government gets money from God and gives it to the churches. You can get money from church — if you go. My Mom does.

An 8-year-old: The man goes out to work to get money from his job. Then he gives it to the woman to spend.

A 12-year-old: The government makes money, in the U.S. Mint.

The many systematic studies that pinpoint and describe the development of thinking in children allow parents to be better teachers and advisers, in money matters as well as other important areas, such as religion and birth. If you know what to expect, you can avoid spending a lot of time trying to get a certain idea across to a youngster who is too young to understand it.

Concepts about money are difficult for children, but if they are to grow up with a proper and realistic understanding of money concepts, they must be taught. The subject is too important to be left to chance

With the foregoing as background, let's look at some of the things children can learn about money at different age levels.

Stages in Thinking

Stage 1: Birth to About 3 Years

For babies under 2, thinking and doing are the same thing. Babies cannot really think, in the sense of holding ideas in mind. A good clue to your child's development into what is generally called thinking is his or her pretend play. When children start playing pretend games—pretending that the teddy bear is going to sleep or that a block is a fast car—it means that they can think about one thing (a car) while they are doing another (playing with a block). That's a good signal that the child has developed the ability to think.

Stage 2: 3 Years to About 6 Years

Thinking in these preschool years is still quite limited. Children of this age are strongly influenced by what they see. "Bigger" and "older" mean the same to them. For example, a person who looks bigger than another must be older. A row of spaced-out checkers looks longer so it must be "more." A child who has a choice between a 3-inch square of cake in one piece and a 3-inch square cut up into several pieces will choose the latter because it looks like "more."

What adults think of as logic does not exist in preschool children. For example, a 4-year-old boy is asked:

Do you have a brother?
Yes.
What's his name?
Jim.
Does Jim have a brother?
No.

These children cannot make the connections—formulate the relationships—between thoughts that would let them think like adults.

Children can, however, begin some learning about money at age 4 or 5, in spite of the fact that logical thinking is not yet a skill that they have mastered.

On a very small scale, you can then begin sharing the family income with them. Give your daughter a small amount of money to spend at the store while shopping. Make it clear that the amount you give her is all she gets. Let her make her own choice of what to buy. If what she wants costs 30¢ and you gave her a quarter, *don't* give her another nickel. Tell her she must choose something else. "The important thing," according to Dr. Carol Seefeldt of the Center for Early Childhood Development at the

University of Maryland, "is to let the child make the choice . . . this builds decision-making skills." Once children learn that money is not magic, that it is not available in unlimited amounts, they will spend their tiny hoard much more thoughtfully. And give them their dime or quarter cheerfully—not grudgingly. No point in starting them off with the negative impression that whatever you give them is an imposition.

You probably won't be able to teach them much about saving—at least not in ways that ensure an understanding of the connection between putting coins in the piggy bank and something they might want to do or buy in the future. For preschoolers, "two days from now" and "two months from now" might mean the same thing. They may collect the coins in order to please you, and they may parrot back to you some of your sayings about the virtue of saving, but a probing dialogue would reveal their lack of any real understanding of the situation. The young child sees money as something that is available when it is needed. Little understanding can yet be expected of where it comes from, its proper uses, or its relative value.

Yet many parents *do* expect the young child to have a greater understanding of the value of money than is reasonable. It is true that what children learn about money must be taught to them, primarily by their parents, but it is also true that expecting them to learn before they are ready simply sets the stage for a great deal of frustration—for both parent and child.

Parents, then, should not expect a young child to appreciate how hard they had to work for the money they give him. They should not expect him to prefer saving part of his allowance to spending it all. They should not insist that whatever money their children have to spend must be spent on something useful rather than something "foolish."

Stage 3: 6 Years to About 12 Years

At about age 6 or 7, most children begin to be able to think systematically and generally about concrete things. Their new logic doesn't let them be fooled by the appearance of a long line of checkers or the height of the water level in a jar.

They come to understand that age and size are two different aspects of living things. Compare the answers of a 4-year-old and an 8-year-old when asked about the ages of two trees, one tall and the other short and thick. The adult asks, "Is one of these trees older than the other?"

4-year-old: Oh yes, the tall one.
Why?
Because it is tall.

8-year-old: The tall one may be older, but that's not certain because tall trees can be old or young. So, we have to know when they were planted.

The greater generality of thinking at this age can be seen by comparing answers to the question: "What is an apple?" Younger children answer in specifics: "It is to eat." School-age children put the apple into its conceptual category: "It's a fruit."

Children of 7 or 8, then, can start learning how to handle money and understand its uses and misuses. They can learn that an allowance, for example, is a given amount of money and that when it is used up, no magic will make it reappear.

But note that there are still some limitations on thinking during these years, and that while children can think logically about concrete things, they cannot think logically about abstract or hypothetical things. So when you want to teach something about money, do it in as concrete a way as possible. Sit down with the child and actually count money or tokens, or do simple arithmetic to get your point across.

As your son grows, look for ways to teach him the value of money in the everyday world. Let him pay for the groceries and count the change for you. Let him pay the bill at a restaurant. Let your daughter pay cash on your next visit to the pediatrician — or your next trip to the hairdresser or carwash. Children need to see that services cost money, too.

Children can now learn that there are limits to the amount of money they can get from their parents — in fact, limits on how much their parents are *able* to provide. They can start learning how to budget what is available to them, and learn the value of saving some of their money for a future use. They can even learn something about earning money, and the relationship between money and working.

Learning money skills is the subject of the following chapter. In it we will explore some of the ways parents can help their kids acquire these skills.

Stage 4: 12 Years and Beyond

Not long after children reach puberty, the final development in thinking begins. Adolescents begin to be able to deal with abstract ideas and to think logically about hypothetical happenings.

By the time they are 14 or 15, then, you should be able to teach your kids anything you want them to know. (In fact, you'll probably find them trying to teach you a few things.) Now they will have no trouble understanding the explanations of inflation, taxes, competition, and the other subjects presented in Chapters 11 through 17, which help explain the economic world they live in. Many younger children—some as young as 8 or 9—will also be able to profit from reading those chapters, since most of the ideas are presented in terms of very concrete examples. You can show teenagers your family's budget and expect them to understand that making a family's finances work often means choosing between difficult alternatives.

If you've done a reasonably thorough job along the way, you won't have this conversation that a frustrated single mother had with her 21-year-old college senior, home for Christmas vacation and armed with knowledge about how to become a financial success:

Son: If the furnace isn't working right, why don't you get it fixed?

Mother: I don't have enough money this month.

Son: What do you do with all your money?

Mother: What money? Do you have any idea what it costs to raise three kids? All I make is $1,500 a month!

Son: But what do you do with all of that?

Mother: You mean *all* of what's left after $400 in taxes and $450 for the house payment? That only leaves $650. Utilities are $75, food's never less than $150 and the car payment is $125. The $300 that's left pays for clothes, gas, insurance, and entertainment, if there's anything left!

Son: Well, you should have invested!

Mother: With what?

Son: I don't know. You just should have invested in something. That's what I'm going to do.

"I guess I didn't do a very good job of explaining things as he grew up," this mother sighs. "The trouble is, he goes out and earns $2,000 to take a trip, and he gets to keep all of it—no taxes, no mortgage, no food bills. He just can't, or won't, see how much it costs to live today."

All parents want to avoid this mother's frustration; we all hope that by the time our kids are 21, they'll have a better, more reasonable idea of the uses of money. But hoping isn't enough. There are certain basic skills that can provide the foundation for a future understanding of money matters that is realistic. These basic skills are discussed in Chapter 4, and Chapters 5 through 10 present some ways to implant good attitudes about money.

CHAPTER 4

MONEY—
SKILLS TO BE MASTERED

Irv Robbins grew up in Tacoma, Washington. His father was in the business of manufacturing ice cream, which he sold to stores. He also had a retail ice cream store. Irv started working in the retail store when he was 6.

The store had a number of large oak armchairs for the use of the customers. Irv's job was keeping them clean and picking up dishes. Irv always looked forward to the times when the store got very busy. Then he was allowed to ignore the armchairs and work behind the counter.

From the age of 6 on, Irv worked in the store. Eventually he got to work behind the counter full-time. When he was 13, he started working in the ice cream factory, where his dad kept him busy with a variety of chores, including stenciling the company's name on the tubs in which they packed their ice cream. One day

Irv was eating lunch with Sabin Swanson, the plant manager. Sabin was eating lingonberries, and Irv suggested that they try mixing the berries with ice cream. Everyone agreed the combination tasted great, so Irv set about convincing his dad to try making lingonberry ice cream. The plant made only a few flavors at that time, so his dad agreed to give it a try. "It was a sales disaster," Irv recalls. "People couldn't pronounce the name of the new ice cream, and were reluctant to try an unknown."

Thirty years later, Irv took another try at making and selling lingonberry ice cream. This time he sold two tons. Irv was now in a position to make any flavor he chose. He was president of Baskin-Robbins, which he and his brother-in-law founded in 1945.

Irv Robbins' story illustrates the value to a child of experiences learned early in life. His memories of the armchairs in his father's store resulted in the armchairs you see today in every Baskin-Robbins store. His early interest in experimenting with flavors led to the 31-flavor concept that his company has made famous. The lingonberry experience produced the idea of letting customers see and taste new flavors before buying.

According to Irv, his father was very influential in his development. In some ways he was very strict. Irv recalls that his father often made him work at the plant on Saturdays. "You work while they play," his dad would tell him. "One of these days, they'll work while you play." When Irv was 13, his father bought him an insurance policy. At first, Irv made part of the payments with the money he earned. Eventually he paid the premiums by himself. The $3,000 he received when he cashed in the policy provided the capital to get Baskin-Robbins started in business.

Children learn in several ways. They learn by observing, they learn by having things explained to them, and they learn by doing. You'll have no success explaining that money is a medium of exchange to a 5-year-old. That fact is learned by exchanging a quarter for a candy bar at the store. Even a 16-year-old will probably not fully appreciate the concept of the cost of borrowing money until he buys a car. When he sees that a $3,000 loan for two years requires repayment to the bank of over $3,400, the lesson is clear.

Parents can provide valuable guidance to children as learning opportunities as these present themselves. If he didn't understand it before, the 16-year-old should now understand the relationship between interest earned on savings and interest paid on money that is borrowed. He can also understand that the bank makes its profit by paying him 5 or 6 percent on his savings account while charging him 11 or 12 percent for his auto loan. And at some point along the way, you can explain to the small child where you get the quarters that pay for her candy bars.

Money Skills

Spending Money

It all starts here. Spending is the first thing a child learns to do with money. A child learns about exchanging the 25¢ for the candy very quickly. Later, when you let children pay cash for your gas or their tennis shoes, they can begin to see how important money is to their everyday lives.

It's much more difficult to teach children that the supply of money is not inexhaustible. You can start by placing limits on what you give them. That introduces the idea of scarcity, and is the initial exposure to the idea that money has value. As children become older, they should be taught how to spend their money intelligently at the grocery store. Some schools teach this, some do not. Boys should learn how to buy groceries, too. Many of them will be doing it for themselves later on. When you take kids shopping for clothes, show them the prices. Point out cases where you can buy two pairs of less expensive pants for the same price as a higher-priced pair. Make them aware of prices on the menu when you go out to dinner.

Spending wisely is a matter of making choices, something at which kids need a lot of practice. So don't tell them how to spend their allowance once you start giving them one. One of the most important reasons for paying an allowance is to give them experience in making choices. Their ability to choose between alternatives improves rapidly once they begin to earn some money of their own. Even a youngster of 6 or 7 will tend to be careful how he spends a dollar if he spent an hour raking leaves to earn it.

Parents sometimes incorrectly assume that kids will pick up many buying skills automatically. However, if you have teenagers, do they know: that stores mark prices down right after Christmas; that the same exact item, from tennis balls to washing machines, is cheaper in some stores than in others; that most major department stores have a "white sale" in January and in August every year, and if you can wait until then, many items are less expensive; that if you want to buy an expensive item, you can find out when it will be put on sale—just by asking? These are facts you can tell them; there's no point in making them learn all this on their own.

No matter how well money is handled in other ways, learning to spend it the right way is vital, and giving advice on wise spending is well worth some effort on the part of parents.

Budgeting

What if kids had budgets, budgets that they prepared themselves and followed? What if all the adults who hate budgets (and too often are unable to use them) had had some practice when they were 12? or 15? If you have a 12-year-old son with a predictable source of income from an allowance, why not help him set up a budget for himself? His budget can show his income and how he plans to allocate it for the next thirty days—to savings, to charities or Sunday school, to items he wants to buy himself this month. Later on, when he is earning some money of his own from a job, he can add in estimates of how much that income will amount to in the coming month.

By the time they reach college, some young people are ready to accept a great deal of responsibility. If their parents have done a good job of teaching money skills, the kids *should* be ready. At this point some parents are able to sit down with their kids and work out a budget for the full college year, covering all expenses that the youngster will take care of, including entertainment, transportation, clothing, and the other college expenses. The parents then write a check for deposit in the student's savings account, and at that point he's on his own. If he spends it too fast, there's no more. Any kid able to handle this kind of responsibility successfully is in very good shape.

Budgeting is often used by families in an attempt to see where all the money goes; however, its greatest value is in planning for future goals. When your daughter comes up with an important goal, that's the time to show her how to budget. If you haven't done it before, you'll have your chance when a teenager wants a car. One girl started thinking seriously about a car when she was 14. She started asking people for opinions on various cars. She compared mileage ratings and even found a chart showing comparative maintenance expenses of different models. She did everything but plan where she would get the money to buy a car. She got to that when she was 15. Then she started worrying. She *had* to get the car when she was 16, but only had about two hundred dollars saved. Her dad suggested a budget.

This young lady's budget was fairly simple, and looked like this:

Weekly Budget

INCOME

Allowance	$ 5.00
Housecleaning (regular weekly customer)	10.00
Housecleaning (misc. jobs—estimate)	5.00
Babysitting (Mrs. Jenkins—Wed.)	6.00
Babysitting (misc.—estimate)	4.00
TOTAL WEEKLY INCOME	$30.00

"If you earn that much every week for a year," her dad pointed out, "you'll make $1,500." It looked as if she would have her car after all—until she did the second half of the budget. Now she tried to remember where she had spent her money over the previous couple of months. Her estimates looked like this:

EXPENSES

Clothes	$12.00
Records and similar items	3.50
Cokes, milkshakes, etc.	2.50
Other miscellaneous	6.00
TOTAL WEEKLY EXPENSES	$24.00
AVAILABLE FOR SAVINGS PER WEEK	$ 6.00

Only $6 a week! And what she had saved over the past couple of months was for a new tennis racket. It wouldn't stretch far enough. Saving all the extra money each month only added up to $300 in a year.

A budget performs no magic. It creates no money. However, it does present the facts so choices can be made. This young lady can do one of three things: find a way to increase her income, spend less on certain items, or forget the car. One approach she can use is to decide how much money she needs and when she wants to have it available. Suppose she decides she'd better have $1,500 cash before she buys her car, and she'd like to have it saved in eighteen months. That means she'll need to save $20 a week for a year and a half.

A look at her budget shows this youngster what might be practical. She now has $6 available to save each week. She can't increase her income by the $14 she needs because she can't spend that much time working. She could probably squeeze in a bit more time babysitting, enough to add another $5 to her weekly income. Then the income figure in her budget will read $35. Now for the spending side. She currently spends $24 a week, and in order to save $20, she can only spend $15. She'll have to spend $9 less each week until the money is saved. Saving instead of buying some of the clothes she wants will help. She knows she can live with fewer record albums. She'll have to watch her money very carefully, but if she does, her budget says she can make it. She can get her car before she turns 17.

One other approach to teaching kids about budgeting is involving them in discussions of your family's budget. The advantages of this approach are discussed in Chapter 6.

Saving

Some kids seem to enjoy saving money. Others spend it as fast as possible. It is not uncommon to find both kinds in the same

30

family, kids who were presumably raised in the same way. In general, however, most kids are more oriented toward spending than saving.

Young people live in a "now" world. The very young child doesn't understand the concept of a future. By the time they are teenagers, however, most parents expect their children to be able to look and plan ahead. But most teenagers also focus on "now." They want to learn to drive, and then they want a car—now. They want spending money to buy a million things. Saving for things in the future is difficult, especially if they did not get in the habit when they were younger.

Fortunately, their attitudes begin to change in the late teens. In one nationwide poll, young people from 15 to 21 were asked if they had saved any money. Sixty-eight percent answered "yes," and a fourth of those had saved over $500. When asked what they were saving for, 42 percent said for an education, 20 percent for a car, and the rest mentioned things like travel and clothes. The fact that 68 percent of these young people had saved some money is reassuring but not remarkable. By this age, young people should have an appreciation of the value of saving for an education or a car, since these represent goals that are both practical and immediate.

Encouraging a 10-year-old to save money is an entirely different process. Such encouragement can, and probably should, start when the allowance begins, as early as age 6 or 7. It's hard to get young children to accept the virtues of saving when there are things they want to spend that money on right now. You can *force* them to save part of it—that's one approach. How much better it would be, however, if you could get them to save voluntarily. One way to begin is to identify something your son wants very badly. Something you might normally buy for him just because he wanted it. Let's say it costs $2.50, and your son's allowance is 75¢ a week. Why not tell him that this is something he's going to have to buy for himself—he'll have to save enough money to pay for it out of his allowance. If he saves 25¢ a week and spends the other 50¢ as it's received, it will take him ten weeks to reach this objective. On the other hand, if he saves 50¢ a week, it will only take five weeks. So watch for opportunities like this. Start with little lessons. They become bigger later on.

Initially, the things children save for should be relatively inexpensive. If it would take your child a year to save enough money to buy a particular item, forget it. A year is a lifetime for a 7-year-old. Two or three months is probably about right, to start. When kids are 14 or 15 and saving for a car or college, it's a different story. Now they're mature enough to go without some of the things they want today and to save for something that will benefit them in two or three years.

Borrowing

In money matters, children observe their parents charge things at stores, at gas stations, at restaurants. In this "day of the consumer," credit has become a way of life. Most people use credit in a variety of ways without giving it a thought. No wonder the youngster who is told, "I can't buy that for you today," responds, "Well, if you don't have any money, why don't you charge it?" Or suggests that you "write a check." The concept of borrowing against the future needs to be clarified so children understand that what is borrowed today must be paid back from future income. This is where practical experience is required. Let's assume your daughter has an income of $1 per week from working, an allowance, or both. Have her sit down with a piece of paper and work out the following figures for herself the next time she wants to borrow some money:

This week's income	$1.00
Borrow 75¢ in advance	+ .75
Now, how much do you have to spend *this* week?	$1.75
Next week's income	$1.00
Pay back 75¢	− .75
Now, how much will you have to spend *next* week?	$ .25

Even a little kid who cannot add or subtract very well can do this exercise with coins. If your daughter's allowance is only 25¢ a week and she wants to borrow 10¢, pay her the following week's allowance in nickels. Let her count out the two nickels she owes you and give them back to you. Now she will begin to understand the concept of repaying borrowed money.

It's probably better for kids to learn to save before they make a habit of borrowing. Borrowing is, however, an almost essential part of our lives and should be understood. However, unauthorized borrowing from brothers and sisters, or a pattern of always having to borrow against future allowances can be setting the stage for some very unhappy circumstances later on. This could create a belief that there will always be someone there to bail them out.

Earning Money

It is interesting that children learn to acquire money (from their parents), to spend it, to waste it, to lose it, perhaps even to save it—all before they learn how to earn it! The ability to earn money involves a much more complex process than that required to save or to budget. The skill of making money is made up of a number of other business skills, skills that can best be learned by actual practice. There is considerable evidence showing that kids who get jobs of their own can learn many of these skills early in the game.

Let's look at several of these business skills and see how kids can learn to use them to make money.

Sales Ability

If you are an adult in the sales business and get on the right mailing lists, you will be buried in an avalanche of invitations to attend seminars, buy books, take courses that will show you the way to sales success. There are, of course, many aspects of sales that can be taught, but the best lessons come from actually selling something to people.

Louis Lundborg, former Chairman of the Board of the Bank of America, began his business career at the age of 8 in Missoula, Montana. His first job was as a newspaper boy, and he began in a somewhat unconventional way. He started with what he describes as "a slightly used" newspaper, which he took to the newspaper's office and traded for a new one. The new one he sold. It was the first of many sales. Lundborg didn't just have a newspaper route as most boys did but bought and sold his own papers as a strictly independent agent. When he was 9, he "graduated" from selling newspapers on the streets to the more profitable sale of magazines.

On his own, Lundborg learned some extremely valuable sales lessons: "I learned early in the game that there were different classes of customers for each of these magazines; for example, a housewife would not be interested in the *Country Gentleman,* but an implement dealer would be; so then I sold the *Country Gentleman* to all of the implement and farm supply dealers in town. Housewives, of course, were good prospects for both the *Ladies' Home Journal* and the *Saturday Evening Post.*"

Selling magazines to the right customers might seem obvious, but many adults in sales waste much of their time trying to sell things to the wrong people. Lundborg sold his magazine business to a younger boy when he reached high school, but not before he had become the most successful *Saturday Evening Post* salesman in eastern Montana.

Another story of early sales success that started with the magazine business is that of Robert T. McCowan, President of Ashland Petroleum. McCowan was selling the *Ladies' Home Journal* at the age of 10, when he discovered one of the principal secrets of sales success. One week he was talking to a potential customer when he happened to mention that there was an article about Eleanor Roosevelt in that issue. That article sold the magazine, so he tried it at the next house. From then on, he looked for articles of special interest in each new issue, and sold them instead of just selling magazines.

According to McCowan, "I turned out to be a top salesman at the age of 10 when I realized you've got to let people know about the benefits of what you're selling them."

Any kid who understands the concept of "selling benefits" at the age of 10 is a kid you'll probably never have to worry about. He'll take care of himself.

Learning to Take Risks

Some people develop the ability to make money to an unusual degree. J. Paul Getty was one of those. He reportedly retired at age 24 after he had made his first million, but he was not satisfied and was soon back in the business of making money. He was ultimately worth in excess of $2 billion. Getty describes his rules for success this way: "Great wealth is due to imagination, ability and a successful risking of capital." At these things Getty was a master, and his preoccupation with business was lifelong.

Getty's comment implies two things. First, in order to risk capital you must have it, and in order to have it you must save it. Saving, therefore, is an extremely important early lesson to be learned. And once some money has been saved, there's nothing wrong with having a healthy respect for keeping it. One of the ways to get rich is to hang on to what you already have while you add more to it. But making a lot of money usually involves taking risks, and a healthy attitude toward risk-taking can be a valuable asset. The kid who sticks his neck out and buys a power power that enables him to mow five lawns in the time it formerly took to do one is taking a risk, particularly if he borrowed money to buy the mower. His risk? That he won't find enough new customers. That he won't make enough additional money to pay for the mower and still make a reasonable return for himself. But if he does find the customers, the risk was well worth taking. Once the mower is paid for, his income can be five times what it was with the same amount of effort.

Are successful people more inclined to take risks than the less successful? The *Saturday Evening Post* (December 30, 1967) published a survey taken to measure people's money attitudes, in which a wide range of people were asked the following question:

"If someone gave you $2,500 tax-free and said you could triple it at the toss of a coin or lose it all, would you take the chance?"

A fifty-fifty chance to *triple* your money is obviously attractive, but just 25 percent of those interviewed said they would take the chance. Of the wealthy people interviewed, however, 42 percent said they would try for it. This difference indicates a greater willingness to take risks on the part of people who have been financially successful. Keep in mind that risk-taking is not the same as gambling. A gamble generally means that your odds are less than even. The kid who bought the power mower took an intelligent business risk where the odds were on his side. Getty did not become the richest man in the world by gambling.

Louis Lundborg bought his newspapers and magazines from the publishers, then went out to sell them. That involved taking the risk that some would remain unsold each time he did it. There are far more opportunities in business for the person who is willing to take some risk than for the person who is not. Kids who want to undertake business ventures that entail some risks should be encouraged. After all, there's no better time to learn what risk-taking is all about than when a kid is young and the stakes are low.

Understanding Competition

If your daughter loses her best babysitting customer to another kid who charges less, she suddenly understands the meaning of competition in a way no book or explanation from you could ever convey. Kids can bounce back from such experiences more readily than most adults, so getting an early understanding of competition can be an important asset later on in the business of making money. Coping with competition is a necessary skill, since competition is so basic a part of the business world.

Competition may be a basic factor in business, but it is the *only* factor in auto racing. One of the most successful members of his profession is Tom Sneva, USAC Champion in 1977. If Sneva is representative, the instinct to compete may often show up early. Tom made money in a number of ways as a kid, but here is how he describes his very first venture:

> My first money making activity was a Kool-Aid stand at the busiest corner on our block at the age of 7. Due to the large number of kids in our neighborhood, there was a great deal of competition for this business. To succeed we had to cut our price per drink and rely on a big volume.

The basics of competition are the same, no matter what the activity, and they can be learned best through experience. Irv Robbins opened an ice-cream sandwich business in the local department store when he was 15. It was open only on Saturdays. He operated out of a small booth near the elevator, which he had talked the new store manager into renting to him. The business was quite profitable until a nearby Woolworth's installed an ice cream counter that was open all the time and put Irv out of business. For him, it was only a minor setback along the way. Almost immediately he began another venture to make money selling ice cream.

The fear of competition keeps many people from trying potentially profitable ventures. Learning to accept competition and to handle it is a useful skill and a good one to learn early.

Applying Business Skills

Some of the skills kids can acquire by working are directly related to money and to business. Others are skills that are also useful in many nonbusiness areas. These include the ability to make decisions, to get help when it is needed, to solve problems, and to deal with failure or disappointments.

The business, sports and community leaders whose stories appear in this book acquired business skills as youngsters which they were able to use effectively as adults. These skills were often acquired in different ways and for different reasons, but the end result was essentially the same. This is illustrated by the following examples:

Albert V. Casey, president of American Airlines, grew up in the Boston area during the depression. His father had been in the construction business, but his business had failed and, as Casey puts it, "each of us had to struggle along as best we could."

When your family has nothing to give you, you earn your own. Here's how Casey describes the way he did it.

> My particular efforts were directed toward door-to-door selling of the most common household objects such as Band-aids, household oil, shoelaces and other items.
>
> Every time I wanted to go to a movie or purchase a personal item, I would pick up my bag and parade the streets until sufficient money was raised.

Unlike Albert Casey, Henry Ford II grew up as a member of an extremely wealthy family. However, his grandfather, Henry Ford, founder of the Ford Motor Company, did not believe that youngsters should be idle just because the family had money. As Henry Ford II puts it:

> I learned early from my grandfather that there is a direct relationship between effort and reward—that you gain no more out of life or a given task than you put into it. When I was told to plan on doing some farm work, harvesting hay

and many other such chores, I didn't exactly welcome the idea. But as I finished the work, I had the feeling that I had accomplishéd something tangible and worthwhile. I had found the relationship between hard work and results. It's important, I think, to find that early in life and to remember it throughout life.

Clearly, the values kids learn in relation to the world of money or work are applicable to other areas as well. As Henry Ford II put it, "I learned early ... that there is a direct relationship between effort and reward." A kid who learns to budget and save is also learning the important skill of self-discipline. The kid who learns to spend wisely has learned something useful about making decisions, about choosing between alternatives.

The starting point for real training is probably when a youngster starts receiving an allowance. The next chapter looks at the allowance and tells how it should be used to start the learning process.

CHAPTER 5

ALLOWANCES—
A SYSTEM THAT WORKS

Jeff's mother is just starting dinner when Jeff appears in the kitchen obviously in a hurry.

"Mom," he says in an urgent tone of voice, "I need five bucks, quick. We're going down to ride go-carts and I don't have any money."

Jeff is 14, old enough to have learned his share of tricks. Part of the strategy is to make it sound like an emergency. Don't give her a chance to think. She might remember the last time you pulled this one on her. This time Jeff senses trouble.

His mother is starting to object: "What happened to the ten dollars you had a week ago? I thought your father told you that had to last until the end of the month?"

Jeff thinks quickly, "This is now, not last week. That ten dollars was at least two record albums, ten Cokes, and half dozen hamburgers ago."

She's still protesting. Time to play his ace: "C'mon, mom. Roger's mom is driving us there and she's in a hurry. Everyone's waiting for me in the car."

Silence. "Works every time," Jeff thinks as he watches the sudden look of desperation in his mother's eyes. Moments later he is racing up the driveway to the waiting car. Somewhere in the distance it seems he can hear her saying, "This is the last time." He'd worry about that later. For now, he had the money.

Now, let's see how Jeff's mother feels. She knows she's been had, but she hasn't the foggiest idea what to do about it. What possible thoughts run through her mind when Jeff confronts her with this situation?

Thought Number One: "He's blown all his money *again*! This time he'll just have to go without."

Thought Number Two: "But all his friends are going. Poor little kid. Maybe we really don't give him enough."

Thought Number Three: "Of course we give him enough money. He just spends it as fast as he gets it. If we gave him twice as much, he'd just spend it twice as fast."

Thought Number Four: "Mrs. Smith's waiting in the car? Good grief! If I don't give it to him, she'll probably think I'm a terrible mother."

Thought Number Five: "Mrs. Smith *might* even think we can't afford it." (This is where she hands out the money.)

A dirty trick? But all kids do it, don't they? Besides, it works just about every time.

Jeff's family does not employ an allowance system. Jeff gets the money he wants by asking for it whenever the need arises. If his parents think the request is reasonable, he gets it. If not, he's not supposed to get it. But, as we have just seen, it doesn't always work that way.

Having no system is a continuing invitation to hassles over money, hassles that could be ended by the adoption of a workable system that both parents and children can live with.

Jeff's parents, however, are frustrated for reasons besides the ongoing conflict, reasons that even go beyond how much money Jeff spends. They can see from Jeff's behavior that he is getting no real experience in managing money properly and that he is learning little about the necessity to budget his funds, make intelligent spending choices, or exercise any restraint in his spending patterns. They're not even sure that he really appreciates the fact that the supply of money may be limited.

Jeff's parents are not the only ones who are concerned. Many others are equally frustrated by their seeming inability to teach their kids the value of money and the basics of responsibility. Here are some fairly typical complaints from parents that deal with these two related subjects. The first set of complaints deals with kids and money:

Our kids have no appreciation of the value of money.

Johnny is constantly begging, asking for money to buy something else every time I turn around.

No matter how much we give our girls, they always want more. In fact, sometimes it seems that the more we give them, the more they want.

It doesn't matter how hard I try, I can't get Jerry to save a dime.

Last month Hank spent more than he had, and I caught him borrowing the difference from his younger sister.

The second group of complaints centers around responsibility:

It's a constant battle to get Joanne to do her jobs around the house. Even taking away her allowance doesn't seem to help.

I'd be happy if Steve showed just a little responsibility. He leaves his bike in the street, loses his lunch money; he just doesn't seem to appreciate the value of anything. Everything we do for him is taken for granted. None of the sacrifices we've made for him seems appreciated.

There is an obvious and close relationship between problems that involve money and those involving responsibility. The kid who shows irresponsibility by "leaving his bike in the street" is likely to be the same kid who has "no appreciation of the value of money." The mother complaining about getting her daughter to do the household chores for which she is responsible has tried to remedy the situation by withholding her allowance.

The complaints listed here would obviously not exist if these parents were achieving their goals in raising their children. Unfortunately, teaching a kid to ride a bike is far easier than teaching him not to leave it in the street. Teaching a youngster how to vacuum is no problem when compared with getting her to do the job every week, even though she has agreed to do it as her share of the family effort.

Let's identify the goals that seem so difficult to accomplish. There are three, and two of them relate directly to money. The first goal is to teach kids the value of money and the related value of the things it buys, like a bike. The second is to teach them money skills, such as saving and budgeting. The third goal is to teach them responsibility for themselves and their own actions—and the responsibilities they have to others, such as to the family. Because all three goals involve concepts that are intangible and difficult for children to understand, the best approach is to expose them to *experiences* that will teach them what they need to learn.

The allowance provides what is probably the single most effective tool parents can use to teach money values to their children when they are young, and its use is strongly recommended. Kids do get money from their parents, whether it is on a random, unplanned basis or on an orderly and predictable basis. The question is: Which is the best way to give it to them? Not everyone agrees. Let's look at the ways kids get money from their parents.

How Parents Give Money to Their Children

There are many different ways parents give kids money, and the six alternative approaches listed below describe the situations in most families; four methods use an allowance and two do not. Many parents may be surprised to discover that the allowance method they use is not really an allowance at all.

Before reading about these methods, answer the following questions for yourself. They represent common dilemmas parents face in deciding how to deal with money and teach responsibility to their kids. If you have trouble formulating firm answers to some of the questions—or find yourself giving some contradictory answers—the rest of the chapter will help you set up a system that works and is fair for your family.

If you pay an allowance, how much should it be?

What factors should you consider in deciding the amount?

Should your kids be involved in the discussion of how much?

Should kids have to work for their allowances, and if so, what kinds of jobs should they do?

If they don't do their jobs, should their allowance be reduced or stopped?

How about paying them for the jobs they do at home instead of giving them an allowance?

If you do pay them for jobs they do at home, does this mean you have to pay them for cleaning their room?

How about giving them an allowance and, in addition, a chance to earn extra money?

The first two methods described below do not involve an allowance.

1. Money Is Given as Needed

Parents use no formal allowance. They provide money to their kids on an irregular, unplanned basis as it is needed or requested. Jeff, whose story starts this chapter, gets his money this way. Most parents want to know in advance how the money the kid requests will be spent, and they are then faced with deciding whether they approve.

2. The Commission System

Parents pay their kids for working at home. Pay is based on actual work done. The jobs that are available for kids to do are posted. They will be paid for each job, and how much they are paid is agreed upon in advance. Most parents assign a value to each of the jobs. Washing the car might be worth $1.75, vacuuming the house $4, mowing the lawn and sweeping the walks $2.50. Rates are set based on what is agreeable to both parents and kids. Some families pay for jobs by the hour and give the kids the responsibility for keeping track of the time. If a kid needs extra money, the jobs are available. If no jobs are done, no money is given to the child.

3. An Allowance Tied to Responsibilities

This system, in some form, seems to be the most commonly used. A regular allowance is paid, normally weekly. Household chores are assigned to be done on a regular basis. If the child doesn't do the jobs, however, his allowance is docked or withheld. Some parents require completion of all tasks before any allowance is paid; others reduce the allowance according to the amount of work left undone.

This is commonly thought of as an allowance system, but actually it is not an allowance at all. It amounts to a regular job for the child, one for which pay is forthcoming when the job is done—just like any other job. This system is almost the same as the commission system, except that it usually offers the kid no means of earning extra money.

With a few subtle changes, however, this approach takes on an entirely different character and becomes the best of all the systems to use: the allowance (no strings) plus responsibility. Those changes, and how they can be made, will be described shortly.

Descriptions of the three methods that involve a true allowance follow.

4. An Allowance with No Strings— No Responsibilities

Parents provide the child with a fixed amount of money paid on a regular basis with no conditions. Many parents use this method as the best way to teach money skills and values. The principal difference between this system and the three just described is that the amount and timing of each payment for kids is totally predictable. No action is required on the child's part to qualify for the next installment.

A wide number of variations on this theme are possible, but they all have the same basic similarity: The allowance is not contingent on anything and is always paid. Two of those variations are described next.

5. An Allowance (No Strings)— Supervised Spending vs. Freedom of Choice

Parents pay the allowance as described above but insist that the child use it in certain ways. Some require that a certain portion be saved and another portion donated to church or charity, with the balance available to be spent as the child wishes. Others want to know exactly how all the money is to be spent, and the child buys only what has been previously approved. The objective of such supervision is to show the child how to spend and use money wisely.

The merits of such supervision are a matter of debate. Many parents feel that the child should make all the spending decisions and that they should intervene only when the child requests assistance. These parents believe that one of the purposes of the allowance is to build decision-making skills.

An Allowance System That Works

Many families use one of the preceding systems, or a variation, in giving money to their kids. Our research also indicates that many families are dissatisfied with the results they are getting with their children. Even the parents who are satisfied with their present method may soon find that what worked with smaller children will not work with teenagers.

Here is an allowance system that works.

6. An Allowance (No Strings)— Plus Responsibilities

Parents who use this system combine the elements of several others. The allowance is always paid and is not contingent on any required behavior by the child. At the same time, the child and parent agree on which family chores the child will be responsible for. Failure to do the work, however, is never punished by reducing or eliminating the allowance.

This approach employs the best features of all the methods described and is recommended for use by any parents concerned about the longer-term best interests of their children. This system works with children of all ages and so eliminates the necessity of changing your approach as the kids become older.

To implement this system, several things are required of the parents who use it:

1. What you plan to do must be explained clearly to the child.

2. The discussion should be two-way. The objective is to reach agreement on a system that is acceptable to all parties.

3. Mutual respect of one another's rights and responsibilities must exist between parent and child. Parents naturally expect this from their children but often forget that children have rights, too, not just responsibilities.

4. Once the rules are set up, they *must* be adhered to with few, *if any*, exceptions.

You can put this system into effect at any point, no matter what the age of your child at the time. For the purpose of description, however, let's start at the beginning. That beginning is at the age of 6 or 7. As pointed out in Chapter 3, kids younger than this are not prepared to deal with concepts such as being responsible or handling money wisely. By age 6 or 7, however, children's thinking abilities have developed to the point where they can begin to learn some meaningful lessons about money. The allowance should now be initiated.

How Much Allowance?

Decisions about the amount of the allowance are based upon several factors. It must be large enough to be of some significance to the child. A 25¢ weekly allowance for a 7-year-old boy means very little when the entire amount can be spent on one Coke or when he has to save it all for two weeks to get a milkshake. You should estimate how much you normally spend buying him such items each week and should give him a comparable amount plus something extra, which he should be encouraged to save for the purchase of special items. (Expenses the allowance might cover are described below.)

One approach, especially with older kids, is to ask your child to work out what he needs for movies, carfare, lunch, and so on, and use the figures he comes up with as a starting point for deciding how much he will get. An allowance based on a child's estimate will probably need revisions, so ask him to show you where the money really went over the first few weeks.

The objectives: To shift decisions on how his money is to be spent from you to him, to eliminate begging on his part, and to start for him the process of learning to handle money.

The amount you pay your child will be influenced by where you live. What is reasonable in one area might not be in another area, where prices are higher. The amount will also be based on what you can comfortably afford, especially as children move into their teens. What your child's friends get may influence your thinking, but it should not be the standard you use. You must pay what seems both reasonable and fair to you and your child. When the two of you do not agree, *you* must decide. The allowance should not be excessive. The purpose of a fixed amount is to teach the child that there are limits to the availability of money, and something about its value. An allowance that is larger than necessary can frustrate this objective.

The parent and child should agree in advance on the kinds of expenses that the allowance will cover. For a 7-year-old it might include all purchases of things like ice cream and gum for a week. At 12, a larger allowance could also cover the child's entertainment, such as roller skating or movies, in addition to purchases of personal items like records and Cokes. As kids grow through the teens, the allowance can be expanded to cover more of the child's basic needs. Some families figure out how much would normally be spent on a kid's clothes in a year and include that in a monthly allowance. This accomplishes two things: It makes budgeting much easier for the parents, since now most of the child's expenses are included in the one budget item, the allowance; at the same time, this system forces the kid to budget carefully. Knowing what she must pay for with her allowance, your daughter can figure out how much additional money must be earned from an outside job in order to afford all the things she wants to have or do. Each parent must decide how rapidly and to what extent this shift of responsibility to the child is made. For some families, the final step is college, and some parents who are paying part, or all, of a young person's college expenses are able to write out one check to their son or daughter at the beginning of the college year and know that the child will still have some money left the following May.

When Should the Allowance Be Paid?

The allowance should be paid weekly—on the same day each week—to younger children, and monthly to kids as they approach their mid-teens. The shift to a monthly payment is not for your convenience but is for the purpose of encouraging more careful attention to budgeting and planning ahead on the part of your teenager. The important thing is that the payment should represent a predictable source of income that the child can count on.

The allowance should *always* be paid, so your child can count on it as a dependable source of income. This means it should never be withheld as punishment or used for the purpose of influencing your child's behavior. This is a critical issue. Withholding the allowance for failure to complete family chores that have been agreed to and assigned converts those tasks into paying jobs and frustrates efforts to teach the child the concept of responsibility to others. It also means that the allowance is no longer a dependable source of income, since it must now be earned before being received. An undependable income makes it more difficult to teach a child to budget, save, or plan ahead. Teaching such money skills is one of the purposes of making the allowance something a kid can count on.

Another reason for never withholding the allowance is this: The money that the child receives should be viewed as his share of the family's income because he is a member of the family, just as he is expected to assume family responsibilities because he is a family member. Sharing the family's income *and* its responsibilities are related but must never be dependent upon one another.

Using the allowance to bribe a child, to encourage good grades, or to influence behavior in other ways has negative implications that go well beyond the issue of allowances, and this misuse of money is explored in Chapter 2. Withholding the allowance as punishment is another misuse of money. The message to the kid is: If you behave yourself, we pay you. Therefore, the reason you behave is for cash.

Once the amount of the allowance has been established, parents must stick to it. When it is all spent, no more should be given to the child until the next regular payment. The parent who weakens on this point might as well forget the whole thing. One way to teach your daughter to save is to explain that if she saves part of her allowance each week, she will have money for something special. If she fails to save and cannot afford the special event, parents have two choices. You can let her miss it, or give her extra money. If she cannot go because she failed to save, a positive lesson will be learned. If you give her the money, the lesson is: If I fail to plan ahead, someone will always bail me out. Parents, should make sure the ground rules are reasonable and then stick to them.

How Should the Allowance Be Spent?

The child should be allowed to make his own spending decisions. Doing so helps him learn how to make choices and spend wisely. It does not mean that you never offer advice or make observations on how the money was spent but only that you do not make those decisions for him.

What the Allowance Teaches— a Summary

In all but a few families the supply of money is limited. If this lesson can be learned early in life, later problems of overspending can usually be avoided. A fixed allowance with no more available once it is spent will introduce this concept to the child.

Planning ahead for future expenditures is necessary for adults. Planning ahead for one week may not seem like much to a parent, but a week is a long time if you're only 7. Knowing that an allowance must last a week starts the process of learning to plan ahead.

Budgeting is something all parents do, even if a formal budget is not used and you do it in your head. It's a matter of deciding where the family's income is to be spent each month. On a small scale (which will increase as they grow older) children can begin to learn how to allocate the money that is available to them. Budgeting is a skill some older children master and use very effectively.

Being a good consumer means obtaining more value from each dollar spent. Parents should let a child make his own spending choices; at the same time, they should use every opportunity to point out ways in which more value can be obtained by looking at alternatives and choosing carefully.

A small portion of the allowance should be identified initially as money that is to be saved for special uses. Even if it is only saved for a couple of weeks and then spent on a desired item, the child can begin to see that some things can never be obtained without putting some money aside for their purchase. As children grow, larger amounts can be saved for longer-term objectives.

Decision-making is a skill that comes only through practice. It is one of the most useful skills adults command. Making choices of any kind is often difficult for a child. Learning to budget, save, plan ahead, and spend wisely all contribute to the child's ability to learn how to make good decisions.

The allowance system described here is designed to foster the development of these money skills, and a child who does not have a fixed, dependable source of income is deprived of the opportunity to learn them. John D. Rockefeller, Jr., was certainly not trying to save money when he decided to pay an allowance to his five sons. According to son Nelson, "We got 25¢ a week, and had to earn the rest of the money we got." To earn part of that extra money he raised vegetables and rabbits. He remembers an ingenious scheme that he and one of his brothers used to get started raising rabbits. "We borrowed a pregnant rabbit, and returned her when the baby rabbits were born and old enough to be on their own."

"We always worked," according to Nelson. All the boys were required to keep personal daily account books. They were required to give 10 percent of their income to charity, to save 10 percent, and to account for all the rest. They had to balance their account books every month and to be able to tell what happened to every penny they earned. Nelson went on to serve as Governor of the state of New York for many years, and, ultimately, became Vice President of the United States. One of his brothers, David Rockefeller, Chairman of the Chase Manhattan Bank, says, "We all profited by the experience—especially when it came to understanding the value of money."

Learning Responsibility

Responsibility is a companion issue to learning money skills. It is a trait that all parents want to develop in their children, but it is often an elusive goal. Complaints about the irresponsibility of their children are among those most often voiced by parents.

Childhood experiences that taught them the meaning of responsibility are often viewed by adults as the most important events of their childhood. Hank Aaron, one of baseball's great superstars and now Vice President of the Atlanta Braves, remembers working at many jobs as a child, including cutting grass, picking and selling blackberries, and being an ice boy. But the things that seem to be most significant to him were the jobs he did helping out at home. "I think every child should learn to have some kind of responsibility," he says, "and learn it at a young age, including responsibilities in the home." Learning responsibility, like learning money skills, requires practice, and there are specific steps parents can take that will start their children along the road to becoming responsible adults.

At the time the allowance is initiated, each child should accept a part of the responsibility for maintaining the family—should begin to contribute to the family effort. The task the child will perform should be a simple one initially. It is to be something for the benefit of the entire family, like setting or clearing the table, taking out the trash, feeding the family pet. *Keeping his own room clean and making his bed don't count.* These are things he should be expected to do for himself. The child should participate in selection of the task for which he will be responsible.

There is no pay for performance of the agreed-upon chore. It is the child's contribution, just as it is mom's to cook dinner or dad's to mow the lawn (or the reverse, as the case may be). Children are the beneficiaries of a wide variety of benefits and services provided by their parents. As they grow, therefore, they should return the favor, in whatever ways they are able to do so. The allowance is just one of the many benefits received by the child. This share, however small, of the family income, he receives because he is a member of the family, and he should be expected to carry out his responsibilities to the family for the same reason.

Failure to perform the assigned chore must not result in withholding of the allowance. To do so destroys any hope of using this system to teach responsibility. Admittedly, it's a tempting device to use to get the trash carried out. Don't do it.

What about letting kids earn extra money at home? Parents who can afford to hire their own kids to do jobs besides their family responsibilities should do so. This is especially helpful for younger children. It gives them a chance to get a little extra money for things they want. It also serves to introduce them to the concept of work and the relationship between money and personal effort.

Once each year, preferably on the child's birthday, an annual review should be held to decide the amount of the coming year's allowance and which family responsibilities the child will assume for the year.

The Rules—A Summary

Here is a summary of the rules that make up this preferred system.

1. The system you will use should be explained to the child at the time it is started.

2. The allowance is initiated at around 6 or 7.

3. The amount should be a reasonable one, and increased as the child grows older when it is expected to cover a wider range of the child's expenses.

4. The parent and child should agree in advance on the kinds of expenses the allowance will cover.

5. The allowance should be paid weekly on the same day each week to younger children, and monthly to kids in their mid-teens.

6. The allowance should always be paid and should not be based upon performance of chores. it should never be withheld as discipline or to influence the child's behavior.

7. Once the amount of the allowance has been established, the child should not be given more money just because he has spent all he had.

8. The child should be allowed to make his own spending decisions.

9. The child should be assigned an agreed-upon chore (or chores), which he will be responsible to do for the benefit of the entire family.

10. No pay is to be expected or received for doing the job.

11. Failure to do the assigned chore must not result in reduction or elimination of the allowance.

12. Parents who are able to pay their kids for doing *extra* jobs around the house should do so.

13. An annual review should be held yearly on the child's birthday to set the allowance and chores for the coming year.

The Alternatives

As a parent, you may be using or may be tempted to use methods other than the one just described. Most other systems have drawbacks relative to the no-strings allowance plus responsibilities one. Let's examine a few of those drawbacks.

When money is given only as it is requested by the child, conflict may not be inevitable, but the stage is certainly set for problems. This approach has drawbacks for kids as well as parents: Having no system puts the youngster in the position of "begging" and the parent in the position of having to make an endless series of individual decisions that may involve: (1) figuring out how much you've already given him this month; (2)

asking what it's for and deciding each time if that's something he should have; (3) even looking in your wallet or purse to decide whether *you* can afford it.

Here's the comment of one mother who thinks allowances are not good for young children: "When they ask for money, they get it, if they deserve it, and if they have a good reason for needing it. I think it's better to know in advance what small children want to spend their money on." This might not be a big problem when children are small, but it is likely to become one with teenagers, and it may be difficult to change the rules later on. The most serious defect of this random method of giving the kids money, however, is that it contributes absolutely nothing to the objectives of teaching either money skills or responsibility.

The commission system—paying kids for work done at home—is a big improvement over the random method. Here a kid will learn something about the value of money and its relationship to personal effort and working. The commission system eliminates begging. If a kid wants something, the opportunity to earn it is available. The money he earns means somethig to him if it's tied directly to his own efforts. Kids like to earn their own money for a variety of reasons, and these are some of the reasons they give: "because it's your own money if you earn it"; "it is a good feeling of accomplishment"; "so that when you are older you have a better chance to earn money."

In spite of these positive aspects, however, there are two drawbacks to a pure commission system. One is that it fails to provide a predictable source of income for the child, making it difficult for parents to teach the child to budget or save. The major drawback is that, taken alone, it does not teach the concept of sharing responsibilities. When a kid on the commission system is asked to help out with something around home, his response is likely to be, "How much will you pay me?"

The problem with an allowance paid only when assigned chores are done is that jobs at home are done for the wrong reason—they are done to *earn* the allowance when they should be done as an expected contribution to the family effort. In the process, another benefit can also disappear. One advantage of the allowance is that it eliminates the necessity to be constantly deciding how much money the kids should get. But if chores must be done to earn it, you're almost back to where you would be without one. Will you pay the allowance if the job is three-quarters done, or half done? How much will they get under these circumstances? What if the kids miss doing their job one week because they have final exams or get invited to go on a trip with a friend? Keeping the allowance separate helps keep things much simpler.

Allowances, then, are useful for parents and kids for many

reasons. But unless they are used correctly, it is possible that little will be accomplished.

The system we have recommended, combined with a positive expectation of success on the part of the parent, offers the best prospect of teaching children the values we want them to learn.

CHAPTER 6

THE FAMILY BUDGET— INVOLVE YOUR KIDS

You've been appointed as the person in charge of the annual company picnic. It's been a very profitable year, so there's more money available than last year. Your job is to spend the money that's been allotted, but no more. To accomplish this, you need a budget. On the "income" side is what the company has given you to spend on the picnic. On the "expense" or "cost" side you'll list how the money will be spent, item by item. Your objective: to break even.

Businesses do exactly the same thing each year. As its starting point, management estimates sales. Then it estimates what it will cost to produce those sales. These costs include rent or mortgage payments on the plant or buildings, the costs of materials, wages and fringe benefits for employees, and taxes. The company's objective, unlike yours for the picnic, is *not* to break even. Its objective is to have some of the money received from sales left over after payment of all necessary expenses—to make a profit.

A family might be looked at in the same way. Each month there is a certain amount of income. With that money, the family's expenses are paid. If the costs of operating the family exceed its income, the difference must come from one of two places: it must be taken from savings or it must be borrowed. And just like a company, a family's objective each month is to have its income exceed its necessary costs—to make "a profit." Of course, families generally don't usually use the term "profit." Economists refer to the family income left over after the house payment, food, clothing, transportation, taxes, and other required expenses, as discretionary income. That excess can be spent on extras, saved, or invested.

If a family were to look at itself in this way—as a business enterprise—it would require a budget, and it is difficult to imagine a family that would not benefit from preparing and using one. Later in this chapter you will find a hypothetical budget for a family of four that you can compare with your own.

What do your children know about *your* family budget?

Ignorance Is Not Bliss

While people are increasingly open in their discussions of subjects like human relations, politics, and religion, money somehow remains a taboo topic. "The taboo surrounding money," according to Herb Goldberg and Robert T. Lewis in *Money Madness*, "was traditionally shared with subjects such as sex, aggression, and death. Today it stands practically alone." These authors quote James A. Knight, a professor of psychiatry at Tulane University School of Medicine. Knight writes that his patients "show far less resistance in relating hatred for their parents or in disclosing sexual perversities than in discussing their money status or transactions. It is as if they equated money with their innermost being."

If this taboo encompassed only discussions with friends, acquaintances, or strangers, there would be no need for concern. But this taboo encompasses the family as well—especially the children. Many parents keep the details of family finances a secret from their children. Some think the children will worry too much about money, especially if the monthly budget is a delicate balancing act. Others keep the children from knowing because they are afraid that their kids will discuss the family's net worth with all their friends. Yet, these same parents may deal with their children openly about other family matters, trusting that openness and honesty instead of secrecy will teach the children to be open and honest.

This same attitude should prevail with family finances. When children are kept ignorant of how much money the family gets and spends, Goldberg and Lewis write, "They are likely to either underestimate or overestimate the family's wealth. They may scrimp unnecessarily or spend recklessly. They will most likely use poor judgment in financial matters. When the time comes to face their own financial transactions, they feel insecure and ill-equipped and uncomfortable about asking for help since they have learned by example that money is a taboo subject."

Children, then, can and should be taught about the family's finances. Far too many youngsters reach maturity with no real idea of the valiant struggle their parents are engaged in to keep things together financially. When the brakes on the family car need to be relined, the children only know that somehow it gets taken care of. New tires, a new washing machine, or new carpeting magically appear. Where the money comes from is not their concern. And unless they are shown what these things cost and the decisions that had to be made about their purchase, children have no reason to be concerned.

Parents who complain that their children's *only* concern is getting movie tickets for this weekend and having some "decent" clothes to wear when school starts in September usually have only themselves to blame for their kids' lack of consideration. Such attitudes generally arise from ignorance.

When children are given a reasonable picture of the family's situation, they will know where the money comes from that pays for movies and clothes. For the parents, there is a selfish and absolutely legitimate payoff. It can get your kids "off of your back." As previously discussed, the child who has a distorted view of what is actually available often makes unreasonable demands on the family's income. But when that child is shown that the new carpeting cost $1,200, which constitutes five months of the family's discretionary income, he is much less likely to insist on three pairs of forty-dollar shoes as basic to his September school wardrobe.

Very young children, of course, cannot be expected to understand the family budget. But youngsters of 8 or 9 can understand enough to have a basic notion of where the family's money comes from and where it goes. And teenagers should be able to understand it all.

One family used the technique of allowing their kids to take turns writing the checks for each month's bills. The parents had no problems saying "we can't afford it" after the kids went through this exercise.

Young children can, however, surprise you. One enterprising

7-year-old decided she would make some extra money by writing a book. She called it *A Cat Book*, a richly illustrated five- or six-page volume with very little accompanying text. After all, how much could she say about her two cats? Three individual "books" were produced, each an original, whereupon she went forth to sell them for 10¢ each. One sale was made at the house next door—and that was it. Her father, obviously pleased with this display of enterprise, tried to buy the remaining two books. "No," she responded after a moment's reflection, "that wouldn't be any new money for the family."

Explaining the Budget

For the typical family, one of the great puzzles to solve is: "Where does all the money go?" Therefore, when a budget is used, it focuses on the spending side and not on income. Yet many kids do not understand the sources of family income. Where the money comes from is as much of a mystery as where it goes. So don't forget to start with your income in explaining the budget to a child. Then you can show them how the money is spent.

Let's assume you have a total family income from all sources of $16,000 a year. Your two teen-age children know that the family's income is $1,333 a month. That seems like a lot. They also know you have bills to pay. But what they can't understand is why there's so little left at the end of the month. The following budget will be different from yours, but let's see what you could show them using this hypothetical budget for a family of four.

Monthly Budget — Family of Four

INCOME (MONTHLY)		$1,333
Less Deductions For:		
Federal Income Tax	$110	
Social Security Tax	67	
State Income Tax	15	
Medical/Dental Insurance	25	
Other Miscellaneous Deductions	20	237
TAKE-HOME PAY		$1,096
FIXED PAYMENTS		
Mortgage on Home	300	
Property Tax	40	
Insurance (Life, Fire, etc.)	35	
Auto Payment (or Boat, etc.)	100	475
BALANCE AFTER FIXED PAYMENTS		621

Food	180	
Household Expenses and		
Repair	75	
Utilities	85	
Transportation	80	
Clothing	100	520

BALANCE AFTER ALL EXPENSES   101

Many of the items in this family's budget are expenses with which the kids are already familiar. They know about the items for food and clothing. They help shop at the store. They also know that utilities cost money too, since they've been reminded for years to turn the lights out when they're not being used and not to waste hot water by standing in the shower for 45 minutes. But what's this item for social security taxes? And why are there so many other deductions before you even get home with your check? They may have known about the mortgage payments, but why $480 a year for property taxes? Where does that money go, and what's it used for? (Some answers to these questions are provided in Chapter 14.)

The "bottom line" is that this particular family's budget leaves them $101 at the end of each month that is not allocated for some specific purpose. When the car is paid off, or if there is no car payment, it's $201 per month.

Let's use $200 per month, and see where this discretionary income might go. Some of the money might be spent on family entertainment like movies, eating out, or even a weekend trip. There's nothing for that in the budget. Some might be used to repair a broken bicycle or to buy some new kitchen curtains that are on sale. Some of it might go into a vacation fund for a family trip next summer. There might even be an item in the budget for allowances. The balance, if any, can go into family savings. Unless, of course, the washing machine quits for the final time this month. To replace it takes all the family's extra money for perhaps a month and a half. Or unless the roof needs replacement this year. Depending on the type of roof, that could take *all* this family's discretionary income for six to twelve months. What if the family needs a new car, or one of the kids wants a new bike?

What can you teach your kids with this "budget review"? First, it shows them in a very clear way that the money supply is limited. It also shows them that parents must make difficult choices as to how to spend what *is* available. This month's decision may be whether or not it's time to start Sharon's visits to the orthodontist. That may cost $1,000 or more over the next two years. Next month it might mean choosing whether to pay for ice skating and tennis lessons for the kids or new drapes for the living room. Each month the choices tend to be different.

Once kids understand this process, it will make family life happier, more livable, *now*. Children in the know are far less likely to make unreasonable demands on the family's resources. Also, children will be able to feel that they are being included in an important aspect of family life.

The budget review is also invaluable training for adulthood. Why should each new generation be forced to "reinvent the wheel," to figure out how to manage the finances of a family on their own? Yet few children ever receive much of the benefit of the painful lessons learned by their parents. One of the most important lessons they can learn is how to allocate a scarce resource like money. Even when they are not making the final decisions, seeing that difficult choices must be made can keep them out of a lot of trouble when they strike out on their own.

CHAPTER 7

KIDS—THEY'RE EXPENSIVE!

"But Mom," Billy, age 12, is complaining, "you know my old bike can't be fixed, and I don't have one single friend who doesn't have a ten-speed."

"I've told you before, your dad has told you, too—we can't afford $150 right now for a bike. You'll just have to wait."

Billy feels that his parents are not being honest with him. His parents are telling him they can't afford $150, when they just bought themselves a new car a few months back for over $5,000. He also feels they are being selfish, buying things for themselves but nothing for him.

A 12-year-old who wants a bike might look at the car as something his parents bought just for themselves. He doesn't stop to think that their new car will probably haul him to a wide variety of activities and will go to the market to buy his food. The fact that it is new means that his parents are assured of getting to work to earn the money for the family.

The unfortunate aspect of this situation is that Billy's parents *are* being honest with him. Right now, they can't afford $150. Buying the car means paying out an additional $115 a month for three years, and their budget was already pretty tight before the car. The trouble is, Billy doesn't know all this. His parents have never told him.

As pointed out in Chapter 6, the children most likely to make unreasonable demands on the family's resources are those who know the least about the family's financial picture. It is possible, however, that even after an explanation of the family budget, a kid still will have only a hazy understanding of the amount of money his parents are spending on him. It might never occur to him that part of the rent or mortgage payment pays for the extra space the family needs because of him — an additional bedroom, for example. The same is probably true of most other family outlays, from utilities to medical insurance.

There is, then, another way to use your family budget for educational purposes, if it seems to be appropriate. You can show your youngsters how much it actually costs to raise them. This includes *all* the costs — not just the cash you give them to spend on themselves.

Let's assume you have a 15-year-old daughter whose demands on your family budget have finally gotten out of hand. You're aware that it costs plenty to support her, but *she* has no idea how much — and you may not be sure yourself. The "everyone has one but me" routine has finally become too expensive. You can't keep up anymore.

You've tried to explain why you can't provide everything she wants. But it hasn't made much of a dent. Her appetite for more and more things grows by the week. She shows few signs that she understands how much money you *do* give her. She seems unable to appreciate the value of money; and she won't save a dime!

Maybe things got to this point because you've never used any systematic approach to the subject of money. She's spent what she could get from you as fast as she got it. Maybe her friends' parents give their kids more than you can afford — or more than you think 15-year-olds should get.

Whatever the reasons, showing her what you're really spending on her every month will at least give her a realistic view of your family's financial picture and her place in it. There will be some families where this approach is not applicable. If your family's income is well above average, your child may not be impressed by the proportion of family income that goes toward the costs of raising him. On the other hand, if there is no extra money at all, chances are that your kids are not making unrealistic demands on the family income; what they have they probably must earn themselves. Most families, however, fall somewhere between rich and poor. Showing the kids what they cost is a way to bring them into touch with the reality of limits.

One caution. Making kids feel guilty about how much they cost must be carefully avoided. The objective here is simply to bring a kid face to face with a reality he seems to be having trouble accepting. The long-term effects of guilt on a child are a poor trade-off for obtaining desired behavior today.

How to Figure the Costs

"... the sheer cost of raising a child is enough to make any potential parent pause—and current parents shudder. At 1977 prices, a family of four, earning between $16,500 and $20,000 a year, can expect to spend $54,297 to support a child to the age of 18, excluding the expenses of higher education," according to *Newsweek's* special report, "Saving the Family" (May 15, 1978). The article goes on to give the cost breakdown for various income levels for "what a family of four would spend over 18 years to raise a child in a northwestern city. Costs include food, clothing, education (except college), and medical care after birth, at 1977 prices."

Family Income	Total Cost per Kid
Under $10,500	$24,727
$10,500 — $13,500	$32,414
$16,500 — $20,000	$54,297

On the next page is a hypothetical budget for a family of four, two adults and two kids. Family income is $18,000 a year, or $1,500 a month. This budget is intended only to be somewhat typical, and your budget may be quite different in terms of how you allocate your income. Nevertheless, these figures are useful to illustrate the cost of raising a child, and if you insert your own figures on the blank budget, you can show a kid what his or her cost is to the family for one month. That amount multiplied by twelve is the annual expense; multiplying that total by eighteen gives the cost of raising a child to the age of 18.

A few words of explanation as to how the family's costs are allocated on this budget.

No cost was attributed to the child for taxes (for the sake of simplicity). No cost was assigned for the car payment, assuming the family would have bought the car with or without kids. However, if it was a new station wagon bought to haul kids and their equipment around in, that would call for a cost figure in the kids' column. No figure is included for contributions. No items in

MONTHLY BUDGET (Two Adults, Two Children)

ITEM	TOTAL FOR FAMILY	FOR ONE CHILD %	COST
INCOME	$1500		
EXPENSES & INVESTMENTS			
DEDUCTIONS FROM PAY			
Federal Income Taxes	130		
Social Security Taxes	75		
Misc. (incl. State Income Tax)	40		
	245		
FIXED EXPENSES			
Rent or Mortgage (incl. Prop. Tax)	340	20	68
Insurance (Property)	20	20	4
Automobile Payment	115		
	475		72
HOUSEHOLD/MEDICAL/AUTO			
Food & Household Supplies	210	25	52
Household Maintenance & Repairs	40	25	10
Utilities: Heat, electric, water	80	25	20
Utilities: Telephone	20	25	5
Medical: Doctor, Dentist, Medicine	40	25	10
Medical/Dental Insurance	30	25	8
Auto: Gas, oil, tires	50	20	
Maint. & Repair	25	20	
Insurance	25	20	20
	520		125
PERSONAL & RECREATION			
Personal Expenses (Beauty Shop,			
haircuts, dry cleaning, cosmetics, etc.)	35	20	7
Contributions	25		
Recreation & Entertainment	60	25	15
Vacations	50	25	12
	170		34
SAVINGS AND INVESTMENTS			
Insurance (Life)	30		
Savings	40		
Other Investments	20		
	90		
	1500		231

MONTHLY BUDGET (Two Adults, Two Children)

ITEM	TOTAL FOR FAMILY	FOR ONE CHILD %	COST
INCOME			
EXPENSES & INVESTMENTS			
DEDUCTIONS FROM PAY			
Federal Income Taxes			
Social Security Taxes			
Misc. (incl. State Income Tax)			
FIXED EXPENSES			
Rent or Mortgage (incl. Prop. Tax)			
Insurance (Property)			
Automobile Payment			
HOUSEHOLD/MEDICAL/AUTO			
Food & Household Supplies			
Household Maintenance & Repairs			
Utilities: Heat, electric, water			
Utilities: Telephone			
Medical: Doctor, Dentist, Medicine			
Medical/Dental Insurance			
Auto: Gas, oil, tires			
Maint. & Repair			
Insurance			
PERSONAL & RECREATION			
Personal Expenses (Beauty Shop, haircuts, dry cleaning, cosmetics, etc.)			
Contributions			
Recreation & Entertainment			
Vacations			
SAVINGS AND INVESTMENTS			
Insurance (Life)			
Savings			
Other Investments			

63

the savings and investments category were attributed to the child as an expense because these items would most likely be there even if there were no children. However, each of the savings and investment items obviously is there as much for the benefit of the kids as for the parents' sake. You might decide how to handle this last section based on what you are saving for.

As for the percentages used on the other items, they are assumptions that probably will not fit any family exactly. Some kids eat everything in sight; others don't. Some kids take care of their clothes; some destroy them. Some mothers run a full-time chauffeur's service. That raises the auto costs. It all depends on each family.

As for the totals, the results for this family are quite similar to the national figures. The monthly total of $236 equals $2,832 for one year, and that gives a total cost of $50,976 as the eighteen-year cost of raising the child. The *Newsweek* figure was $54,297.

This budget does not include some potentially significant items. For example, it includes no provision for ten-speed bikes, trips to Europe, or cars for the kids. These are extras, and the money—if it is to be spent—must be found in one or more of the existing budget items. The largest potential cost that does not appear, of course, is college.

According to *Newsweek*'s figures, the 1960 cost of one year at a private college was $1,528. The 1978 cost was $4,363. If costs continue to rise in this way, a four-year education at a private college will soon be a $20,000 outlay, or $40,000 for a family sending two youngsters through school. Costs at state colleges and universities are somewhat less, but the costs are shown simply to point out that adding college to all the other expenses of raising kids makes them a large investment indeed.

Remember that the objective of showing a youngster how much he costs is not to make him feel guilty about asking for a dollar. It is to introduce a youngster who seems to feel he is not getting "his share" to some fundamental realities. If this can be properly accomplished, perhaps a more orderly approach to sharing the family's money can be initiated.

The Total Providers

In spite of the squeeze that inflation exerts on budgets, to-day's average American family lives better on a higher real in-come than has generally been the case in the past. Along with the higher living standard, however, has come a feeling on the part of many parents that they should be able to provide for all of their children's needs. This proves to be an impossible undertaking for most families, probably because the "needs" of children might be described as "open-ended." Still, any suggestion that parents are not able to be the "total providers"—that the children have unmet needs—causes many of these parents to view themselves as failures.

Parents have rights, too. After all, if the business of raising kids meant taking on a whole list of responsibilities, financial and otherwise, plus transferring all of our rights to the children, who would be interested? The objective is to balance your responsibilities to your children with the responsibilities you have to yourself. Spoiling children by being overly responsive to their "needs" can have an unintended result. "The spoiled child is not a happy creature even in his own home," according to Dr. Benjamin Spock.

Dr. Spock was describing infants' behavior, but buying older children everything they want can be expected to yield the same result. If all a 12-year-old's friends have a ten-speed, a parent should not feel guilty telling him he'll have to earn the money to buy his own. In fact, a strong case can be made for not giving him the money, for letting him earn it himself, even if you'd never miss it.

Parents should not defer living their own lives until their children are raised. Many parents, however, deny themselves luxuries for years, saving money to pay college costs for children who may have little interest in applying themselves when the time arrives. Taking that long-anticipated trip to Spain, or buying a camper or a new home, should not cause feelings of guilt on the part of a parent. If you can afford to send your kids to college, by all means do so, but don't feel guilty if you can't.

As Ann Landers puts it in an article entitled "Parents: What Do You Owe Your Children?": "You do not owe them every minute of your day or every ounce of your energy. Nor do you owe them round-the-clock chauffeur service, baton twirling lessons, horseback riding lessons (and $90 boots), singing lessons, summer camp, ski outfits, and ten-speed bikes, a Honda or a car when they turn 16—you don't owe them a trip to Europe when they graduate from high school."

The conclusion: Rights and responsibilities are a two-way street. It is possible for families to live together under circumstances where the rights of all family members to share in the family's income are respected and observed, where there are mutual responsibilities that are fair to both parents and children.

CHAPTER 8

SINGLE PARENTS—
MULTIPLE PROBLEMS

Margaret was married at age 24. She continued to work another two years until the birth of her first child. From that point on she stayed home. Thirteen years later, at the time of her divorce, Margaret had three children aged 11, 10, and 7. She retained custody of the children after the divorce and was awarded the house, which was located in an expensive neighborhood. She considered selling the house but was reluctant to move the kids away from their friends; also, she discovered that she could not rent any reasonable alternative for as little as the mortgage payments on the home.

Margaret went back to work, and after eleven years out of the job market, considered herself fortunate to find a reasonably good job. But even with her salary and child support payments, the family's income suffered a substantial drop.

Initially, Margaret avoided discussing any changes in the family's financial situation with the children, preferring not to worry them about such things. The problem was that everything else in their upper-income neighborhood stayed the same. Her children's friends and their spending patterns remained the same, so her children continued to take their tennis lessons, weekend trips, and go to summer camps as if nothing had changed. In less than one year, however, Margaret was forced to admit that her assets had dropped sharply. There was simply not enough money to maintain their former standard of living. Margaret was forced to do what she should have done at the beginning. She was forced to be honest, to tell her kids what the situation actually was, to include them in the family partnership.

Facing up to the Changes

There is a strong temptation for any individual to "carry on," even in the face of economic reversals. As in Margaret's case, it may be a reluctance to admit to the children that circumstances have changed. But beyond that, few people willingly reduce their standards of living. For the single parent, however, facing reality is usually a necessity, and one that should be dealt with as quickly as possible.

One of the economies of marriage is the elimination of one person's rent or mortgage payment. Separation reverses that process, so a decline in the overall availability of money is likely no matter who takes the children. This decline in resources is usually accompanied by additional expenses. If it is the father who has custody of the children and they are young, he will face new expenses in the areas of child care and perhaps housekeeping. If the mother takes the children and she has not worked for several years, what she can earn, even with some child support payments, will seldom permit her the same level of spending as before. One mother remarked, "I haven't worked for over eight years. Do you have any idea how little I can make until I get some more experience?" But even a woman who worked during the years she was married will experience a substantial drop in income once her husband's contribution is no longer available. Yet the single parent has many, perhaps most, of the same living expenses as a two-parent family.

Obviously, for most single parents honesty with their children is at a premium; the new reality must be shared. But there are important benefits beyond economic survival that can result from sharing matters of family finance with the children. A child who has a realistic picture of the family's situation is less likely to make unreasonable demands on the family's resources. One recent study concludes that there is less fighting about money in those families where children participate in (or at least listen to) family talks about money management. Inclusion in discussions of family finance will also provide the child with a sense of participation, a feeling of being a member in the family partnership. The lessons they will learn—that managing a family's money involves making difficult decisions, plus the realities of what it costs to live—are things they will need to know as adults.

The Osmond family, most recently represented on television by Donnie and Marie, followed the practice of making each of the children a member of the "family board of directors" when they reached the age of 8. Columnist Jack Anderson interviewed the parents for *Parade* Magazine (August 27, 1978) and, according to Mrs. Osmond, "On family night, we would discuss finances." All the family's business was open to the kids, and they had their say about how the money was spent. "At a very early age, our children were learning the business of mortgages, grocery bills and financing."

The benefits that can result from an open discussion of family money matters will accrue to any family, but economic realities indicate that these benefits are of even greater importance to the family headed by a single parent.

The focus to this point has been adjustment to change. But not all single-parent families experience change; many of today's families start off being single-parent families from the beginning. These include an increasing number of single men and women who adopt children, and women who have children with the intention of raising them on their own. The number of single-parent families continues to increase. One child in every six now lives in a single-parent family, and it is estimated that, of every ten children born in the seventies, four will spend at least part of their childhood living with one parent. An example of this pattern is offered by James A. Levine, writing in *Psychology Today* (June 1978). He cites the case of an 8-year-old named Susan who, after a month of second grade in a suburban school, told her mother that she felt "funny" because there were no other children like her in her class. "Like her" meant that she was from a single-parent family. However, when Susan and her mother went over the class list together, they discovered that twenty-one of Susan's thirty-three classmates came from single-parent families.

Obviously, the single-parent family that comes into being for reasons other than death or divorce does not face the same difficult financial *transitions*. However, it is also true that where there is only one parent, no matter how that came to be the case, financial flexibility is reduced because there is only one possible income. For all single-parent families, both the benefits of an honest discussion of money matters and a sharing of family responsibilities by the children assume even greater importance than in two-parent families.

The Necessity of a Budget

Putting together a workable budget is a valuable starting point for the single parent. In your budget, child-care expenses may be a major item. Your personal entertainment budget may be higher as a single person than if you were married. When your children are old enough to understand, your budget will help them see where the money is spent. A 9-year-old, for example, may be too young to stay by himself, but he is certainly old enough to understand that you have to pay a babysitter. Allowances can be put in the budget as well.

The allowance, in fact, might prove to be a significant budget item if you follow the practice that a number of families have found extremely useful as their children grow older. One woman describes it this way: "We give the kids an allowance large enough to cover almost all of their expenses. This includes enough money to buy their clothes in addition to the normal things allowances cover, such as their own entertainment and buying things that they need. If they want anything else, they have to earn the money themselves."

Determining the size of an allowance that will cover all these things might be difficult at first, but doing it will greatly simplify budgeting and will virtually eliminate the badgering for additional money that most parents experience.

The Partnership

A single parent needs to form a working partnership with the kids. This partnership goes well beyond giving them a frank and honest appraisal of the financial picture. Cooperation is needed in many areas. A 5-year-old can keep her own room clean. She can make her own bed, perhaps not to your standards, but perfection need not be a requirement. By the time she's 7, she'll have it right and will be helping at other things as well. The older the child, the greater the responsibilities that he or she can and should be assigned.

The single parent should make sure the children understand that privileges and responsibilities go hand in hand. Their privileges include participating in the family's activities and sharing in the family's income, even if there is very little extra cash left over at the end of the month. As the children mature, they should be made to understand that their share is not measured solely in terms of the size of their allowance. It is also measured in terms of a roof overhead; a utility bill that has been paid so that the television, radio, and lights work; food in the refrigerator for breakfast; and a pair of tennis shoes. Most kids really never appreciate these things. They are just there, taken for granted because they've always been there. Items like these are easy to identify but there are many more, so many that it's worth listing a few of the more significant ones in case you are feeling guilty about asking your 12-year-old to clean her room, wash the dishes, and help with the laundry.

Someone in your household has to perform the following tasks in order that your family may operate. If you're doing it alone without any help, then:

> You have to do the shopping—for food, clothes, and other necessities.

> You must prepare the meals—possibly including school lunches.

> You have to set and clear the table, wash the dishes, and clean up the kitchen after each meal.

> You must do the laundry so that everyone in your family has clean clothes to wear.

> You have to clean the house or apartment.

> You must provide transportation once your kids have friends and activities that are outside your immediate neighborhood.

> You are in charge of coordinating trips to the doctor, dentist, piano lessons, and Little League practice.

> You are also in charge of paying the bills and trying to balance the checkbook.

> You may even end up feeding the dog and the fish.

This list represents only a part of what you do in your spare time, while you are not working at and getting to and from your full-time job.

The partnership with the kids the financial questions central to this book. The old adage that says "Time is money" applies here. Many single parents with a full-time job and a few extra dollars a month try to hire outside help for housecleaning and chores, even if it's only for one or two days a month. If the kids really help out around the house, that money can be left in the family for extras—entertainment, lessons, sports equipment. A full day of household help costs a lot of money these days, and an extra $25 or $50 a month can buy a lot of family fun.

Single parents who cannot afford outside help will do the housework themselves until the kids are old enough to help. They have no choice. However, once the kids can take over part, or even all, of the household duties, they can make a real contribution to the family's income. The parent who comes home from a hard day at work only to face cooking and housework is not likely to turn in as good a performance on the job the following day, and promotions and raises are normally based upon performance. In many jobs, such as sales, where there is a direct relationship between effort and income, the contribution the kids can make is even more obvious.

Parents who feel guilty about asking for some help from their kids should reexamine the preceding list, and then reexamine their feelings. Can you think of any reason the children should not help? How else will they learn to become responsible individuals? And how else will they learn the skills they will need as adults? So even when money is not a factor, giving kids responsibilities at home is important. It can also teach them something about the relationship between time and money.

Any kid who knows exactly what his responsibilities are for the week must learn to budget his time in order to accomplish everything he wants to get done. If he wants to go somewhere on Saturday, he'll have to have the lawn mowed or the carpet vacuumed by Friday. If he wants to earn some extra money, he'll have to work that in. If he fails to plan ahead, missing the Saturday trip will help him remember the next time. Learning to budget time is at least as important as learning to budget money. And make sure you don't succumb to "It's easier to do it myself." If you do, only one thing is certain. You will continue to do that task yourself. Take the time and invest the energy to teach the child to do something and do it right.

The short-term advantages of getting the kids to join the family partnership are yours. You are getting the help you need. But the longer-term advantage is theirs. They are learning things they need to know. They are also learning the meaning of cooperation and that there is more than one kind of sharing: there is fun to be shared, but there are also jobs to be shared. The real world is like that.

Dealing with Individual Problems

The response you get from your children to the partnership idea may vary from child to child. You may have a daughter who is naturally sympathetic and cooperative, who actually asks you if there is something she can do. Your son may drag his heels; if he cares about your plight at all, he hides it so well you can't tell. One mother describes her pair of kids as follows: "Hank is 13 and he's a real hustler. He does the dishes every morning, seven days a week, takes the trash out on Wednesday, and does all the yard work—twice a month during the summer and monthly in the winter. But he does lots more things too. He always needs something, so he's always looking for ways to make extra money at home. I let him wash the car, things like that. Last summer I paid him 25¢ a bag for getting a lot of ice plant out of the backyard. My daughter Rhonda is 15. I pay her $20 a month to keep the house clean, but she never quite gets it done. She has a million excuses. Sometimes she's just too busy, sometimes it's homework, sometimes a friend called on the phone. But there's one thing about our arrangement that really frustrates me. It's not just that I have to do the work she doesn't get around to doing, but when she doesn't earn the $20, she calls her Dad on the phone and ends up getting it from him."

There are three problem areas in this mother's relationship with her daughter. The first problem is quite simple—this mother works full time to support the family and needs her daughter's help. The second problem involves her ex-husband, who is seriously undermining the mother's position every time he gives his daughter money she should have earned at home doing her assigned jobs. The third and most serious problem, from a long-term point of view, is that the daughter is forming some bad habits. The message she is getting from her father is that if you're sloppy about carrying out your responsibilities, it's okay, someone will come along and bail you out. This mother's best first step in solving her problems with her daughter is to have a serious talk with her ex-husband. He may not care that his ex-wife has to do her daughter's unfinished chores, but he should have some interest in seeing his daughter grow up to be a responsible adult.

This mother might consider using the following approach with her daughter. It is a technique that can be used if it is used carefully, one that has been used successfully by some parents in cases where logical explanations and requests for help—even patriotic appeals to the necessity for mutual support within the family—fell upon deaf ears. This technique can be used when a child simply refuses to carry out any family responsibilities whatsoever. It involves the selective withdrawal of services that are provided to the child. If your son won't keep his room clean, don't drive him to soccer practice. After all, if he doesn't have time to clean his room, he doesn't have time to play soccer. If getting your daughter to set the table and help do the dishes proves to be so frustrating that you've given up trying, see how she likes cooking her own meals and doing all her own laundry for a while. The objective, of course, is simply to get the child's attention. Each parent must decide what it is that will accomplish that goal. Once the child is listening, it may be possible to have a talk about the mutual responsibilities and support that members of every family must give each other if they are to live together.

The Other Parent

Relationships with the absent parent often create difficulties for the one who has the children. "I always feel like the heavy," says a divorced working mother who is trying to raise two children. "The kids ask me for something and I say no. Then they go to their father, and he steps up like the big hero and buys it for them." Some degree of cooperation must be obtained from the other parent, usually the ex-husband. It's not that he should never buy anything for his kids or that he should never give them any money. What is important is that his gifts do not directly counter what the mother is trying to accomplish.

Some mothers resent the fact that, while they have to scrimp and save just to get by, the kids' dad can come along and take them on an expensive trip, one she simply couldn't afford. From her point of view, he gets all the glory while she gets all the work. It's a problem with no easy answer. It hardly seems reasonable for the mother to deny the kids a trip just so she can avoid feeling resentful. It's probably better to accept things for what they are, to be happy that the kids have a chance to do some things that they would otherwise miss.

If you are the absent parent, the one who does not live with your children, a realization on your part that money and love are not substitutes for one another will go a long way toward solving the types of problems under discussion. Spending large amounts of money on your children when they are with you will not convince them that you love them. It may, in fact, have the opposite effect. So give your ex-spouse a break. She (once in a while, he) is probably struggling to do the best job she can in raising your kids. Don't make it tougher by taking actions that provoke feelings of resentment in your ex-spouse, because these feelings are likely to spill over into the relationship you have with your children.

The best possible solution for difficulties between single parents and their former spouses over the children and money is to attempt to reach agreement on some basics. Probably the most important issue involves giving the kids money. If a mother is attempting to teach the kids to handle money responsibly by paying them an allowance and requiring them to budget in order to get things they want, extra money from dad when the kids run short will only frustrate the mother's efforts. Kids will never learn important lessons in responsibility if help is only a telephone call away. Ex-spouses who agree about what things the kids should learn can be asked to cooperate and make sure that money or gifts do not frustrate efforts being made to teach the kids valuable lessons.

Comments on Child Support

Child support for the single parent exists for a particular reason. Not all children understand this reason. As they grow older, in fact, many come to believe that the child-support check should be for their personal use. One mother who was raising two boys was confronted by the older on this question. She responded, "Okay, at the end of the month I'll write you a check for half of the child support I receive. In return, you will write me a check for one-third of the rent, utilities, food, and other expenses that we have in maintaining our family." A quick calculation by this youngster led him to conclude that this would be a very bad deal, and nothing more was heard from him on the subject.

It simply must be made clear to kids that child-care payments are for the principal purpose of paying rent, buying food, paying for gasoline for the car, and the like—not for buying tennis rackets, riding boots, ice skates, or Cokes. Of course, some of those things may well be purchased, if there's extra money. But kids should be told what the check is all about. Parents whose children are giving them problems on this score should go over the family's budget with them as recommended in the preceding chapters. Many single parents seem to have a problem spending any money on themselves when they are receiving child support. Should you feel guilty if you treat yourself to an evening out when earlier in the day you have told your youngster that the family cannot afford ice skating lessons right now? You shouldn't! Ice skating lessons are a luxury. That evening out may be essential to your mental stability. So treat yourself and don't worry about it.

When college is part of a family's future plans, an unusual problem arises that few parents seem to properly anticipate. Take the case of Beverly, divorced and raising one son, Jeff. Jeff was 17 and a high school senior. His father sent a child-support check for $200 each month. In addition, he had agreed to help Jeff with college expenses.

In the year Jeff became 18, two things happened: the support checks stopped, and Jeff started college. His father now sends the $200 directly to Jeff to cover school expenses.

Where does this leave Beverly? If Jeff lives at home while he goes to school, her expenses remain exactly the same, but her income has dropped by $200 a month. Even if he lives at school, that only reduces food expenses somewhat. The $200 had been used to help make the house payment, pay insurance premiums, and cover the many expenses of maintaining a home.

According to one prominent firm of attorneys that specializes in divorce, women tend to have an emotional commitment to keeping things "as they were"—to maintaining the home as a place the kids can come back to. Unfortunately, this commitment often extends well beyond the time when the women will be receiving the outside financial assistance they have come to depend on. "Failure to anticipate what will be happening financially during these years is the largest single problem our clients come up against in the years following a divorce," notes one member of the firm. "Sometimes it is difficult to look that far ahead, but it is essential if unpleasant surprises are to be avoided."

Parents, therefore, should look ahead to this period and make some decisions on how they will handle the situation in advance. When the kids stay with the mother, she must be prepared to sell the home if circumstances dictate that is what must be done.

The Balance Sheet

This chapter's focus on problems of the single parent may have created the impression that there is no other side to the equation, no reward to offset the frustration, no joy to counter the pain. Any parent reading this chapter knows better. Raising a child, in spite of the difficulties of doing it alone, is a unique and rewarding experience. It is hoped that in pointing out some of the possible pitfalls along the way, those hazards can be avoided and the experience can be even more rewarding.

CHAPTER 9

HIS KIDS, HER KIDS— WHOSE MONEY?

In an Iowa town in the late sixties, a seemingly routine event occurred—a divorce. Taken alone, it probably would have been accepted and soon forgotten by the town residents, except that it set off a rather extraordinary series of subsequent events that will be long remembered.

It all started when the mailman's wife left him to marry someone else. The someone else, however, turned out to be the local minister, who, in turn, left his wife, and the two departed for parts unknown. The minister's former wife then married the assistant minister who, in order to accomplish this, had to first divorce his wife, who then left town as well.

But what happened to the kids who were involved in this drama of musical chairs? The mailman and his wife had a 17-year-old daughter and an adopted son, age 12. The daughter left home, and the son stayed with his father, who moved to California, remarried, and had a child by his second marriage. a new stepfamily had been formed. The minister and his wife had one daughter still living at home. She stayed with her mother when her mother married the assistant minister. As a result, the minister and the mailman's wife took no children with them when they left town. The assistant minister had an 8-year-old daughter. She moved with her mother to Wyoming: a new single-parent family had been formed. Left behind were the assistant minister, now married to the former minister's wife, and her 16-year-old daughter, making up another new stepfamily.

Whatever Happened to the Typical American Family?

The story just recounted represented a major drama for a small town but one that might go largely unnoticed in many areas of the country. Families are in a period of change. The conventional, or traditional, view of the American family is a father who goes off to work in the morning, leaving a mother at home to raise the children. The reality of this conventional view of things is fast disappearing. In fact, fewer than half of today's families can now be described in these terms. Even among intact families, at least half the wives now go off to work in the morning, along with their husbands.

In the United States today nearly four first marriages in ten end in divorce. More than three-fourths of the divorced men and women remarry within three years. Where children are involved in these remarriages, the new families might best be described as "stepfamilies." Estimates of the number of stepchildren living in such families today range from 15 to 18 million. These new families take a variety of different forms: kids who live with their mother and their new stepfather; those who live with their father and a new stepmother; children of both parents living in the new family; and, finally, any of these three forms plus children that result from the new marriage. Whatever the combination, these new parents must deal with the subject of money as it relates to their children under a new and often complex set of circumstances.

According to popular belief, "Love conquers all."

This myth, an ever-present hazard in a first marriage, is still a potential hazard the next time around. Taboos surrounding the subject of money are not easily dispelled, and the idea often persists that a discussion of money demeans the relationship between two people in love. Fortunately, many people who remarry *do* have a realistic appreciation of the need to discuss this subject. They have had some experience with money problems the first time around. However, this time there's a new element—the children. How the new couple will relate to the children on the subject of money is one of the biggest potential sources of conflict that lies ahead of them, but it is one subject that is often completely ignored.

It has been estimated that 40 percent of second marriages end in divorce within four years. According to a study done by Lillian Messinger and published in the *Journal of Marriage and Family Counseling* (April 1976), the reasons for failure of a second marriage are quite different from the reasons for a first divorce. The reasons most often given by men and women for the failure of their first marriage were: the partner's immaturity, sexual difficulties, and a personal lack of readiness for marriage. A variety of other reasons were also given, including interference by in-laws and differences in social interests and values.

In sharp contrast to these findings, *the two reasons most often given for the failure of second marriages were children and financial problems*. All other reasons given were significantly less important than these two.

Changes in Economic Circumstances

When the family situation changes, the economic situation is likely to change as well. The new stepfamily may have more money to spend on its children, but there's just as good a chance that it will have less. The case of Frances is somewhat typical. Frances and her children were living quite comfortably before she got divorced. Frances remarried soon after her divorce was final, but her new husband's income did not permit the family to live in the style they had followed during the previous marriage. Her kids had grown accustomed to getting the things they needed, and most of the things they wanted. Now they were being told, "If you want that, you'll have to go out and get a job." Some resentment is likely on the part of Frances' kids, even if they receive a full explanation of the change in circumstances. With no explanation, however, such resentment seems assured, and it is likely to become a serious problem.

Frances can adjust to the change, since it was her decision to make it. The children, on the other hand, did not make the choice, and they need a clear and forthright explanation of why the family's circumstances have changed.

It might be assumed that stepping up financially would cause no problems. After all, having more is certainly a more pleasant experience than having less. One couple, however, found quite the opposite, and their experience demonstrates that it is important to explain changing circumstances to children whenever they occur.

Carol had been divorced for a number of years, and her two

boys had been getting along with relatively little money. When Carol remarried, the boys found themselves relatively "rich" in comparison to their former circumstances. With the new family had come a new home, a new neighborhood, and new friends. Most of their friends came from fairly wealthy families. By the boys' standards, their friends had a lot of money to spend on themselves.

The boys' attitudes began to change, although the change was not obvious at first. Initially, the parents found it increasingly difficult to get the boys to do their chores around the house. The larger amount of money they now had to spend on themselves only seemed to increase their appetite for more and more things. As they acquired more things, their responsibility toward the things they already had seemed to decrease. Bicycles and skateboards were misplaced or broken. Library books gathered dust in their rooms as the fines mounted.

Tension between the mother and stepfather increased. The stepfather felt that it was important for the boys to earn some of their own money so they would acquire a more responsible attitude. The mother felt that, since the money was available, the boys should have it. Phil and Carol's stepfamily ended up in divorce.

According to Phil, disagreement over how to raise the boys, principally on the subject of money, was the major ingredient in failure of the marriage. By the time Phil and Carol came around to making a real effort to repair the damage, their positions on raising the kids were so far apart that compromise proved impossible. "It wasn't that we didn't discuss things before we got married," Phil recalls. "We had long discussions on a variety of different subjects, including family finances. When I look back, it's amazing to me that the one thing we forgot to discuss was how to raise the kids—especially on the subject of money. For some reason it didn't occur to us that this would be important."

This couple's experience supports the findings that the two major causes in the failure of second marriages are children and money. When possible, the new family should reach agreement on these critical subjects before the marriage takes place. When that is not possible, an acceptable common ground should be arrived at by the stepfamily as quickly as possible.

A Stepfamily's Unique Problems

In any new stepfamily, the chances are probably very good that the two parents have different ideas on how to raise children. Where money is concerned, one may believe in allowances while the other feels that it's best to give money to the children as they need it. One might feel that the children should be paid for getting good grades in school, while the other is certain that kids should be expected to get good grades without being "bribed." One might believe in giving the kids money for whatever they need, while the other thinks that kids should earn some of their own money for extras. Chances are also good that economic circumstances will be somewhat different for members of the stepfamily than they were before; that is, there may be considerably more or less money available for the entire family, including the kids, than there was in the past.

The "conventional" family (a mother and father living with their own children) has the obvious advantage of being able to evolve what both parents consider a reasonable approach as the children are growing. The stepfamily, however, does not have this time. There is pressure to make a wide variety of decisions as quickly as possible about the rules under which the new family will operate. Among the most difficult of these decisions are those that deal with money.

A stepfamily encounters some unique obstacles in its efforts to establish an orderly set of rules. Psychologists Emily and John Visher (in "Common Problems of Stepparents and Their Spouses," *American Journal of Orthopsychiatry*, April 1978) note that conventional families have an inherent stability that enables them to maintain equilibrium while resisting interference from the outside. The stepfamily, on the other hand, is subject to interference from the outside, principally ex-spouses, who are involved in the family but over whom very little control can be exercised. For example, will Valerie's wealthy father agree to spend less on her this Christmas to avoid jealousy on the part of her stepsister? Or, will Freddie's father forget to send the child-support check this December, as he did last year?

One threat to the stability of the stepfamily rests in the subject of family loyalty. Unlike conventional families, according to the Vishers, "in which children will usually exert much effort to keep their parents together, stepfamilies are often fragmented because the children, either consciously or unconsciously, wish to separate their parent and stepparent, with the fantasy that their natural parents will then be reunited."

One means of counteracting these feelings on the part of children is to include them as participants in such things as family financial planning. If including the kids in such activities is important to a conventional family, it is absolutely vital in the step-family, especially where money is concerned. Family meetings are probably the best way to accomplish this objective. Properly handled, such meetings offer all members of the stepfamily an opportunity to express their views on a variety of subjects that might otherwise grow into serious problems later on.

One final way to overcome the stepfamily's unique obstacles is for the stepfamily to develop and follow a set of rules that are acceptable to all family members—including the kids. Uncertainty and confusion are typical of any family with no firm guidelines, and uncertainty is one thing that the youngsters in a stepfamily do not need, since in many cases they are already confused and uncertain as a result of their parents' divorce.

Many conflicts can be solved within the stepfamily, especially if a reasonably open exchange of feelings is established. But not everything is within the family's control. Two such sources of potential problems are child-support payments and relationships with ex-spouses.

Child-Support Payments

Resentment over child-support payments can arise both between adults and between children and parents. In some cases, child-support payments are both received and paid out, but in unequal amounts. A mother might receive $200 a month to provide support for her two kids, while her husband pays out $450 to his ex-wife for his two kids. To the woman's children, this exchange may seem very unfair. The reasons for the unequal payments should be explained to the kids in terms they will understand. They can be told that there are courts and judges who decide such matters, that it is not their stepfather's decision to provide that amount of money for the support of his kids. The children can also be made to understand that their stepfather is not deliberately withholding income from his new family. Unfortunately, even though the mother in this case understands the reasons for the difference, she may find it difficult not to resent the inequity in the payments and the effect it has on her own family's standard of living.

Problems with Ex-spouses

Money is often a source of conflict between the absent parent and the stepfamily. Let's take the case of a mother whose children live with her and her new husband. They have agreed to raise the children according to a set of rules that make sense to them, including how money is to be handled where the kids are concerned. They have told their 15-year-old son Jerry that he can go to summer camp if he earns half the money himself.

Jerry, however, returns from a weekend with his father and announces that dad will pay for his camp. This offer places the stepfamily in an extremely difficult position. Whether they wanted Jerry to earn half the money because they could not afford to pay the entire sum or because they wanted him to learn certain values by working, the ex-husband's offer to pay has the effect of undermining control at home.

The case of Michelle illustrates another potential source of problems. Michelle has one daughter, Annie, from her former marriage, and a boy and girl from her present marriage. Michelle's ex-husband is quite wealthy. Whenever Annie visits him, he spends a large amount of money entertaining her and buys her expensive gifts, which Annie brings home with her. Michelle and her husband cannot afford to spend that much on the other two kids, and they are concerned that the other children will feel neglected or resentful.

Both of these cases involve what the stepfamily sees as excessive spending by the ex-spouse. In many situations like this, a successful middle ground can be worked out if all the adults concerned sit down and talk it out. Even when two of the adults retain some feelings of bitterness from the preceding marriage, a conference can work if the stepparents make it clear to the ex-spouse that they assume he has—as they have—the best interests of the child as the object. In the case of Annie, if the gifts received from her natural father create resentment on the part of the half-brother and half-sister with whom she lives, the net effect on Annie may be more negative than positive. This father should probably find some other way to express his affection for his daughter. He might decide to spend more on entertaining her than on gifts, since the other children see the gifts he buys her but not the entertainment. If he can understand that those gifts are not important to how Annie feels about him, perhaps he can be persuaded not to send them home with her. Perhaps he can also be made to understand that the gifts cause the other kids to feel resentment, and such feelings end up being harmful to his daughter.

The Family Conference

The advantage of resolving differences before they become problems is obvious. Existing stepfamilies, however, cannot go back and work everything out in advance. The existing stepfamily must simply deal with things as they come up. One of the most effective ways of handling problems or potential problems is through the family conference. Such a conference would normally be conducted in two stages: first, a discussion between the parents and then a conference that includes the kids.

Many of the important questions can be settled between the parents, and the more points upon which the parents can agree in advance, the better. For example, the parents should decide in advance whether or not to use allowances. Then let the kids help decide which of their expenses it should cover, and how much it should amount to. Parents might decide that each child will be assigned responsibilities but let the children make the decision as to which job each one of them will do. As the children grow older, their wishes and feelings should be given increasing weight in coming to decisions that affect them. No set of rules works well unless it is generally agreed to by all participants.

The key to a successful family conference with the children is a real intent on the part of the parents to let the kids help make some of the decisions. The child who helps establish the size of his own allowance and agrees to what things it should pay for is more likely to live within his budget than a child who has had no say in these matters. But the family conference has value beyond deciding the details of such things as allowances and family responsibilities. The children can be included in discussions of major family decisions such as buying a new home or a promotion that would involve moving to a new city. Family relationships such as the problem of Annie's gifts from her father can be discussed in order to get feelings out into the open. Resentment over matters involving money is less likely to become serious if all members of the family have an opportunity to express their feelings at regularly held meetings of this type.

Being Fair

Parents often struggle with decisions on how to be fair to their children. In many cases, the children will make a better decision on what's fair than the parents are able to make by themselves. One couple whose second marriage combined a child from each side recalls having an extensive disagreement over the payment of allowances. Because one child was a boy, one a girl, and they were different ages, the parents were unable to come up with what seemed to be equitable allowances. It seemed as if each one of them was fighting for his or her own kid. These parents were discussing their dilemma with a friend, when the friend said, "Why don't you ask the kids?" Since the parents were unable to reach agreement themselves, they finally called a family conference and presented all the alternatives they had discussed to the kids. The two children solved the problem very quickly, in terms that satisfied both them and their parents.

Some things parents will want to decide themselves. Whether or not to pay an allowance might be an example. But when it comes to which of the children's expenses the allowance should cover, it's smart to include kids in the discussion.

In many stepfamilies, treating the children fairly becomes somewhat complicated since there are so many "family" influences outside the immediate family. When one stepparent's children live with the family and the other stepparent's children live with his or her ex-spouse, the children's perception of fair treatment might be quite different from that of the parents. One stepfamily that included the wife's children was visited periodically by the husband's children. On those occasions the family made an effort to do something special, sometimes an outing or going out to dinner. Both these parents were astounded when her children asked, "Why do we only do special things when they come to visit?" To this couple it had seemed quite natural to plan special things when his kids came to visit, since such visits were not frequent. This couple pointed out to the kids who were living at home that they were forgetting many of the special things they did together as a family in his kid's absence. They also reminded these children that when his kids came to visit, all the kids were included in whatever the family did. They pointed out that planning something special was a very natural thing for them to do under the circumstances, and in no way represented favoritism of any sort.

Staying in touch with the feelings of children is a full-time job. Sometimes, as this couple discovered, uncovering those feelings can yield some surprises and head off problems before they become serious.

Living with His Kids and Her Kids

The problems of a stepfamily are complex enough, but when each parent in the new stepfamily brings along one or more children, there are special considerations. It's entirely possible that one set of kids is stepping up financially, the other stepping down. Changes in economic conditions can be difficult enough for youngsters in a stable environment, but the children in the new stepfamily have many changes to deal with all at once. What will the family do if the mother has always paid her kids a generous allowance and discouraged, perhaps even prohibited, her kids from working to earn extra money, while the father has always felt that a kid will never appreciate the value of a dollar unless he earns it? It seems obvious that one of them has to change. Some approach must be adopted that is acceptable to both parents and both sets of kids.

When children from two different families are joined together in a new stepfamily, they not only need to feel they are receiving equal treatment, they also need a clear understanding of the rules. "Publish or Perish" is a good policy for parents to adopt.

Write out the rules and post them as a reminder. Include responsibilities as well. Then all members of the family know where they stand.

Adjusting to Change

Children do not welcome changes. They want things to stay the same. When a new family is formed, however, changes are inevitable. Parents and stepparents must give special attention to helping the children understand the nature of the changes and the reasons for them.

The best time to make decisions relating to how the new family will operate, especially where the children and money are concerned, is before the family is together. The next best time is as soon afterwards as possible. What you decide is probably less important than that you establish a set of guidelines within which the children can operate comfortably. Rules that are followed by everyone provide at least some certainty during what might otherwise be a very uncertain period for youngsters.

Where money is concerned, an approach to the rules — a philosophy of raising kids — that is confident, consistent, and fair will provide an essential element of stability in a child's world. The children may not welcome change, but it is important for parents to help them understand it when it happens.

CHAPTER 10

ALREADY IN TROUBLE? — THERE IS A WAY OUT

Ruth's son Kevin was 9 when Ruth was divorced ten years ago. Since that time Ruth has worked full-time and raised Kevin with no financial help from her former husband. Kevin is now 19, in his first year of junior college, and still living at home. Ruth feels that Kevin should get a part-time job to help buy food and pay for other expenses. She has told him so, and, although Kevin agreed that he would look for a job, several months have passed with no evidence that he actually intends to start working. "Kevin is an adult now," Ruth says, "and he's old enough to take care of himself. I'm not even asking him to do that — only to help me out a little. I'd like to be able to do some things for myself now, things I've put off for the last ten years because there wasn't enough money."

Ruth's problem did not appear overnight. She looks back and admits that she was probably overly generous with Kevin during the years he was growing up. Rather than encouraging him to work for the extra things he wanted, she tried to provide them herself. She wonders if it's fair to Kevin to change the rules now.

The real question is: Is Ruth being fair to herself in going along with things as they are? The answer is no. It is Ruth's turn, and she is entitled to change things. Kevin may not like the changes his mother feels are overdue, but change often involves some initial discomfort. The alternative is for things to forever stay the same, even when a situation has become unacceptable. There's nothing wrong with deciding that there is a better way to handle a subject like money with your kids than the way you are doing it now.

Assuming that a change should be made, how can the change be most easily and comfortably accomplished? Answering this last question is the subject of this chapter.

In Ruth's case, there was no major or dramatic change in circumstances. Her situation evolved gradually to its current unsatisfactory status. In some families, however, the trouble arises suddenly because of an unexpected change in status. That happened to Don and Shirley, who have three kids, ages 16 to 20. One is in high school, one in college, and one works full-time. All three still live at home. About eight months ago, Don's company moved to another city. Don chose not to move, but he has not yet found another job. At first, Don and Shirley were not too concerned. Don expected to be working again right away, and they had several thousand dollars of savings available. As the months passed, however, their concern increased.

According to Don, it was only he and Shirley who were concerned; their three kids went right on as if nothing had happened. The 16-year-old still asked for money to see a movie or buy clothes. The 18-year-old still expected the same level of help to pay her college expenses, including all costs for the car she drove to and from classes. Even the son who was working expected to find dinner on the table every night, but he never thought to help out with household expenses.

Before his company's move, Don had had a good job and had always taken pride in the fact that he took good care of his kids. When he lost his job, he was unwilling to face the fact that he might not be able to support them at the same level as before. No family discussion of the change in circumstances was ever considered. Now Don is increasingly "frustrated and disappointed that the kids don't seem to care," but he has not yet been able to tell his children that the money is almost gone and that he needs their help and understanding.

Don and Shirley's problem, like Ruth's, represents only one area of potential conflict between parents and their children. A whole world of other problems exist for many families. In most cases, families face such difficulties because they neglected to take certain steps when their children were young.

Secrecy was the immediate cause of Don and Shirley's dilemma. Their expectation that the kids would understand and offer to help out was probably unreasonable since no family discussion of the situation had ever occurred—the issue had never been raised. Openness about family money matters is the best possible way to keep problems such as this from getting to an advanced stage.

For many families, the crisis period occurs as the kids move into their teens. Sometimes referred to as the nation's largest independent leisure class, today's teenagers spend billions of dollars each year—most of it obtained from their parents. While it is true that little kids also cost money to raise, they don't *spend* much money. The little you do give them to spend hasn't much impact on your budget. There is no real pressure to teach them good money habits. But as they approach the teenage years, the pressure begins to mount.

The most obvious pressure is for more spending money. They "need" more clothes, and the clothes they want are increasingly expensive. They also "need" stereos, cosmetics, magazines, trips with their friends, and a lot more. And even all these costs seem relatively minor when compared with the costs of a "needed" car. Handling this stage has always put parents to the test. But today, the effects of taxes and inflation combined with youngsters' rapidly growing demands mean that many families actually find their standard of living threatened.

The question many parents ask is: If we've always given our children what they needed, how can we *now* tell them that if they want more, they'll have to get a job? In fact, how can we tell them that from now on there will be *less* than before? The families best able to adjust to changing circumstances and financial pressures are those that, early in the game, were able to evolve a consistent and workable relationship between the parents and the children with regard to the family's money. Such families will experience far fewer money-related problems through the teen years.

But what about the family that did not start early? What about parents whose kids are older now but show no evidence that they appreciate what their parents have done for them, no understanding that there are limits to the family's resources, no interest in behaving in a responsible manner where money is concerned? For these parents, is it too late? The answer is NO! It is not too late. It is always possible to change the direction of things, even though reversal of the trend often *seems* out of the question.

One reason behind the failure of parents to act is fear of the possible consequences. People tend to avoid change whenever possible. Shakespeare observed this human tendency in Hamlet's famous soliloquy on suicide. The risk of change, he said, ". . . makes us rather bear the ills we have than fly to others that we know not of." Parents' relationships with their children where money is concerned may range from uncomfortable to intolerable, but too often nothing is done about it for fear of even greater difficulties than those now faced. Change often does require courage, but when family relationships are deteriorating, the risks associated with making changes are less than the risk of doing nothing.

Changing Things

Let's examine a series of steps that you can take to make changes in family relationships — specifically those relationships involving money and children. The steps themselves are easy to understand. It is a bit more difficult to come to certain decisions, which must be made in order to carry out the process. Most difficult is the necessity to follow through on decisions that are made.

The steps consist of a series of two conferences. The first is the parents' conference. (Single parents can work out the needed items alone, or they can enlist the support of a trusted friend or ex-spouse.) There are several items on the agenda. The starting point is to define what is happening now. What is the condition (or conditions) that is causing the distress? For example: you've never had an organized allowance system. The kids have always asked for money when they needed it. When you felt that their requests were justified, you gave it to them. That worked fine until recently, when the amounts requested seemed to double overnight. Your protests that they are spending too much money are met with replies that indicate they think you have plenty of money and you're just being stingy. That's not the case, and they need to understand that the money supply is limited.

Here's another example. Your kids have always had an allowance — in fact, a large one that includes most of their expenses. This year, however, the cost of living has shot up at the same time your company has eliminated the overtime you've been used to earning. Your budget is being squeezed. You've had to cut back. The kids should have to cut back too, but you don't know how to tell them.

One more possibility. Your kids used to help out around the house, but gradually it has become more and more of an effort to get any work out of them at all. Sometimes it's homework, sometimes a dance, sometimes a friend who dropped by. The excuse varies, but the result is the same. Their spending needs keep going up, but their contribution has dropped to zero. You've given up asking them to help out. It's not worth it. And you're coming to resent every nickel you give them to spend.

Whatever the problem is, it should be clearly defined and written down. Now what is the desired situation? What set of conditions can be defined, again in writing, that would restore relative peace and contentment to the family setting?

You now have a description of where you are, as well as where you would like to be. Now you must decide what specific changes must be implemented in order to establish the desired set of conditions. This can be a difficult step. In some cases the answers will be fairly obvious, but in others it may be necessary to do some research. You may, for example, want to talk to other parents who seem to have been successful in dealing with the situation you face.

Once you have decided what must be done, it's time to set up the rules. Some of the rules will probably be firm and not subject to change. Others can be general and the subject of further discussion.

Now it's time for a conference with the entire family—parents and kids. Here, the situation should be presented as seen by the parents, the problem as well as the desired result and the proposed means of accomplishing it. To the maximum extent possible, the kids should participate in final decisions on the goals to be sought and the means of their accomplishment, since rules are generally effective only when they are agreed to by those involved. In the event agreement cannot be achieved on a point considered essential by the parents, it should become part of the rules as well. Kids should not have veto rights on rules that are felt to be necessary.

The final steps include writing out those rules that are adopted, posting them, and following them. Rules must be reasonable to be effective.

Parents must be especially careful to observe their own obligations. In effect, the process described here results in a family contract between parents and kids. In any contract, both sides have obligations. If a kid violates the agreement from time to time, it can usually be overlooked. But if parents fail to live up to the contract, it becomes worthless.

In summary, the steps start with a meeting of the parents, who must accomplish the following:

Define the problem (where are we?)

Describe the desired condition (where would we like to be?)

Decide what needs to be changed (how will we reach the objective?)

Establish the rules.

The next step is the family conference. The objectives:

Review the situation, objectives, and proposed solutions with the kids.

Finalize the rules in a form everyone can live with.

Finally, the rules must be posted and enforced.

Going through these steps without writing anything down will almost certainly prove futile. Writing out the problem, the objectives, and possible solutions is essential. Defining a problem on paper is quite different from just thinking about it, or even discussing it. Writing requires a rather precise definition of things. In some cases, it can expose previously unrecognized problems or suggest solutions.

Don't skip writing things down to save time!

It might be said that the family that follows the foregoing procedure has established a "family contract." There are two principal parties to the contract—the parents and the kids. The contract must be honored by both parties for it to work, and it is most important that the parents honor their obligations. A family is basically a self-contained economic unit with a certain amount of income and certain basic needs. It also is made up of a group of people, all of whom would usually like to have more things than is possible. Living together in peace requires living under some system that is considered both reasonable and fair by *all* participants.

The foregoing exercise provides a way Ruth can get her message across to Kevin, a way she can let him know in clear terms that she feels it is now her turn. It is also a technique that Don and Shirley can use to help them overcome their reluctance to discuss their dilemma with their kids, and to let those kids know that immediate changes are essential. Following these steps might not yield the perfect solution, but it can represent a way out for parents who are not sure which way to turn.

INFLATION, TAXES, AND OTHER MYSTERIES

To Parents:

One of the most neglected areas in the education of most people is economics; there are few economics classes given in high school, and few college graduates ever receive any formal training in it. Yet probably no other subject has a greater impact on our daily lives. Most adults eventually learn some things about our economic system by participating in its workings. A lot of that learning, however, is through trial-and-error—with sometimes costly errors.

Kids can and should learn some basic economic facts of life. They don't have to learn abstract economic theories or mathematical models. But kids as young as 10 can be made to understand a lot through simple facts and concrete examples. That is what the following seven chapters offer. They explain things like: why profits are important; where jobs come from and how new jobs are influenced by profits; how competition works; why people pay taxes, and how the taxes are spent; what kinds of things cause inflation and how inflation affects us; the role of saving and investing in the economy and the ways kids can invest.

The chapters are written in language that kids can understand. You may want to just give the book to your kids and let them read these chapters. If you think your kids are too young to understand the information themselves, you might want to read through the chapters so that you can explain things to your kids yourself.

To Kids:

School teaches you basic skills. To be successful as an adult, you'll need to know how to read, write, and spell. You'll need math both for many adult jobs and for getting things done in everyday life, just buying things or balancing a checkbook.

There are, however, many things you need to understand that you will not learn in school. Take a look at the following list of questions. See how many you think you can answer.

Can a business be started using other people's money, and why might someone loan money to you to start one of your own?

Where do jobs really come from, and where is the best place for kids to find jobs?

How important is it to you that other people's businesses make a profit, and why?

If you have a small business of your own, do you know how to tell if you're making a profit?

How much of the money that the Ford Motor Company gets from the sale of its cars is kept by the owners of Ford? Would you guess that, of

each $1 of sales, Ford's owners keep 4¢, 12¢, 50¢, or 70¢?

Do you know who owns your local telephone company, and who owns Disney and McDonald's?

Who decides which items to put on the shelves of the clothing store, record store, or supermarket where you shop?

Do taxes affect the price of the things you spend your money on?

How can a company cut prices on the things it sells and yet make more money?

Do you think anyone will pay you for letting them use your money? If so, how much might you earn, and why?

Why do you think people who save money pay less for some things they buy than other people pay?

Do you know how you can become one of the owners of McDonald's or Jack-in-the-Box or Eastman Kodak or Coca Cola?

Answers to all these questions and many more will be found in the following seven chapters. These chapters are written to be understood and used by young people, and designed to do important things for you. They will help you understand many of the events going on around you today, things that people are talking about, like inflation and taxes. These things affect you and your family, and you should understand them.

CHAPTER 11

PROFITS—
WHY ARE THEY NECESSARY?

The sign on the main gate of the steel mill reads, "CLOSED."

They put the sign up at the end of the day last Friday. Everyone in town knew it was coming. Some families had already moved away. But most of the residents of this town don't know where to go, where to find a new job and a new home.

The steel mill has been here for more than forty years. In those years, it has grown old and tired. Now it cannot be run at a profit. Other, newer plants have taken this one's place. Another new business might move to this town and provide jobs again, or maybe the people here will just gradually move out.

One thing is clear. Without profits, there are no jobs—in this town or any other. Without profit a business dies.

But profits do a lot more than just keep businesses alive. Let's look at some questions about profits with answers directed to a kid's point of view.

What Are Profits?

Profits are the most important reason that people start businesses in the first place. There are, of course, other reasons, too. Some people like the freedom they have when they run their own business, when they are their own boss. Others like the excitement. But if there is no hope for profit for a new business, it will not be started.

Let's assume you're a kid who needs some extra money this coming Christmas. You've decided to earn that money by making wreaths for people to hang on their front doors during the holidays. You can get all the pine branches you need for the wreaths free, but you must buy the ribbon and other decorations. Your costs add up to $1 for each wreath, not counting your work. You decide to start carefully, make a couple, and see how much you can get for them. Suppose people tell you they will buy your wreaths for $1 but no more. There's no profit for you at that price. Will you keep making them? What price do you need to make it worth doing? What if you could sell them for $2.50? That's a profit of $1.50. So the wreath-making business is attractive at a price of $2.50 but not at a price of $1.00. If you can't make some money, why do it?

Here's a simple way to look at profits: "Profits are the amount left over after a business has paid all its expenses and bills." Every business works the same way. If the money it takes in during the month is more than the amount that has to be paid out during the month, that month was profitable.

But someone about to start a new business has some problems. He doesn't know if the new business will ever make a profit. It might lose money. It is estimated that more than one-third of all businesses make no profit at all in any given year. And each year many thousands go bankrupt for various reasons. When each new business starts, however, the objective is to be profitable.

Let's look at the case of Mr. and Mrs. Smith. The Smiths have just retired, and the money they saved during the years they were working is now in a savings account where it is earning them 7 percent interest. They are considering starting a business of their own in order to increase their retirement income. Let's suppose that Mr. and Mrs. Smith decide that their growing community needs an ice cream store. There is a building for rent on a busy street that looks like a perfect location. The closest ice cream store is more than a mile away.

The first thing the Smiths must decide is this: If they take their money out of the bank and invest it in their new ice cream business, can they make more than 7 percent? If they think the money will earn less than 7 percent, they will leave it in the bank.

If they think they can make exactly 7 percent, they are still better off in the bank since there is little or no risk in having it there. But there *is* risk in any new business. They could lose *all* of their money.

In this case the Smiths decide the store might earn them 12 percent on their money, and they decide to go ahead. Once they get started, here's how the Smiths will tell how much profit they are making. All of their income will be from the sale of ice cream. Using that money, the Smiths must first pay for the ice cream they buy from the factory that makes it. Next they must pay the employees they hire to help them. Then they pay their rent, insurance, and utilities on the store itself. What's left over is for them. That is their profit. If the ice cream store is the right choice of businesses, if the store is in a good location with plenty of customers, and if the Smiths are able to hire good employees who work hard, their profits will be good. The risk is that there will not be enough customers each month to pay the costs. In that case, the Smiths will lose money. Before long they will be forced to go out of business and someone else will rent the store to try another kind of business. The Smiths' customers will have to go someplace else to buy ice cream.

Our economic system is often called "the profit system," but it would probably be more accurate to call it the "profit and loss system." When you have your own business, you might make a lot of money, but you might not. When the Smiths went into business, the owner of their building made a profit by renting it to them. The ice cream factory made a profit by selling them ice cream. The young people they employed to work in the store got jobs that were not there before. The people who live in the Smiths' community had a place to buy ice cream when they wanted it. For all this, the Smiths are entitled to a profit. But because they might lose the money they invested in the business, they ask for a profit that is greater than what they could earn on a *safe* investment like a savings account.

What Difference Do Profits Make to a Kid?

Profits make a big difference. The only reason any kid would invest all the time and effort needed to start his or her own small business is to make a profit.

But how about the profits of other businesses? Is it important to *you* for them to make a profit? You bet it is! Every movie you see, every record album you buy is available for you to enjoy *only* because the movie or record company is in business trying to make a profit. The products they make are available to you only as long as the companies that make them stay in business. And to stay in business, they must make a profit.

How about the Smiths' new ice cream store? Before it opened you had to go more than a mile if you wanted ice cream. Now it's just a few blocks. You might even get a job working in the store. Those are two good reasons for you to want the Smiths to make enough money to keep their store open.

So profits *do* make a difference to kids, and profits are important whether they are your own or someone else's.

How Much Profit Do Most Businesses Make?

Many people think business profits are much too high. Business says they're too low. Who's right? As an adult, you may well be part of the business world, so you should understand how much profit businesses actually make.

Over the past ten years many surveys have been taken on the subject of profits. One survey asked teenagers where they think the money goes that is received by the average manufacturing company when they sell their products. About 67 percent thought that the owners kept at least 60¢ of every $1 they took in. Another 23 percent thought the owners kept 80¢ or more. The fact is that the actual amount of profit available to the owners of the average company is between 4¢ and 5¢ from each $1 of sales.

But teenagers can't be blamed for not knowing. No one has told them. And it's not just kids who are confused. A labor consultant asked the same question of a number of corporate personnel officers. A personnel officer is a corporate executive in charge of hiring people. He should certainly know about profits. Yet it was found that even *this* group believed profit margins were 33 percent. At the time this survey was taken, the real answer was 4.2 percent.

Where Does the Profit Go?

Companies make their money by selling a product or a service to customers. A service is something that you use, but you can't put it in your pocket or take it home with you. A service you might *buy* is a ride in an amusement park. A service you might *sell* is washing your dad's car or mowing the neighbor's lawn. Things like lawn mowers and cars are products, and they are made by people called manufacturers. A manufacturer like the Ford Motor Company sells its cars and trucks to dealers. The money the Ford Company receives for all the cars and trucks it sells in a year is called "sales." The question is: What do companies do with all the sales dollars they receive? The best way to find out is to look at a real company. We'll look at Ford.

In 1977 Ford had the biggest year in its history. Both sales and profits made all-time records. Total sales were more than $47 billion, a figure so huge that it is impossible for most adults to appreciate—and out of the question for kids. But we can see what Ford did with all that money by looking at just $100 in sales, one tiny piece of all those billions of dollars.

Ford's largest single expense is for materials that go into making the car. Ford is not in the steel business, so the company buys its steel from people like U.S. Steel. Ford doesn't make tires either, so it buys them from Firestone, Goodyear, or Goodrich. It buys fabrics to upholster seats, headlights and tail lights, screws, nuts, and bolts—all the things you need to make a car or a truck. The company must also maintain the factories in which it builds its cars. On these it must pay property taxes, and it must also pay for utilities. Companies like Ford also spend a great deal of money designing and testing their new products. And the ads you see on television are not cheap. On all of this, Ford spends $63.06 out of the $100 of sales.

The next piece of that $100 goes to Ford's employees, the workers who build the cars. That amounted to $29 in 1977, leaving $7.94 in profits, before the payment of income taxes to the federal government. The government's share was $3.51, which amounted to 44 percent of Ford's profits. So we finally arrive at what's left for the owners of the Ford Motor Company. They get $4.43 for every $100 worth of sales—or do they?

The owners of a company like Ford get their share of the profits in the form of dividends, which are paid in cash four times a year. But very few companies pay all of their profits out in dividends. If a company paid all of its profits out, it could not expand; that is, it would be unable to grow.

It turns out that for each $100 of sales in 1977, the owners' (stockholders') cash share of the profits was 95¢. The company kept $3.48 to be spent on the business.

It's up to the management of Ford—the people who run the company—to spend that $3.48 in the right places. If they make the right decisions, sales and profits of the company should continue to grow in the future. As sales grow, several other things also happen. First, Ford will have to build new production plants. Along with the new plants come new jobs, and these new jobs would eventually be added to the 479,300 employees Ford had in 1978. Building the new plants provides jobs for the construction industry, and after they are built, additional property taxes are available to support schools and local governments. As profits go up, more income taxes are paid to the federal and state governments. Finally, the owners of the company will expect higher cash dividends in the future.

It is sometimes said that owners of American business take too much for themselves and leave too little for their employees. Remember that in the survey mentioned earlier, most of the teenagers thought the owners kept 60¢ or more of each sales dollar. Now we see that the owners of Ford in 1977 received less than 1¢ in actual cash for each dollar of sales. On the other hand, the workers at Ford received 29¢, or more than thirty times as much. The money left to be reinvested in the business is left there to create more for everyone in the future—more profits, more jobs, higher dividends. When a company is profitable, healthy, and growing, everyone wins, including the public, because a successful company is obviously providing products that people want.

Who Are the Owners of Ford?

Ford has 335,400 different owners. These owners are called "stockholders." We'll discuss stock in a chapter on investing, but for now, let's just take a look at who these people are or might be.

You can be one of the owners of the Ford Motor Company. Let's see how, using the price in July 1978. If you had some money saved, you could have taken about $47 to a stockbroker and bought one share of Ford Motor Company for yourself. That would have made you one of the owners. You would not have been a very big owner, since there are 119 million shares of Ford stock. But you *would* be one of the owners, and the company would pay you part of the profits they make a long as you owned the stock. Your share of the company's profits for 1979 would have been about $3.60. That's about 7 1/2 percent of the $47 you invested—a pretty good return. Your $3.60 would have been only part of the profits for your one share, and the company would have kept the rest to help its business grow in the future. If it was successful, the price of your stock should have gone up, and the company would be able to increase the size of the check they send you each year.

Lots of people, then, own Ford. People just like you. Most of them own more than one share, but everyone has to start somewhere. It's important for you to understand that the people who run Ford, just like the people who run Walt Disney Productions or McDonald's, do not own the whole company. Companies have a chairman and directors, a president and vice presidents. These people usually own stock in their own company. They may own a lot more than one share, but each of their shares is exactly the same as yours. You're an owner just as they are. They just own more than you.

So who owns Ford? Ford has more than one-third of a million owners, and you can be one of them if you want to—and you have the price of one share.

If I Started My Own Business, How Much Profit Could I Make?

Almost any new business that someone starts requires money. The money you put into a business to get it going is called your investment. When you start your own business, you are investing in yourself, hoping you're getting into the right business at the right time and that you'll make a lot of money. If it's a hot dog and hamburger stand, you'll need money to pay rent, you'll have to buy equipment to prepare the food, and, of course, you'll need a starting supply of hamburger meat, hot dogs, buns, and so on. What you spend on all of this is your starting investment. If your business is successful and six months later you expand so you can handle more customers, the additional money you spend also becomes part of your investment. One of the best ways to see how well you are doing—how profitable your business is—is to compare your profits with the amount you have invested. It's very difficult to guess how profitable a new, small business will be before it gets started. Some make a lot of money. Others lose money and disappear. But we can look at two large, well-established companies, see how they did in 1977, and see how their profits compare to the total amount of money invested in them.

A & P, with 1900 stores, is the world's second largest chain of grocery stores. The grocery business is always a competitive one, but 1977 was a particularly tough year for the company. Based on the total amount of money that had been invested in A & P since it got started (not counting money they had borrowed), profits in 1977 amounted to only seven-tenths of 1 percent—less than one cent for each dollar of investment. On the other hand, Levi Strauss, the company that makes Levis, had a very good year in 1977. The company earned 28¢ for every dollar of investment. This does not make Levi the best company to buy, or A & P the worst, but it does show that there are large differences in what companies can make, especially companies in different businesses.

Every time you go to the store you are "voting," voting for someone's product. If you buy a pair of Levis, that's a vote for them instead of a vote for one of the other companies that make jeans. You, and the millions of other people who buy jeans every year, are the ones who decide which companies will be successful. If Levi continues to make jeans that people like and buy, they will continue to be successful. If people stopped buying Levis, the Levi company would have to change or it would go out of business.

When you open your hot dog stand, if you put it in the right place and make the "best hot dog in town," you'll make a lot of money. Your profits are the reward you get for providing something people are willing to pay for. But in a small business, just like a big one, the final decision is not yours. If you do not provide something people want at a price they are willing to pay, your business will not be a success. In our economy, the customer has the final vote.

Then, Profits Are Important to Everyone?

The American system gives you the freedom to go into business with any product, idea, invention, or service you think people will be willing to buy. And the buyers have the freedom to make you rich or ignore you. It's often hard to appreciate just how much this profit system of ours has done for us. It doesn't mean that everyone in this country is rich. It doesn't mean that however, that most of us accept much of what we have as being "just normal," never realizing that in many places in the world many of the things we have but never notice are considered luxuries. In this country, 95 percent of our households have full plumbing facilities, but in East Germany, less than half of all the homes or apartments have toilets, 40 percent don't have private baths, and 15 percent don't even have running water.

In your own home, running water is something you expect—just as you expect the sun to come up tomorrow morning. It's not a thing you think about. But many people in this world have no faucet to turn on. Water and plumbing are luxuries not available to them.

Nearly all American families have refrigerators, radios, and television sets; more than 90 percent have telephones; 92 percent have washing machines; 80 percent have at least one car. More than 60 percent of all American families own their own home. In 1974 Americans bought 31 million major appliances, 11.5 million new cars, 8 million color TV sets. You may think it's like this everywhere. It's not! What we have and enjoy is largely due to the productivity of American workers. The United States has one-twentieth (5 percent) of all the world's people, yet we produce one-fourth (25 percent) of the entire world's goods and services—the things people buy.

Why is this true? Probably the most important reason is that our system is designed to pay more to those who produce more. Workers who can produce more each day can be paid more. Companies that produce more each year can increase their profits.

Agriculture is probably the best single example of our ability to produce. The Bushman of Africa spends almost all of his time getting the food he needs to survive. In the underdeveloped countries of the world, people spend 60 percent of their money on food alone. In Russia, about 40 percent of income goes for food. In Great Britain it's 30 percent. Yet in the United States it's only 18 percent. In 1974, 3.25 million farmers produced enough food to feed this entire country and leave a lot left over to ship to the rest of the world. In South America it took 23 million farmers to feed approximately the same number of people. That year, 39 million Russian farmers were unable to produce enough food for their country, and the Russians were forced to buy a large quantity of our wheat to make up the difference. The ability of our farmers to produce lets us all live better. What we do not have to spend on food we have available to spend on other things.

Conclusion

So profits *are* important for everyone in an economy like ours. The search for profits provides us with growth, new products, and the investment required to create new jobs. It gives you the freedom to go into any business you choose, and, if you are successful, to make as much money as you are able to make.

As President John F. Kennedy put it, ". . . in a free enterprise system, there can be no prosperity without profit. We want a growing economy, and there can be no growth without investment that is inspired and financed by profit."

CHAPTER 12

JOBS — WHERE DO THEY COME FROM?

Joe, 10 years old, lived in Whitesboro, Texas. His folks had friends in Dallas. Each time the family went to Dallas, Joe bought a supply of yo-yo strings, which were hard to find in Whitesboro. He paid a dollar for a dozen, but he could sell them back home for 25¢ each.

So those trips to Dallas were always profitable ones. Joe spent most of his yo-yo string profits, but he always made sure he had a few dollars left to buy more on the next trip to Dallas.

When he was 11, Joe got a paper route that gave him a steady source of income. And that year he saved enough to buy a heifer for $70. He kept the cow for two years, letting it graze on a neighbor's pasture, and finally sold it for $262.50. Since he had made almost $200 on his first try, Joe decided that raising cattle was a good way to make money. He got another chance when the local barber had two heifers for sale for a total cost of $200. When this pair had put on enough weight to be sold, Joe got $900 for the two. Joe took the $900, got a loan from the bank, and bought 18 Black Angus cattle. Now, at age 16, he was really in the cattle business. The following year he sold his small herd for enough to buy a Chevy Impala.

It took him six years, but this enterprising youngster from Texas managed to turn $70 into a new car—a pretty good record for a kid starting at age 11. Joe remembers that he always made money when he was young, while other kids around him did not. "It's a lot better if you have encouragement from your parents" is the way he puts it. That sounds like pretty good advice to parents who want their kids to get off to an early start. Joe learned a lot about working and jobs at an early age. Some kids, however, are uncomfortable with the world of jobs and business because they do not understand it, so let's look at a few questions on the subject of jobs.

Where's the Best Place to Find a Job?

One of the best ways to get a job is to create your own. That's how most kids make their money. If your neighbor shovels the snow off his own walk and driveway, and you convince him that he should pay you to do it, that's creating a new job. If you start doing laundry for working mothers and single people who don't have time to do their own, that's another new job. And if you decide to make Christmas wreaths for people to hang on their front doors, that's still another.

In each of these cases you have gone into business for yourself. You are your own boss. But the important thing is that you went out and discovered something you could do for other people that they would pay you for, or found something to sell them that they would buy. There were no "help wanted" signs, no ads in the paper for you to answer.

So the first place jobs come from is you creating your own—going into business for yourself.

The second place you can find a job is to replace someone in an existing job. Suppose the kid who works at the local gas station quits, or maybe gets fired, and you get his job. That happens every day in businesses all over the country. People leave one job to find another, and when they leave, they leave a vacancy for someone else to fill. This does not represent the creation of a new job. It's just people changing places.

The third source of jobs is new jobs that are created by businesses that are growing, or by new businesses just getting started. Suppose there's been a lot of new construction in your area and many new families are moving into the homes and apartments that have been built. Now there's a new job for a paper boy. Or a new Jack-in-the-Box may have been built in your neighborhood. If you're one of the first ones to apply, you might end up working there. Businesses that are growing provide most of the new jobs in this country. The more profitable these businesses are, the faster they grow. And the faster they grow, the more new jobs they create.

Why Can't the Government Just Hire Everyone Who Needs a Job?

To answer that question, you have to start by asking another question: Where would the government get the money to pay everyone? The government *has no money* except the money it takes as taxes from business and from individuals—most from individuals like your parents. Once you earn enough to pay taxes, some of the government's money will come from you, too. If the government hires people just so they'll have a job, it has to pay those people with the money it takes from your parents and from the company your parents work for.

But what if the government, instead of raising taxes so it could hire people, lowered taxes instead? Then companies and people would have more money to invest, and the new investments would create new jobs. The people with the new jobs would pay taxes, too. And the new taxes they would pay might even give the government more income.

That seems like a better way to do it.

What Can a Worker Do to Increase His Pay or Profits?

There are two important ways that you can increase what you make. The first is by improving your skills—becoming better at the job you do. The second is by your employer (or you, if you are in business for yourself) investing in new tools that let you produce more in the same amount of time.

Improving your skills means you have learned how to get more work done in an hour or a day. Both managers and workers know that when more work is done, more pay is available. The same thing is true if you're a kid in your own business. If you can mow a lawn in forty-five minutes, while it takes another kid an hour to do one the same size and you both get paid the same amount, *you'll* make more than he will. If you can make $1 an hour for walking a dog, two customers and two dogs at the same time will earn you $2 an hour.

But there are limits to how fast you can push a mower or how many dogs you can handle at once. Tools can't help you with dog walking, but they can help you with mowing a lawn. The proper use of tools is the second way to increase the amount of money you can make. Buying a power mower will let you do a larger lawn, or more lawns, in the same amount of time.

Modern businesses provide tools of many kinds to save labor and increase the output of their employees. Here are a few examples of what all this means to us.

A coal miner using hand tools could once produce only about three tons of coal a day, but when power tools become available, production went up to ten tons. Today, with even more modern equipment, production in some mines is as high as 35 tons per day for each man.

Cotton is an even better example than coal. After cotton is picked, the fibers must be removed from the seeds. When it was done by hand, it was a very time-consuming job. A man could clean only about one pound of cotton fiber a day. Then a machine called a cotton gin was invented. Using a hand-operated cotton gin, one man could then clean 50 pounds of cotton per day. The addition of steam or water power allowed production to rise to 1,000 pounds per day, per man.

Tools have been extremely important to farmers in the development of their ability to produce greater quantities of food. Back in 1830, farmers raised their food using hand tools and animals. When a farmer's plow was pulled by a horse, it took him 57.7 hours to plant and harvest 20 bushels of wheat. In 1896, farmers started using tractors, and that same farmer could then plant and harvest 20 bushels in 8.8 hours. By 1940, using all power equipment, the same job could be done in 4.1 hours.

If you are the farmer who has made the effort to learn and keep up with the latest and best ways to produce food, you have improved your skills as a farmer. And if you've saved money and invested in the very latest machinery available, you have provided yourself with the tools you need. Using your tools and skills the best way you know how, you work hard to make as much profit as you can. If all of this means you produce nine times as much food in a year as another farmer, you should be able to earn a lot more money. With your profits you can buy more land and expand your business. To do this, you will need to invest your profits in additional farm machinery and to hire more workers to run that machinery for you. You are reinvesting your profits in hopes of making even greater profits in the future, and you are creating new jobs.

The same thing is true of a nonfarm business or factory. When a growing company invests money in new production facilities, it creates new jobs. And that's expensive. The land, buildings, and machinery to create just *one* new job in a typical industry today cost $38,000 to $40,000. One new job for a production worker in a factory requires an investment of $52,000. In petroleum refining, the business of taking the oil we get from wells and turning it into gasoline and other products, the investment to create each new job is $200,000.

That takes a lot of *saving!*

Where Does All This Money Come From?

Before any money can be invested, someone must save it. When a company like Ford makes a profit, if it pays all the profits out to the owners, there are no savings. So Ford pays only part of its profits to the people who own its shares. The rest is savings that can be reinvested in the business.

Another source of money is borrowing. The money available to be borrowed often comes from the savings of people like you or your parents. If you take half the money you earn from babysitting and put it in a savings account at a bank, it doesn't just sit there. The bank uses it to make loans to other people or to businesses. In other words, the bank puts your money to work. For the use of your money, the bank pays you interest, maybe 5 or 6 percent per year. If the bank now takes the money from many other small savings accounts and adds it to yours, there's enough to make a loan to a business. That business is now able to invest the money in new tools, in hopes of making a profit from their use. (The bank makes a profit, too, by charging the company maybe 10 or 12 percent interest for the loan.) The tool might be a $700 typewriter, or a $15,000 truck. In the process, a new job has been created for a secretary or a truck driver. His or her profit is in the form of wages from that job.

But it all started with you and the other savings accounts like yours. Because *you* saved, the bank had money. Because the bank had money available, the company was able to get a loan. The loan purchased a new machine that provided one new job.

There's one other place companies get the money they need to create new jobs. Companies sell stock to people who want to invest. Investors who buy a share of a company's ownership do it

107

in hopes of making a profit for themselves. In this case, too, the money must be saved before it can be invested.

All this works for a kid just as it does for a large business. If you want to make more money waxing floors, you can buy an electric floor polisher and do it faster. If you are delivering your papers on foot, you can invest in a bike and deliver more papers. If you decide that renting surf mats at a lake might be a good summer job, you can invest in surf mats. In each case you need money (called "capital") to invest in your business. If you've already saved enough waxing floors or delivering papers, you can just buy your floor polisher or bike out of your profits. If you don't have enough, maybe your dad will "invest" some money in your little business. Or maybe he'll loan you all, or part, of what you need, if he has some extra money saved.

So there are three places a business can get money for investment. The first is from profits that are kept in the business and not paid out to owners. The second is from borrowing. The third is from people who are willing to invest in the company's future. In each of these cases, the money must first be saved by someone. And just as important, the company must be profitable (unless it is just getting started). Without proits, the business can save no money for reinvestment. Without profits, the bank will not make the loan. Without profits, or a belief there will soon be profits, who would invest in the company? No matter how you look at it, it all gets back to profits.

But Don't New Machines Sometimes Put People Out of Work?

It happens, but usually new machines create more jobs. It's because of these machines that we are able to enjoy the luxuries that we have. You probably would not enjoy being forced to haul wood and boil water before you could take a bath. And how would you like to do your homework using only a candle or a lantern? Many candle and lantern makers were put out of business once homes had electricity. These people were forced to go into other businesses when the demand for their products disappeared. But if the introduction of electricity put many people out of work for a while, it also created new industries, new places to find jobs. There were plants building steam boilers and generators to make electricity and plants manufacturing copper wire to get the electricity into our homes. There was coal to be mined to provide the energy that was needed.

Finally, what if a company buys a computer? That computer replaces lots of people, and many of them have to go elsewhere to find work. But some of them can be trained to operate the computers. Once they have been trained to do this, they will receive more pay for their work because they are more highly skilled. If the computer improves the company's profits, those profits may be invested in new machines out in the shop, making more jobs for production workers. The computer's purchase also provides more jobs for the people who make them. IBM, the world's largest maker of computers, employs about 300,000 people.

So the purchase of one new machine *can* cause a temporary loss of jobs for some people, but it usually creates more jobs somewhere else. The fact is that most of the money invested in new tools and plants is spent by businesses that need them to expand, and these growing companies provide most of the new jobs.

A recent five-year study compared six very large companies with five young companies that were growing rapidly. The five small companies formed 35,000 new jobs in five years. The six giants formed only 25,000 new jobs, in spite of the fact that the sales of the six large companies were thirty-seven times as great as the sales of the small ones. Money invested in tools by these small companies did not eliminate jobs, it created them.

Conclusion

So where do jobs come from? Most new jobs come from young and rapidly growing businesses that are profitable. As these businesses seek to increase their profits by growing, they must invest in new offices, plants, and equipment. The money from these investments must be saved out of profits or obtained from other people who invest in the company or loan it money. The money that is invested by the company creates new jobs. Before the government can provide jobs, it must first collect taxes. The more people a government employs, the more taxes must be collected. The more taxes a government collects, the less money *you* have, the less your parents have, and the less the companies that you work for have. The result? Less money for business to invest in new jobs.

CHAPTER 13

COMPETITION—
IS IT GOOD FOR US?

The battle started in the living room on Saturday. Five kids were involved. On Sunday the struggle was still raging, but only three kids were left. Why did they have to start in the middle of everything, right in front of the TV set? No one dared walk near that part of the room for fear of upsetting things. It lasted till Tuesday, when, much to the family's relief, one player had finally won the game—we had a winner!

The kids were playing Monopoly. The objective of the game is to outmaneuver your competitors: To end up with all the money and force all the other players into bankruptcy.

The man responsible for the mess in the living room is Charles B. Darrow of Germantown, Pennsylvania. Darrow was one of the victims of the Great Depression of the 1930s. He worked out the details of the game to amuse himself during the period he was unemployed. Before the Depression, the Darrows' favorite vacation spot was Atlantic City, New Jersey. When it came to naming the streets in the game, those in Atlantic City were the ones he chose.

The first Monopoly sets were hand-made. Darrow gave them to friends and sold a few to a Philadelphia department store. The game was an unexpected success. Soon he was unable to keep up with the orders. He arranged for Parker Brothers to take over manufacture and sale of the game. Now Monopoly outsells all other games, not just in the United States but throughout the Western world. Today it is published in fifteen languages and twenty-five foreign countries.

Why is this game so popular? Perhaps it is because competition is an important part of life in most Western industrialized countries including the United States, and it affects the lives of kids as well as adults. Competition is often criticized as a process where only the biggest and most ruthless survive. However, this is not the case. Competition operates according to rules, just as the game of Monopoly does. Here we'll look at competition to see how it works in the world of business and how it affects the world of kids as well.

What Is Competition?

> "RENT!! You landed on Boardwalk and I have a hotel.
> You owe me $2,000!"

You are competing in one way or another from the time you are born. Once you are in school, you compete with others for good grades. If you go out for basketball, first you compete with others to make the team. Then the team competes with the other teams in your league for the championship. Each team is one of the competitors.

In some ways, this is similar to business. We often find one company that makes the best products in its industry, has the best salesmen and the highest sales, and makes the most profit—one company with hotels on Boardwalk and Park Place. But sometimes it's three different companies. One with the best products, another with the highest sales, another that is the most profitable. It is possible, in other words, to have many winners in business. Just because one company is the *most* successful does not mean that other companies in that industry are unsuccessful. In some businesses, there are hundreds of companies that are able to compete successfully. How many stores sell clothing in your community? Or groceries? Is there more than one gas station in your town? In each of these cases, one may be the largest, but another may make the most profit.

Who Chooses the Winners?

"GO TO JAIL — Go Directly to Jail. DO NOT PASS GO. DO NOT COLLECT $200."

In the game of Monopoly there *must* be losers. But, as we have just seen, in business there can be many winners, not just one. That does not mean every new business survives. Many do not. In the real world of business there are also losers — in the long run probably a lot more losers than winners.

Let's take another look at sports. In many schools the football season is a major event. Lots of kids try out for the team. You know who selects the football team. It's the coach. And you know who picks the actors and actresses for the school play. That's the drama teacher. But in the game of business who makes the selections?

The answer is *YOU!* You, your parents, your neighbors, the owner of the business down the street — everyone in this country who decides to buy one thing and not to buy another. If you go to the store to buy a game, when you decide which one to buy you have also made a decision *not* to buy. If it's a choice between Yahtze and Scrabble and you choose Yahtze, you have cast one vote for the company that manufactures that game and one vote against the manufacturer of the Scrabble game. The makers of Monopoly, Yahtze, and Scrabble each receive many votes every year. They are among the winners. That's why those games are almost always on the shelves at your store. But there are other games on the shelves that you only see for a while. Then they disappear because not enough people buy them. Those are the losers. They are the ones that did not receive enough votes.

Your parents vote for companies in the food industry each time they go to the store. First, they vote for the store they like best. That's the place they shop. Once inside, they have several choices of almost everything they buy. They buy the products they like best, or the ones they know you like. When they get home with the groceries, you can see how they voted. For them, the things they brought home were the winners.

Competition, of course, is not restricted to businesses or sports. When you go out looking for a job, you are competing with every other kid who is looking for a job at the same time. You may go to the newspaper office and tell them you would like to deliver papers. You're likely to find ten or fifteen kids in line ahead of you. Or you might get lucky and arrive on the day they need someone. A recent conversation with a manager of a McDonald's went like this:

Is there much competition for the jobs you have available here?

Yes, but our problem is finding good employees.

Then there are plenty of kids interested in working and it's just a question of finding the good ones?

Oh, there's no shortage of kids who are interested. We have hundreds of applications. But finding good workers is difficult.

This brief interview illustrates two kinds of competition. First is competition for the job; there are hundreds of kids applying but only a few jobs available at one time. But the competition does not stop there. Once you get the job, you are competing to keep it. If you never smile at the customers, make mistakes on the cash register, move slowly while others move fast, there are many others eager to take your place.

Maybe you lose the job. But you're not out of the game yet. You just lost one turn. Hopefully, you learned something in the process.

What Good Can Come Out of Losing?

> "PAY POOR TAX OF $15"

Losing a job is not a pleasant experience, but sometimes it's the best thing that can happen to you. If you learned your lesson well, you'll probably be a winner next time.

It's exactly the same with companies. Sometimes companies get into the wrong business. Or they get into a business that changes and they are unable to keep up. Let's look at the case of a small electronics firm that got into the business of making hand-held calculators. When Electronics, Inc., got started, calculators sold for $99.95. The company was successful from the very beginning because the people who started it knew the electronics business very well. The company and its sales grew rapidly. However, other companies were getting into the business at the same time, and soon prices started coming down. Electronics, Inc., lowered its prices, and even though it made less money on each sale, the company was selling a lot more calculators and remained profitable. Then some large companies got into the business. Prices dropped to $19.95. One day Electronics,

Inc., realized it could not sell its products for $19.95 and still make money.

The company had two choices. Some companies faced with this situation might fire all their employees, sell their buildings and equipment for whatever they could get, and disappear. But two of the engineers at Electronics, Inc., had been fooling around with electronic games. Two of the games were very popular with all their friends. Everyone in the company was playing with them on coffee breaks and during their lunch hours. The company made a decision. It started manufacturing and selling games.

Change does not guarantee any company's success, but this company did well. Electronics, Inc., ended up in a business where it could make a profit. The company was forced to go out of the calculator business, but it did *not* have to go out of business altogether.

If a Company Is Losing Money, Why Doesn't It Just Raise Prices?

"Grand Opera Opening. COLLECT $50 FROM EVERY PLAYER for Opening Night Seats."

Wouldn't it be nice if it was that easy? It's not! Companies cannot raise prices just because they want more money for what they sell. It's a lot more complicated than that. In a competitive economy like ours, two things set prices for most companies — costs and competition. You can't sell your products for less than it costs to make them or you will lose money. So you need to charge more than costs. But how much more are you able to charge? It's pretty hard to charge more than your competition is charging. If your prices are too high, customers will buy from other companies.

Here's how competition works to keep prices down. Suppose Post has come up with an idea for a new breakfast cereal. No one's ever made one like this before, so Post decides to test it in a few stores. It costs them 60¢ to make each box, and Post decides they will charge the store 90¢. People like the new cereal. It sells so well that Post increases production, and soon it's on the shelves of every supermarket in the country.

Meanwhile, Kellogg's is not ignoring what's going on. They figure they can make any cereal Post can make and maybe even make it better. Kellogg's waits to see how the new cereal sells. Once it becomes obvious that it is popular with shoppers, they start making a cereal that is similar. The salesmen for Kellogg's go to the store managers and say, "We'll sell you *our* new cereal for

80¢. That's 10¢ less than Post's." Soon Kellogg's new cereal is appearing on all the grocery shelves, and Post's sales are dropping. But Post is not going to sit quietly while Kellogg's steals their market. Their response is to cut the price of each box to 70¢, 10¢ lower than Kellogg's price. Kellogg's matches the price cut.

Now we've arrived at the point where the price will probably stop dropping. Neither company will cut the price to 60¢. That's what it costs them to make the cereal. At 70¢, each company makes a profit of 10¢ a box.

The point is, in pricing its products, a company must sell somewhere between two prices. One of these prices is the one that is high enough to make them a profit. The other is the one that is low enough to get them the business. If they sell below their cost, they lose money. If they sell above the price offered by their competition, no one will buy. It's as simple as that.

What Good Does Competition Do?

"ADVANCE TOKEN TO NEAREST UTILITY. IF UNOWNED, YOU MAY BUY IT FROM THE BANK. IF OWNED, PAY OWNER TEN TIMES THE AMOUNT SHOWN ON DICE."

Competition keeps prices down on almost everything you buy, and it is the major factor in setting prices. Even when prices are rising, without competition they would rise faster and higher. But companies compete in other ways that are of benefit to you. They also compete to provide the highest-quality products and the best service.

If there are three supermarkets near your home and they all charge the same prices for food, where will your mother shop? Chances are she'll shop at the one that provides the best service, the one that has the most courteous checkers, provides kids to carry her groceries to the car, and always has a clean floor and neat shelves. Your mother is voting with her checkbook. She's voting for the store that does the best job of running its business.

Kids compete, just as businesses do, on the basis of quality and service as well as price. You may get a job cleaning out your neighbor's garage because you are willing to do it for $1.50 an hour when some other kid wants $2. But that's only the first time around. If you do a sloppy job or do poor-quality work, you won't be invited back to wash the windows. And even if you leave the garage spotless then show up three hours late to do the windows, you are not providing good service. It takes all three: high *quality* and good *service* at the right *price*. That almost always spells success. Provide all three and you're a winner.

The consumer gets the prize in the game of competition. In the case of the hand calculator, the price came down for two reasons. The first was a change in how the calculators were made. The second reason the price came down was that more companies were getting into the calculator business. This added competition forced the price down so low that some companies were unable to compete; those who did stay in the business only made a small profit on each calculator but they sold enough of them to ensure that the company remained profitable. The buyer benefited from both events.

Is It Fair When a Big Company Runs a Little One Out of Business?

> "You owe me $1500 rent.
> If you can't pay me, you're out!"

No, that would not be fair, if that were the way it worked. But it's not. Companies do go out of business for all the reasons we discussed, but just as in Monopoly, the game of competition has rules. In Monopoly, the rules are not designed to keep everyone in the game. And the rules in the competitive game are not set up to keep everyone in business. They are, however, designed to make everyone play fair.

Large companies could run little companies out of business very easily if there were no rules. Let's assume that you live in a neighborhood where there is only one small grocery store. Then a large supermarket chain decides to build a store nearby. When the supermarket is ready to open, its manager could go over to the little store and check prices on everything. Then when he opened his store, he could mark everything at very low prices in hopes of getting all the business. But suppose some people continued to shop at the small store. The supermarket manager could then cut his prices even more, and start selling his food at a loss because this chain's other stores are operating at a profit. At some point, everyone would stop buying food at the small store and the supermarket would have all the customers to itself. The small grocery store would have to go out of business. Now the supermarket manager could raise prices without worrying about competition. In fact, he could charge more for things than the little store had charged before, and shoppers like your mother would be forced to pay the higher prices because there would be only one place to shop.

This would be described as "unfair competition," and there

are laws that prohibit it. When a company uses unfair tactics like this, there are courts to enforce the rules.

One highly competitive business is the record industry. Records are made from plastics, which are made from chemicals that come from petroleum. So we could say that competition in the record business starts with oil companies competing for the best spots to drill wells. The competition continues as oil is made into chemicals, and chemical companies compete to sell to the record companies. The next step is competition among the artists. Without a record company to make and sell their records, a rock group, soloist, or orchestra earns nothing.

Before the artists can make a dime, the record companies must sell the records to the stores who sell them to you. Record companies compete with one another in many ways. Getting the best artists on your label is very important. Another way the record companies compete is through advertising and promotion. They send free records to all the radio stations that play music. They advertise in magazines, on the radio, and on television. The more popular the album becomes, the more they can sell to the stores.

The final step is competition between record stores. Most popular albums are priced on the jacket at $7.98. But you seldom pay that price. Stores that sell a large volume of records often price them at around $5.99. In a special sale, prices might be cut as low as $4.99. Record stores also compete by advertising to get you into their store and by keeping a good selection of popular albums in stock so you can always find what you want.

So the record industry, just like the supermarket business, is a very competitive one. Yet there are many companies making and selling records. And many retail stores that sell records to kids like you. They exist side by side, large companies and small ones, all with the same opportunity to make a profit.

Conclusion

The benefits that competition provides are much greater than the cost. It operates to provide the best possible products and services at a reasonable cost. And while it is true that not all businesses survive, anyone who tries is a winner in some ways, even if he fails. The lessons learned by trying may make the next attempt a big success. The athlete who does not win the gold medal must be considered a winner when compared with those who were not willing to try.

Excerpts and quotations from MONOPOLY® GAME, © 1936 by permission of Parker Bros.

CHAPTER 14

TAXES – DO THEY NEED TO BE SO HIGH?

At 5:32 P.M. on May 11, John Jones returned home from the plant. He spoke to no one but marched straight to the drawer where he kept all his records and papers, spread them out on the dining table, and started working on something. At 6:40 he stood up, put the papers away and announced he was going for a walk.

John was back for dinner at 7:15. He sat down at the table and said to his wife, "Martha, tomorrow will be my first day at work this year."

It was a trick of some kind, Martha was sure of that, but she always went along. "What do you mean, John?" she asked.

"I mean that as of 5 o'clock this evening, I haven't earned one single cent for myself, for you, or for the kids so far this year, that's what I mean. None of what I've earned so far is mine."

"What do you mean, not yours?" chorused his wife and three kids. This sounded serious. "Not mine," John repeated. "We don't get to keep any of it."

"Who gets it?"

"The tax man gets it, that's who. Starting tomorrow, it's ours. But January till May is a long time to work just to pay taxes to the government."

A long time, indeed! According to a 1978 estimate by the U.S. Chamber of Commerce, the "average American" was expected to work until May 11 of that year—or 131 days—just to pay his federal, state, and local taxes. That works out to about 2 hours and 45 minutes of each 8-hour working day for the entire year.

Taxes have been something adults complained about, a distant thing from the lives of kids. But that's changing. In many parts of the country today, taxes are a current topic of discussion in the classroom and at the dinner table. Frustrated taxpayers in more than one state have voted to lower their own taxes. More and more people are asking the question, "How much government spending is enough?" The "message" they are sending to their elected officials is that government spending has already gone too far.

Government spending has increased more than tenfold since 1950, to a total in 1977 of $621 billion. In 1950, government spending at all levels accounted for about 21 percent of all national expenditures. But by 1978, government spending accounted for 33 percent of the total. A look at just one federal agency shows where some of our tax money is going. The Department of Energy had a 1978 budget of $10.5 billion. For 1979 it is estimated at $12.6 billion. This budget is larger than the 1976 profits of the 18 largest oil companies in this country combined. Twenty thousand people work for this one government agency alone.

The subject of taxes and the connection between government spending and the taxes we pay are confusing to youngsters. Let's look at taxes from several different angles and see if the subject can be made more understandable.

Why Do We Pay Taxes?

For many centuries, humankind has realized that it is efficient to hire specialists to perform certain tasks for the common good. If each family had to depend on its own members to fight fires, who would save their house if it caught fire during their vacation? Few people could handle a fire even if started when they were at home. The answer to this problem is to have a fire department supported by everyone in the community.

Tax-supported services of one kind or another have become an accepted part of our daily lives. We rely on such services without even thinking about them. Kids, however, seldom realize the wide range of things available to them that are paid for when their parents pay their tax bill.

Let's look at a few from a kid's point of view.

All of us live in a town, a city, or a country that is run by what is called a local government. Not all of these local governments spend their money in exactly the same way, but here are some services normally provided by the taxes they collect.

Schools — The public schools are built with tax money. Taxes also pay the salaries of teachers, counselors, custodians, and coaches. Taxes pay the light bill and pay the bus driver's salary and buy gasoline. Running the schools is very expensive and, for many people, school taxes are the largest part of their local tax bill each year.

Schools provide a good example of two other things you should know about taxes.

The first is that taxes are paid by all taxpayers, even if they do not use the services provided. This means that families with no children pay school taxes just as do families whose children use the schools. Let's assume three families live on the same street in your town. One family has no children, the second sends its kids to a private school, and the third has ten kids, all in public school. If all three families' homes are worth about the same amount and their incomes are similar, they will all pay about the same amount in school taxes. If your parents are sending you to a private school, they are paying twice: first, for the tuition at the school you attend; second, taxes to operate the public schools you do not attend.

Many people never use the public library, but everyone's taxes support it. It's the way our tax system works.

The second thing about taxes that can be learned from looking at school taxes is that the money to support one activity or service can come from several different sources. In your community, most of the money to support the schools might come from property taxes on homes and businesses. Your state might pay part of the bill, and many special programs are paid for by the federal government. The money, however, all comes from the same place. It is collected from businesses and from people like your parents, no matter who *seems* to be paying the bill.

Here are some of the other services that tax money provides:

Libraries — Taxes build them, buy the books, pay the salaries.

Streets and highways — Taxes build and repair them.

Buses and subways — The fares you pay almost never cover the costs. Taxes make up the difference.

Police and fire protection — Taxes pay for police and fire stations, police cars and fire engines, and salaries.

Recreation facilities —Taxes pay for the cost and operation of playgrounds and parks, of public tennis courts and swimming pools, of Little League and soccer fields. State taxes pay for larger state parks, and the federal government operates the National Park System with federal taxes.

Public health services and hospitals —Taxes support these in a variety of ways, depending upon the nature of the service provided.

Public assistance —Taxes help support many people who are unable to take care of themselves without help. Among these are the blind, the disabled, and a variety of other groups of people.

Taxes we pay to the federal government are spent on hundreds of different activities. Among the largest are those for public assistance (welfare), social security, and the cost of supporting our military forces.

You can see that government provides many things for many people. What too many of those people forget is that the government has no magic source of money. No local, state, or federal government has money of its own to spend. Everything government spends must first be borrowed from people or taken from them in the form of taxes.

How Much Does Our Family Have to Pay?

For each family it depends on the amount of income earned and on local tax laws. Almost all families pay federal income taxes, social security taxes, and property taxes. Some states also have state income taxes and sales taxes. If yours is an average American family, more than one-third of your family income will be paid out in some combination of these taxes each year.

Why Can't the Government Get Its Money from Big Business?

It does. One large company, Libby-Owens-Ford, makes a number of products, including window glass for homes and automobiles. In 1977 the company paid taxes of about $76 million that was sent to various governments, compared with profits that year of $59 million. (It also took $68 million out of its employees' paychecks for taxes.) Many people assume that it's better to tax business than to tax individuals. In the following example, we can see that it doesn't work that way.

Patti is going into the lemonade business. She has it all carefully planned in advance. Her location—across from the Little League field. Her customers—her brother Tim and his Little League teammates. Her costs—5¢ a cup, for lemons, sugar, and cups. Her selling price—10¢ a cup. Her profit—5¢ a cup.

Patti's business is a success. The team thinks 10¢ is a good price for lemonade, and Patti thinks 5¢ is a good profit for her efforts.

Patti will pay no taxes on her lemonade profits. She won't make that much money. But what if she did? Let's see what would happen to Patti's little business if she had to pay taxes just as other businesses do.

And let's see who ends up paying the tax bill.

Patti is told by the tax collector that she will have to give him half of everything she makes. Since she only makes 5¢, that means the government will take 2 1/2¢ leaving *her* only 2 1/2¢ after she pays the taxes. "It's not worth it," she thinks. "Why should I go to all that work for only 2 1/2¢?" Then she has another thought. Why not just charge more?

So Patti raises the price to 15¢ a cup.

Now she has 10¢ left after paying for her supplies. The tax man gets half of that—5¢—so she has 5¢ left for herself.

Patti is back where she started. But Tim isn't! Now, he and his friends must pay 15¢ if they want lemonade. They're mad at Patti. And Patti is mad at the tax collector.

They might as well all get used to it. That's the way things are. Business taxes are *not* really taxes on business. They are taxes on consumers, just like Tim and his friends. The price of *everything* includes taxes. It's part of the price of tennis shoes, hamburgers, record albums, and sewing machines.

But the lemonade story is not over yet. Tim and his friends, just like Patti, are too young to pay income taxes yet. But if they *did* have to pay taxes, just as adults do, they would probably pay one-fourth of their income (25 percent) to the government in the form of income taxes. Now, out of each 20¢ they earn there will be 5¢ in income taxes, leaving them only 15¢ to spend on themselves. That buys one cup of Patti's lemonade for 15¢.

So taxes make a big difference. Without taxes, Patti could sell lemonade for 10¢, make a 5¢ profit, and everyone was happy. Now, to make the same 5¢, Patti must charge 15¢, and Tim, to get the 15¢, must earn 20¢.

Companies don't really pay taxes. People pay taxes. Taxes are just one of the costs of doing business and are included in the selling price. You pay the company's taxes for it everytime you buy something. It can't be any other way.

Why Not Get the Money from Rich People?

That sounds like a great idea, unless you happen to be rich. The fact is that if taxes were raised on people with high incomes, it wouldn't mean much to the government at all. It wouldn't lower the taxes your parents now pay by enough to make much difference. The Tax Foundation, Inc., did a study to see how much additional tax revenue the government could get if it raised rates to 100 percent on all taxable yearly income over $32,000. That would mean that whenever a person had earned $32,000 in taxable income in one year, the government would take everything he they made for the rest of the year. Those new taxes would have brought the government an additional $12.5 billion in 1973, but the government's budget in that year was nearly $250 billion. All that new money would have run the government for *less* than 3 weeks.

Right now you may be washing windows, babysitting, or hauling trash to make a few dollars every week, but you don't plan to do that when you're an adult. When you're grown you'd probably like to make a lot of money. You might be thinking about becoming an airline pilot, a doctor, a lawyer, president of a college, a congressman, or even a stockbroker. You might start a business of your own that is very profitable. You can make more than $32,000 a year doing any of these things, and many others. But if the government took everything over $32,000, would you try to make $50,000? Would you try to make $100,000?

There's one other big problem with "taxing the rich." One of these days you might decide to go into business for yourself—not just a small business, but one that requires a lot of money to get started. You may have saved part of it yourself, but where will you get the rest? Not from a bank. They are not in the business of lending money to companies that are just getting started. Most of the money invested in new businesses, like the one you want to start, comes from individuals—from people who can afford to take the risk that you might fail and the investment would be lost. But if taxes on people with high incomes were so high that no one could ever get rich, there might be no place to borrow the money you need to get that business started. Wealthy individuals (you might be one someday) perform a very useful function in our economy. In the hope of making large profits, they are often willing to take large risks. Many of the new products you enjoy are made by young companies that were started with the money from people who could take risks. If no one had the money to take these risks, these companies would never have been started.

There is just no way to avoid paying taxes. Taxing the rich doesn't work. That won't raise enough to make much difference.

Raising the tax on business won't work either, since we all pay those taxes whenever we buy anything. So one of these days you'll start paying your share too.

When Will I Have to Start Paying Taxes?

Once your taxable income passes $2,200 a year (1978 rates), you will start paying at least 14 percent of that income to the federal government. However, since taxes are part of the cost of everything we buy, every kid like you is actually "paying taxes" when you spend your first 25¢. It didn't even start there. Taxes were part of the cost of the baby food your parents bought for you from the very beginning. Taxes start when you're born — and stop when you die.

Conclusion

No large group of people can live together without some type of organization. In today's world that organization is called government. Governments, however, cannot operate without money, and each government must take that money from its people in the form of taxes.

Who decides how much the government should take? These decisions are made by the people we elect to represent us; primarily in our state legislatures and in Congress. Once you begin voting, you can cast your ballot for representatives who agree with how you feel about spending and taxes. From that time on, decisions about the taxes you will pay will be partly up to you.

CHAPTER 15

INFLATION—
WHAT'S IT ALL ABOUT?

In May, 1978, the McBride family decided to have Mexican food for dinner. A search of the pantry produced a dusty can of refried beans. The can was bulging at the seams and obviously was too old to eat. Kim had to go to the store for a new can since the dinner was her idea. The old can was still on the kitchen counter when she got back, and she noticed the original price stamp on the lid.

"Look at these prices," she exclaimed to her mother. "How old *is* this can?"

"I'd guess it must be six or seven years old," Mrs. McBride answered. She looked at the prices. The new can cost 49¢. The old can was marked 19¢.

That evening at dinner there was only one subject of conversation—inflation. Mr. and Mrs. McBride were already quite aware of how fast prices were going up. But for Kim, age 19, and her 17-year-old brother Danny, this big jump in the price of something like beans was a shock.

Mr. McBride was very pleased that the subject had come up. By the time dinner was over, both of his kids seemed to understand their family's situation much better. They were beginning to understand that inflation is not just something you read about in the paper. It was something that was costing their family real money—every day.

In addition to the discussion of economics, the whole family enjoyed the dinner enough to fix it again one month later. Danny came home with a confused look on his face: "Didn't the refried beans cost us 49¢ before?" he asked. The new can cost 57¢. That was 8¢ more in just thirty days. Kim and Danny arrived at the same conclusion at the same time: "If we're going to have refried beans again, we'd better buy a whole case right now."

What Is Inflation?

When you pump air into your bike tire, you are "inflating" it, making it bigger. You "inflate" a basketball or soccer ball when you fill them with air. If the kind of inflation that causes prices to go up was that simple, it might be easy enough to stop. Unfortunately, it's not. There are several things that cause inflation, but the final result is the same: prices go up and up.

When prices go up, the value of your money goes down. Your dollar is worth less. Here are some prices from the New York City area to show what this means. In 1974, with $1 you could buy one Baskin-Robbins ice cream cone for 30¢, a pack of Clorets for 20¢, a ride on the subway for 30¢, a pack of M & M's for 12¢, and mail a letter for 8¢. All this could have been yours, if you had one dollar in your pocket back in 1974.

However, four years later things were different. In 1978, the ice cream cone was 50¢, Clorets were 27¢, the subway cost 50¢, M & M's were 25¢, and the postage stamp was 15¢. That adds up to $1.67.

The dollar in your pocket still looks the same. But it only buys the subway ride and the ice cream cone now. You still need another 67¢ to get the rest. So your dollar is *worth less*. For you, that's what inflation is.

126

What Causes Prices to Go Up?

There are two kinds of inflation. Sometimes it's hard to tell them apart, but they are different, and each kind has been given its own name. One kind results from too much money; the other happens when certain costs increase faster than production. We'll look at them separately and try and explain them in ways a kid can understand.

Here's what the dictionary says about inflation: Inflation is a "relatively sharp and sudden increase in the quantity of money or credit or both relative to goods available for purchase. Inflation always produces a rise in the price level." All that means is that if everyone has more money, but there are no more things to buy than there were before, prices will go up. People will simply pay more for things they want. This kind of inflation is named "Demand-Pull" inflation. People want more things than are available. The higher *demand pulls* prices higher.

If you have $2 in your pocket and a friend of yours offers to sell you his yo-yo for $1, you know you'll only have $1 left if you buy it. But if you have $100 in your pocket, you could pay him $2 for the yo-yo and never miss it. You'll still have $98 left. You've got more money, but there's still only one yo-yo. Let's see how it might work if everyone had more money all at the same time.

We will assume that the government is going to double the supply of dollars all at once. Every individual, every businessman, every church, every kid—everyone gets his money supply doubled. You get an extra $5 to match the $5 you have in your pocket. Right now you have $275 in your savings account. You've been saving it to buy a Moped that costs $350. Your parents are also saving money. They want to pay cash for a $5,000 car. They've saved $3,000 so far. Suddenly your parents' savings account has doubled to $6,000, and your savings account contains $550. You have enough for your Moped, and your parents have enough for their new car. That night your dad says, "Tomorrow night we'll have a new car and you can get your Moped, too." This is too good to be true. You thought it would take at least three months more to save enough money to buy it.

The next day you all jump in the family's old car and head for the automobile dealer. But when you get there you find there's a line of people waiting to buy cars. "Looks like a lot of other people had the same idea we did," your dad says. "We'll go over and you can get your Moped first. Then we'll come back here." However, there's a line at the Moped dealer, too. The Moped dealer has been going crazy all day. There was a line waiting when he arrived in the morning. By 9 A.M. there were more people in line than he had Mopeds to sell, and he was on the phone calling the distributor looking for at least another hundred. He was too late. Every Moped that the distributor had was gone. The dealer looked outside; the line was getting longer. His salesmen were selling them as fast as they could write orders. The dealer suddenly realized that once his entire stock of Mopeds was sold, he might as well close. There wouldn't be anything for him or his salesman to do until they could get another shipment. He made a decision. He would raise the price from $350 to $400. Maybe the extra profit would come in handy while he was waiting for things to get back to normal. The dealer came outside and announced to everyone in the line that the price was being raised to $400. You and your dad looked at each other. Was it worth $400? Why not? After all, you had $550 in your savings account now, and that was more than enough to cover the higher price. Then the dealer made another announcement. He only had fifteen Mopeds left. "I'll pay $450," someone shouted. The dealer shrugged his shoulders, "Might as well make it while I can," he thought. "Okay, the last fifteen go to the highest bidders."

Maybe you got your Moped, and maybe you didn't. That depended on how much you were willing to pay. Maybe your dad got his new car. Maybe he had to wait until more cars could be built and shipped to the dealer.

The same thing that happened to you and your dad was happening to people all over the country. Everyone had twice as much money, but there were no more things to buy than there had been before. As a result, everyone was willing to pay a little bit more to get what they wanted than they were willing to pay the day before. The price increases worked their way all the way up and down the line, and within a year almost everything cost twice as much as it had a year before. All the new money had disappeared. All those new dollars that seemed like such a wonderful gift had vanished. When it came to buying things, those dollars were now worth only 50¢. Everything was back to normal. Things seemed the same as they were just before the new money arrived, but they were not at all the same for many people. We'll discuss that after we look at the other kind of inflation.

The second kind of inflation is called "Cost-Push" inflation. This happens when wage costs, or other costs, such as materials, go up. Then, just to keep its profits the same, a company is forced to raise prices.

As an example, we'll take a company that makes bathing suits and sells them for $10 to department stores. The department store sells the bathing suits to customers for $15. In this company, one worker can sew ten bathing suits in a day. That will result in $100 of sales each day for each worker. Part of the $100 goes to pay for materials such as fabric and thread, part for rent and other company expenses, part for workers' wages, and part for profits.

What happens to the price of bathing suits if each worker is still making ten suits per day, but the workers demand a wage increase? Once the company increases everyone's wages, the cost of making each bathing suit is higher. In order to keep profits the same as they were before, the company must now raise prices. If the stores have to pay more for the suits, they will raise prices, too. Once the workers' wage increase works its way up to the department store, you will pay $16 or $17 for the bathing suit that used to cost you $15. So wage increases without any increase in production cause inflation.

Could this company's workers get a wage increase without pushing prices higher? Yes. Here's how. Suppose this company or its workers figure out a way in which each worker can produce twelve suits in a day. Maybe the company invested in new sewing machines that were faster. Maybe the workers figured out a better way to do things in the factory. It doesn't matter. What does matter is that if a worker makes twelve suits each day that sell for $10, sales have gone from $100 to $120. Part of the $20 of new sales goes to pay for materials. The rest is available to increase the pay of the workers and increase the company's profits. In other words, increased production means wages can go up, and profits can go up, but bathing suits can stay at $10. If there's no increase in bathing suit prices, there's no inflation.

Almost everything that causes inflation fits into the two types we have mentioned above. One example of something that causes costs to go up is government regulations. When the utility company that furnishes your home with electricity is forced by the government to install pollution-control equipment, your parents pay a higher utility bill to pay for that equipment. New safety rules at factories increase costs and prices. Higher social security taxes increase the costs of everything you buy. According to General Motors, by the early 1980s the cost of every one of their cars will be $800 higher because of government regulations. When you pay higher prices for the things you buy because of new rules by the government, that's part of "cost-push" inflation.

There's nothing you can do as a kid that will cause inflation by increasing a company's costs. But you can help cause inflation yourself just by thinking that prices are going to keep going up. You remember the McBrides and their refried beans? Both kids said, "If we're going to have refried beans again, we'd better buy a whole case right now." If every family made that same decision at the same time, what would happen to the supply of refried beans? And what would happen to the price? If too many people rush out to buy new homes, new cars, and extra cases of refried beans before the next price increase, that pushes prices higher. And when workers expect prices to keep going up, they demand larger wage increases just to keep up. Once everyone gets involved in the game, it is very hard to stop.

What Does Inflation Do to Our Family?

It depends on how fast your income is rising. If your family's income is going up a little faster than prices are rising, you can keep up with inflation, but you can't get ahead. Here's how it works.

If your dad earned $10,000 in 1960, he would have paid about $1,360 in federal income taxes. To buy the same things in 1978 that your dad's income bought for your family in 1960, he had to earn $22,671. His income tax on that amount would have been almost $4,000. That's about three times as much in taxes on a little over twice as much income. In other words, taxes go up faster than your income. Let's look at exactly how much someone like your dad had to make in 1978 to buy the same things you could buy in 1960 and see where the money goes.

In 1960 he earned $10,000. He paid $1,362 in income taxes, leaving $8,638 for his family. In 1978 he had to earn $22,671. Out of that, $3,935 went to federal taxes. It looks like he has a lot left, but prices have more than doubled since 1960 and inflation has stolen $10,098 from his annual paycheck. He still has $8,638 left over after inflation and taxes. So, even though your dad's income has more than doubled since 1960, you really have no more money than you had in 1960. Inflation and taxes took every nickel of the extra income.

Your family, then, may not be living any better now, but at least it has kept up with the price increases. You are able to live as well as you did before. Unfortunately, this is not true of everyone. Some people cannot increase their income as fast as prices go up. People who are retired often live on monthly checks that will stay exactly the same each year until they die.

Frank Martinez is one of those people. When he was 30 years old, Frank and his wife decided to start saving money for the day Frank retired. The amount they decided to save each year was $1,000. Frank and his wife did save $1,000 a year, even though it meant going without many things they wanted to buy. Frank retired at the end of 1977 at age 65. Frank and his wife were very pleased. Their investment of $1,000 each year plus interest at 6 percent totaled nearly $120,000. They had many plans for the things they were going to do over the next few years. But they hadn't counted on inflation.

In 1978, the year after Frank retired, rapidly rising wages and other costs plus a large government deficit (a "deficit" is when the government spends more than its income) resulted in inflation of around 7 1/2 percent. When Frank looked at prices in the stores, he knew that the interest income he would earn on his $120,000 would buy a lot less in 1979. But Frank forgot to look at the $120,000 he had saved. In just one year, the year 1978, the actual value of his savings had dropped by almost $8,500. In one year, inflation had wiped out as much money as he had been able to save in *eight and a half years!*

Inflation destroys people's savings. The people who are hurt the worst are those who are retired. For them, it's too late to replace the money. It's just gone.

In What Other Ways Does Inflation Affect a Kid?

Since prices go up everywhere in the country during periods of inflation, we can look at a few other items from the New York area list and see how much their costs went up between 1974 and 1978: a *TV Guide*, from 15¢ to 30¢; a can of Coca-Cola, from 20¢ to 40¢; a McDonald's milkshake, from 40¢ to 59¢; developing a 36-exposure roll of Kodachrome film, from $3.95 to $5.15; Band-aids (100), from $1.13 to $1.98; a slice of pizza, from 35¢ to 50¢. All this in just four years.

One of the fastest-rising expenses during the inflationary period between 1960 and 1978 was the cost of a college education. In 1960 the average cost for each year at a private college was $1,528. If you had been born in that year and your parents had started saving for your college education, they'd have planned to save about $6,000 by the time you were 17 or 18. However, in 1977 or 1978, when you were ready to start college, one year in a private college cost an average of $4,363. The $6,000 your parents carefully saved would then take care of *less* than 1 1/2 years of college, not the four that they had planned on.

You can see that inflation affects you in many ways. Families like yours used to struggle to get ahead. In times of inflation they struggle to keep up—just to stay even. You pay the price of inflation every time you buy a milkshake or a pack of gum. You pay the price when you buy a pair of skiis or a soccer ball. The used car a teenager plans to buy costs him more, and he may have to change his college plans—go to a less expensive school or maybe work for a year or two before he can even start.

Most of all, you need to understand that inflation is not something that happens only to *other* people. It happens to everyone, including you. And you must keep it in mind whenever you do any planning for the future.

How Can Inflation Be Stopped?

Most of the things that can be done to stop inflation must be done by the government. G. William Miller, appointed head of the Federal Reserve Board in Washington in 1978, says that this country can curtail inflation if we will do several things:

The government must not "feed" inflation by running big deficits. This means the government should not, over long periods of time, spend more than its income. *You* can't spend more than you have without borrowing it and then paying it back. Neither can your parents. But the government can, and has been doing it for years. Government deficits result in the same thing that happened in our Moped example, where the supply of money was doubled, except that it's not all done in one year. It happens more slowly but it keeps pushing prices higher and higher.

Investment should be encouraged. This means that the actions taken by the government should encourage people and business to save and invest their money. For example, some of the tax rules can be changed to make it easier for companies to save enough to buy more modern tools.

The government should get rid of many rules and regulations that are not needed and hurt profits.

These are a few of the things government can do. If they are done, inflation might not disappear, but prices should rise much more slowly. Then business could plan ahead and invest the money that is needed to create new jobs. New tools that let our workers produce more would then help us sell more things to other countries that we make here at home. The cost of living and taxes would stop going up so fast that people on pensions have to sell their homes to survive. Workers would not have to ask for large raises to keep up with price increases.

Conclusion

Having some basic understanding of the causes of inflation and how it affects you is a very important part of understanding economics. It's even more important when you start planning for things you want in the future.

CHAPTER 16

SAVING—CAN A NICKEL BE WORTH A DIME?

Here comes another lawn mower! This one's being pushed by a kid named Ron. Ron grew up in the Los Angeles area. His family had enough money to get by on, but very little extra. Like many kids, Ron wanted lots of things his family could not afford to buy him, so he started doing jobs around his neighborhood. The job he liked best was mowing lawns, for two reasons. First, he made more money mowing lawns. Second, lawns had to be mowed every week, and once you got a customer it became a steady job. So in 1956 at the age of 12, Ron decided this was where he would concentrate. He also decided he'd better get a power mower, not just because it was faster but because at least two of his neighbors did not have mowers of his own. They depended on whoever mowed their lawns to bring his own. Ron's dad thought the mower sounded like a good idea and agreed to lend him enough money to buy it if he could find a good used one. The mower cost $35, and Ron was in business.

Ron worked very hard for the next three years. He spent most of his spare time on the job and saved most of what he made. By the time he was 15, he had nearly $1,500 in his savings account. Then an unusual opportunity came along. Someone offered to sell his dad an old house for $5,700. The house needed a lot of repairs, but Ron's dad felt it was worth much more than that. Ron's dad wanted to buy it, but this time *he* was the one who didn't have enough money available. He knew Ron had it, however, and suggested that they become partners in buying and fixing up the house. Ron's $1,500 would pay for the down payment and most of the materials they needed. Ron agreed.

For the next several months, Ron and his dad spent almost every weekend working on the house. It took about $1,000 for paint and materials, plus a lot of hard work to get the house ready for sale, and Ron's dad came up with the extra money they needed for repairs. The house turned out to be a very good investment. Ron's dad had been right. It sold for $13,000. Their costs for the house, including the repairs and other costs, were about $7,000. They made $6,000. Ron's half of the profit was $3,000.

Ron had taken a risk with his $1,500. If his dad had guessed wrong on the house, he might have lost some money. But now Ron had his $1,500 investment back, plus a profit of $3,000. That $4,500 was the money that paid his way through college.

Your dad may never buy a run-down house to fix up and sell. Today there are few houses left for anyone to buy at $5,700, even if they need lots of repairs. *Your* chance to make some money will come in some other way. But you never know when an opportunity will come along. If you are ready because you have money saved, it could make a big difference to you. It did for Ron.

Are There Any Other Reasons for Saving Money?

Most kids save money to buy some particular thing that they want. But that doesn't mean saving every dime you earn. It means spending part of what you earn and saving what's left over for something in the future. If you want something expensive, and you want it badly enough, you'll save more.

One important reason for saving money is so you will have it available for emergencies—for things you didn't expect. Your parents may have told you that you should save money "for a rainy day." That's one of the reasons they save money. It's important to have something extra when the car breaks down and needs expensive repairs, when there's an unexpected illness in the family, when the roof needs to be replaced, or the refrigerator wears out. When you're young, these problems are your parents' and not yours. Your problems don't involve that much money—unless you get a car.

Almost all teenagers seem to want a driver's license the minute they are old enough to drive. As soon as they can drive, the next objective is a car of their own. If a car is part of your future plans, saving had better be part of your present plans. Cars are expensive. Buying your car is only the first expense. Your first car will probably be a used one, and on used cars, things break. Suppose you're earning $200 a month at a part-time job and the automatic transmission on your car stops working. Your repair bill could easily be $400 or more. That's every dime you will earn for two months, with nothing left over, even for gas. Once a year you'll have a sizable bill for automobile insurance. These are things you have to plan for if you own a car. It's one example of "saving for a rainy day."

But there's a second use for savings. It's the one we discussed in the example of how Ron used his savings. It's called "saving for opportunities." That's an even better reason to save. Your "opportunity" might be as simple as a friend who gets a new stereo for Christmas and is willing to sell you her old one cheap. If you need a stereo and have the cash, you'll save a lot of money. Your neighbors might buy a new car and let you buy their old one. The local jeans store may be moving to a larger location and have a super sale. Someday you might even have a chance to invest in something that could make you a lot of money. A chance like Ron had. That might never happen to you, but one thing is for sure. If you have nothing saved, the greatest opportunity in the world won't do you any good at all.

How Much Should I Save?

Having a goal—something you really want—makes saving much easier. That's just as true of adults as it is of kids. So the amount you should save depends on what you are saving for and on how quickly you want to get it. If you're 9 years old and saving for a pair of skates, it doesn't really matter how fast you save your money. Whenever you have saved enough, you'll buy the skates. Sometimes, however, time is very important. If you're 12 years old and you want very much to go to a summer camp that costs $400, it's too late to start saving in May. If you decide *this* summer that you want to go next summer, you have a whole year. You can pay for next summer's camp by saving about $35 a month. If you don't decide until December, you'll have to save almost $70 a month. Planning ahead is even more important if you're thinking about college. It's not only more expensive, but it goes on for four years. While you're in college, you can earn money during the summers and maybe even work during the school year. So you don't need to have it all saved by the day you register for your freshman classes. But if you're going to pay your own way through college, you'll need to have a lot of money saved by the time you start. That means you'll have to start saving several years ahead, and that requires some careful planning.

"There's a thing called "interest" that will help you save toward future goals. When you put money in a savings account at a bank, a savings bank, or a savings and loan, they will pay you interest. Interest is payment for the use of your money. If you owned a house that someone else lived in, they would pay you rent for use of the house. When you put money that you own into the bank, the bank pays you rent for the use of the money.

We've talked about it in earlier chapters, but just to make sure you understand it, let's look again at why a savings institution wants to pay you interest. Let's suppose that on January 2 you take $1,000 and deposit it in a savings account that will pay you 6 percent interest. That means that in one year they will pay you 6 percent of $1,000, or $60, for the use of your money. The savings and loan takes the money from your account and several others and lends it to a neighbor of yours who is buying a new home. That neighbor will pay the savings and loan 9 percent interest. On your $1,000, that amounts to $90 a year. Out of that, the savings and loan has paid you $60 interest. The $30 difference is kept by the savings and loan to cover its costs and to make a profit. So the use of money has a value. If you lend money to someone else, they pay you. If you borrow money from someone else, you pay them.

Interest you might earn is not important if you're saving money for a pair of skates. The amount of money is not large enough and the time is not long enough. But when you get to the point where there's more money and a longer period of time involved, then interest makes a big difference. To see how interest can make your money grow, we'll assume that you invest $1,000 each year for thirty years in some way that earns you 6 percent per year and that you don't take out any of the money or interest earned for the full thirty years. (We will ignore the effect of taxes.) At the end of the first year your account is worth $1,000 plus $60 interest, or $1,060. Now you put in your second $1,000 and start the second year with $2,060 in the account. The second year is different from the first because this year you will also earn interest on the $60 that you earned the first year, and that will keep happening each year in the future. At the end of five years you have invested $5,000, but your account is now worth $5,975. You've earned $975 in interest, and it's beginning to add up. By the end of the tenth year you have put $10,000 into the account and its value is $13,972. Now it's growing even faster. Finally, here's what your account looks like at the end of thirty years. You have invested $30,000. The account is worth $83,802. The *interest* you have earned on your money totals $53,802.

Now we have three reasons that saving is a good idea:

Some money should be set aside for emergencies, for expenses that come up that you didn't expect.

Some money should be saved for opportunities, special things that come along that you can take advantage of if you have some cash.

Finally, whatever you save will earn money for you until you need it.

If I Borrow Money, Do I Have to Pay Interest?

Yes. It's a two-way street. If people will *pay you* for the use of your money, you have to *pay them* for the use of their money. The first large amount of money you ever borrow might be to buy your first car. We will assume the following: You buy a car for $3,000 and make a down payment on the car of $1,000; the other $2,000 you borrow from the bank. You will make monthly payments, and the bank will charge you 10 percent interest for the use of its money. When the bank figures out how much you will pay them each month, they divide the $2,000 you borrowed by twenty-four months. That comes out to about $83 a month. Over the two-year life of the loan, you will have to pay them about $220 in interest, and that, divided by twenty-four, is around $9 a month. Your monthly payment is $83 plus $9, which adds up to $92.

Now let's look at another subject you should understand very clearly before you ever borrow any money. When you borrow money, you must pay it back. It doesn't matter why you borrowed it or what happens to you after you borrow it. Let's say you've been driving your $3,000 car for a couple of months and it quits running. Your dad's mechanic says it will take $250 to get the car running again. You don't have $250 since it took all your savings for the $1,000 down payment, and since your car payments are $92 a month, that takes most of the money you earn.

Your car might sit in the driveway for six months before you save enough money to fix it. But the bank doesn't care that you can't use your car. They want their $92 every month, whether you can use your car or not.

Let's look at a much worse situation. Banks require that you insure a car when they give you a loan to buy one. But suppose that a bank did not require you to buy insurance or that you borrowed the money somewhere else and forgot to insure your car (a very dangerous thing to do). After you've had the car just one week, you drive some of your friends to a football game. When you come out, the car is gone. It's been stolen. If the police are unable to find the car and you have no insurance, you have lost the $1,000 you saved to buy it. But that's not all you've lost. You still owe $2,200 to the bank, or to whomever you borrowed the money from. You still have to pay it back, even though you have nothing to show for it. You'll be making payments for the next two years on something you never got to use. Your dad might forget about $10 he lent you, but the bank won't forget the $2,200—ever.

One additional point on borrowing money. When do you *own* your car? Is it when you buy it, or when you've finished paying for it? The answer is, you own it when you buy it. If you have an accident, you didn't damage the bank's car, you damaged your own. But if you stop making payments to the bank, it won't be yours for long. The bank has the right to take your car away from you and sell it in order to get the money you owe them if you stop making payments. Maybe you'd better have more than $1,000 saved before you buy that car. Maybe you'd better have a few extra dollars "for a rainy day." After all, what if you lost your job a month after you bought the car? How would you make the next payment, or the next two payments? If you have some *extra* money saved up, that could be used to make your payments until you have another job.

So there are many uses for savings and many good reasons for you to save, starting as early as possible. None of us knows what will happen to us in the future. Having some money in a savings account is one of the best ways to be prepared for problems — or opportunities — whenever they come your way.

CHAPTER 17

INVESTING—
NOW THAT YOU'VE SAVED
IT, WHAT'S NEXT?

Jerry and his younger sister Beth moved to a small town in
Connecticut when Jerry was in seventh grade. Their dad worked
for a large insurance company, and so did one of their neighbors,
whose son Steven was in the seventh grade also. Jerry and Steve
became good friends.

For several years Steve's dad had raised a few chickens as a
hobby. When his responsibilities at work increased, he asked
Steve to take over the job. When there were extra eggs, Steve sold
them to the neighbors, and his dad let him keep half of the

money. He made a little money that way, but never enough. Steve wanted to have more chickens so there would be more eggs to sell, but there was no more room in their yard, according to his dad.

One day while Jerry and Steve were trying to figure out a good way to make some money, they decided there was plenty of room to raise chickens in Jerry's yard. His house backed up to a small creek with nothing but woods on the other side. Jerry's dad said it was okay with him if they expanded the business, as long as the boys did the whole thing themselves.

The two boys went into the egg business. It cost them $60 each to get started. That paid for enough lumber to build a chicken coop, wire for a fence, a supply of feed, and some new baby chicks. They moved Steve's chickens across the street to their new home behind Jerry's house and got started.

Over the next two years the egg business grew rapidly. They found that fresh eggs were easy to sell, especially if they charged the same price as the stores. They got new customers as fast as they could produce more eggs. Each day they fed the chickens and gathered the eggs. Twice a week they delivered the eggs to their regular customers. When they got too busy, Beth would help them with deliveries. After paying for feed, the boys were each making between $75 and $85 a month.

Then Steve's dad was transferred. Steve would be moving away. But what about the egg business? It wouldn't be fair to Steve if he just left his half of a successful business to Jerry without getting something for it. After all, he had a lot *invested* in it after two years.

Let's see what the boys actually did have invested since the time they had started. At the very beginning they put in $120 cash. Most of that money built the chicken coop and fenced the chicken yard. The chicken coop was their "production plant." Without it, they could not produce eggs. The rest of the money was spent on chickens and feed.

What else did they have invested? As sales of eggs increased, part of their profits was spent on lumber and wire to build a larger production plant, and part went to buy more chickens. All these expenses were profits that were reinvested in the growth of the business and must be added to the original $120.

Were there any other investments? How about the time and energy spent getting regular customers who would buy their eggs? And the same for building chicken coops and fences. There's plenty of hard work involved in getting any new business going. Once a business is established and making a profit, it is worth much more than one just getting started. Would *you* rather buy Steve's half of the egg business when it was only half a dozen chickens, a pile of lumber, and a roll of wire, or after all the work had been done and you knew you would make $80 a month from your half?

In business, there is a word to describe the extra value a business has after it has become successful and has customers. It's called "goodwill." Steve and Jerry's business is worth *more* than just the lumber, nails and wire, the chickens and feed. That extra value is goodwill.

Putting a value on a small business is not easy. This is how the boys figured it out. They had spent $200 as they went along. With the original $120, that meant they had a cash investment of $320. The time involved in building chicken houses and putting up fences was worth at least $100. Now, if another $100 was added for goodwill for all their steady customers who would buy in the future, the total value of the business was $520. Half of that was $260. Anyone who bought Steve's half could make that much in about three months. That seemed like a fair price to both of them.

The easiest solution would be for Jerry to buy Steve's half. The problem with that was it took two kids to run the business. Jerry didn't have enough time to do it all by himself. He needed a partner. Otherwise he'd probably have to sell half the chickens. Steve needed to find some other kid who (1) was interested in the business, (2) had time to take over half the work, and (3) had $260. It also had to be someone Jerry could get along with, since he would have to work with Steve's replacement.

These are some of the problems that can come up in selling a small business. Of course, many are owned and run by one person or a husband and wife, but many others are owned jointly by more than one person or family. Finding a buyer can be difficult, and new partners often find that they do not agree on how things should be done.

Jerry and Steve solved their problem when they realized that Jerry' sister Beth was interested. She was a hard worker, knew all about taking care of the chickens, and knew all the customers. Jerry ended up lending her the money to pay Steve. She paid back what she borrowed plus interest from the money she made as her brother's new partner.

All three of these youngsters learned some important lessons about investing in a business and figuring out what that investment is worth later on. Let's look at some questions on this subject.

How Many Ways Can a Kid Invest Money?

If you have any money in a savings account right now, you're already investing. Remember that saving is the first step. A savings account is your first investment. Once you've saved enough money, you have the choice of investing in someone else's business or investing in your own.

Jerry and Steve each chose to invest $60 of what they had previously saved and use it to start their own egg business. They invested in *themselves*. For them it was a good investment. Once they really got going, they were making more each month than the amount of money they used to get started. Part of what they made went back into the savings account to replace the $60 and let their savings grow even more.

Many of the previous chapters contain examples of kids who invested in themselves. You might buy a power mower or floor polisher to do the job better and faster, a bike to deliver papers, or a sewing machine to hem skirts and dresses or make clothes you can sell. These are all investments in your own business, in yourself.

But you can also invest in someone else's business, like Mattel's, Eastman Kodak's, Ford's, or Coca-Cola's. You invest in businesses like these by buying shares of stock.

Where Do Shares of Stock Come From?

When you buy a share of stock, you receive a stock certificate, a piece of paper that shows that you are one of the owners of the company.

Originally, stock is sold by a company to investors. In most cases the company is selling its stock to raise the money that is needed to get started or to expand. Jerry and Steve might have done the same thing when they got started. We'll use their egg business to show where shares of stock come from.

We know that Jerry and Steve started off slowly by investing $120, then put an additional $200 into their business later on. Let's start back at the beginning and assume that, instead of starting gradually, they want to start by investing *all* of the money at the very beginning. That means they need $320 right now. They don't have that much money in their savings accounts, but some of their friends might be interested.

The boys decide to split their egg company into ten equal shares. They need $320, so if they sell each share for $32, they'll have what they need to start. Jerry and Steve each buy two shares themselves. That leaves six. Steve's dad and Jerry's mom each buy one. Beth buys one. That leaves three, which they sell to three of their friends. They now have the money to get started.

What will each of the company's shareholders get from their investment? Since there are ten shares, each share will receive 10 percent of the profits. The owners of one share will receive 10 percent, and Jerry and Steve will each get 20 percent of the profits, since they each bought two shares.

Who will run the company and do all the work? That's Jerry and Steve. They are the "management." For doing all the work, they expect to be paid. They decide on $65 a month for each of them. Buying feed is the only other big expense. That's $40 a month. Sales of eggs bring in $210 a month. Sales minus costs equals profits. Sales are $210 and costs are $130 for labor and $40 for feed—a total of $170. That leaves a profit each month of $40 to be divided among the owners. Each share then gets $4 since there are ten shares. Steve and Jerry each get $8 from their two shares. The $4 that the boys' egg company pays to its owners each month is called a "cash dividend." It's the way companies share their profits with the people who have invested in their stock—their stockholders.

Doing it this way is good for everyone. The two boys got their business started much faster because they had all the money at the beginning. Each month they pay themselves $65 each for their work and earn $8 as their share of the profits.

Their investors should also be happy. For $32 they make $4 a month. This means they will have all their money back in just eight months, but after that they will keep on getting the same $4 each month as long as they own their shares. If they hold a shareholders' meeting, they might even decide to take only $3 a month and put the other dollar into a savings account so the business can keep growing. That's the way large companies do it. When enough money is saved, the boys can build more chicken coops and buy more chickens. They might have to hire someone like Beth to help them. If they do it right, profits should go even higher.

That's an example of where stock comes from. That's why companies sell it and why investors buy it.

How Can I Buy Eastman Kodak?

The ownership of the Eastman Kodak Company is divided into several million separate pieces. Each piece is called a share. You can go to a stockbroker and buy as many shares of the company as you want. If you had done it in 1978, you might have paid $55 for each share you bought.

After you buy your shares, the company will send you your "stock certificate." If you bought two shares for a total of $110, your stock certificate would show that you own two shares of Eastman Kodak stock. Your shares of stock are exactly the same as the shares everyone else owns. If the president of the company owns 2,000 shares, he owns a thousand times as much as you, but each of his shares is the same as yours. You are both owners of Eastman Kodak.

How Do People Decide Which Stock to Buy?

Let's start with the choices you have. There are large companies and small companies, well-established companies and brand new companies, companies with high-priced stock and some whose stock price is quite low.

First, we'll take a look at the big companies. In a game of poker the blue chips are always worth more than the reds or the whites, and among stocks the largest, best-established, richest companies are called "blue chips." Good examples of "blue chip" companies are Eastman Kodak, American Telephone, and General Motors. In addition to giant corporations like these, there are many other high-quality companies that are not that large. Examples would be Levi Strauss (the maker of Levis), Disney, and McDonald's.

At the other end of the scale are many small companies, most of them with names you have never heard. Some have been in business for a number of years; some are just getting started. You might hear about one of them because one of your parents or neighbors works for the company or because the company is located near your home.

How will you know which is the best one for you to buy? Part of the answer depends on what you want. In most cases, the objective of a kid is to buy a stock that will go up in price, making the investment worth more in the future. A cash dividend check is normally not too important. That will be something you need years from now when you retire. For now, let's assume that your only interest is buying a stock that will grow in value. There are several things that can help you decide which stock to buy.

First, you have to decide how much risk you want to take. Any stock that can go up in price can also go down. Companies can get into trouble and lose money. If you are not willing to take much risk, you will buy a large, well-established company like American Telephone. American Telephone is less likely to go down in price than most other companies, or, if it does go down, it will probably go down by a smaller amount. On the other hand, the prices of many other companies might be expected to go up much faster. So your first choice is deciding how much risk you want to take. If you decide you want to try and make a lot of money on a stock, your best choice is probably a small company that is growing rapidly. There's more risk in these, but there's also the chance of a much larger profit.

Next, you look at the individual companies. Suppose a new jeans store opens in your neighborhood, and most of the jeans they carry are Levis. If you think jeans are becoming more popular and that Levis will remain one of the most popular brands, buying Levi Strauss might be a good choice. On the other hand, McDonald's may have just opened a new store in your neighborhood. Like Levi, McDonald's is obviously still growing. That might be a good stock for you to buy and hold for a few years.

Another way to select stocks is to watch for things that might make the company more profitable in the future, some event or new product that comes along. Eastman Kodak provides two examples. First was the introduction of their instant camera to compete with Polaroid. Suppose you got one of these cameras for your birthday and liked the camera so much that you thought it would be very successful and make Kodak a lot of money. That's a reason you might buy the stock. Second, let's suppose you heard your dad describing how much he liked the new Kodak copier he had in his office. If a lot of other people feel the same way, Kodak sells more copiers and the stock should go up in price. Either piece of information would be a reason to consider buying the stock.

One new product that made a huge difference in a company was the release of *Star Wars* by Twentieth Century-Fox. If you had been one of the first kids to see *Star Wars* and had thought it could make the company a lot of money, you could have bought a share of stock in Twentieth Century-Fox for $16 to $18 in May of 1977. In June of 1978, the stock was selling at $40 a share. You'd have been right. *Star Wars* did make a lot of money for Twentieth Century-Fox. And if you had bought the stock, it would have made a lot of money for you.

Some people invest in stocks because they like the company's products. You can't invest in Crest toothpaste or Tide detergent, but on the package you'll see that both are made by Proctor & Gamble. You *can* invest in that company's stock. You might decide to invest in the company that makes your favorite breakfast cereal. If it's Cheerios, you'll buy General Mills. If it's Rice Krispies, you'll buy Kellogg's. If Jack-in-the-Box is your favorite restaurant, you'll find that the Jack-in-the-Box restaurants are owned by Ralston Purina, the company that makes Purina cat chow and many other products. So when you're thinking about investing in stock, you might find it interesting to look through the shelves in your own home. See which companies make the products you like best. It's a way to get some good ideas.

How Much Money Can People Make Buying a Stock?

You might make a lot of money buying a stock, but you could lose money, too. Let's assume it's December 1968. You've been following several stocks and finally decide on two you like better than all the rest—McDonald's and Mattel. You have $1,000 to invest, and since you can't decide between these two, you decide to put $500 in each stock. The price of Mattel is around $30 a share, and McDonald's is around $10. Your $1,000 buys you 17 shares of Mattel and 50 shares of McDonald's. Profits for McDonald's were higher in 1969 than they were in 1968. In fact, McDonald's has made more money every year since 1968, and profits still appear to be climbing. Mattel's profits also went up in 1969, but after that the company ran into some problems. Profits dropped in 1970, and in 1971 the company lost money. Mattel was not profitable again until 1975. The difference in profits made a big difference in the stock prices. In mid-1978, Mattel was around $11 a share and McDonald's around $60. The $500 investment in Mattel had dropped to around $185, but the $500 that was put into McDonald's was worth $3,000.

As you can see, buying the right stock can make quite a difference. Many successful investors buy shares in good-quality companies when they think the price is reasonable and hold onto them for many years. One of the best ways you can invest is to buy a few shares and add to those shares later or when you have more money.

What the stock market and the prices of individual stocks will do over the next ten or five or even one year is not known. Over the past thirty or forty years, the prices of stocks have generally gone up, and investors who have purchased good-quality stocks over this period have generally done well. In the savings chapter we showed how money grows from the interest that is earned over a period of years. To see how investing in a large group of stocks has done over a long period of time, we can look at the record of one investment company that started business in 1934. This company is a mutual fund, which takes the money of many investors, puts all the money together, and invests it in the stocks of many different companies they think will do well. Over its forty-three-year history—to December 1976—this mutual fund bought and sold the stocks of many hundreds of different companies. If you had been twenty years old in 1934 when this company started, and had invested $250 to get started and then added $100 each month for the entire forty-three years, you could have retired at the end of 1976, at age 63, with a very sizable amount of money. The total you invested would have been

$51,750. Upon retirement, your account would have been worth $1,192,463.

There's probably no one who actually did this. Many people start investment programs, but few, if any, stick to them for more than forty years. You don't need as much as $100 each month to be an investor. But starting young and investing more when you can is one of the secrets to success in investing.

What If People Want to Sell Their Stock?

Once you buy a stock, you can sell it whenever you want to. This is the principal difference between owning shares in McDonald's and owning one-half of the egg company in your friend's backyard. We already discussed the problems Steve might have in selling his half of the business he shared with Jerry. For that kind of business it's hard to find just the right buyer. In fact, you might not find a buyer at all. Anyone who bought half the business also had to help run it. But once Jerry and Steve had divided their business up into ten equal shares, those shares could be sold more easily. People could own part of Steve and Jerry's company without doing any of the work. And with the company ownership divided into shares, when Steve has to move away he can sell his two shares to anyone who is willing to buy them. He might sell them to Jerry, Jerry's sister Beth, or someone else. Steve's dad can sell his one share to Jerry's mom or dad. In fact, now they don't even have to sell them. They can keep the shares and remain part-owners of the business, no matter where they live. Jerry can send them their share of the profits each month.

If Jerry's dad buys the one share owned by Steve's father, how much should he pay him? The original price was $32, but if Steve and Jerry had been keeping some money in the business so that it could grow, and profits were now $6 per share instead of $4, the shares should be worth 50 percent more. That would make each share worth $48 instead of $32. That's really what choosing companies to invest in is all about.

It should be pointed out that if Steve's father sells his share to Jerry's father, the boys' egg company is not involved in that sale. One investor has sold his share to another investor. The same thing is true if you buy a share of Disney stock. You're not buying it from the company. You're buying it from some other investor who wants to sell it. When *you* sell that share, you'll sell it to someone else who wants to buy the stock. You will not sell it back to the company.

Having stock in the hands of investors solves all of these problems for a large company. The people who invest in their stock do not have to look for a seller. Every day thousands of their shares are bought and sold through stockbrokers in the securities markets of this country. Every day you can look in the paper and see the prices of stocks you own or might buy. When you're ready to sell, the same thing is true. You don't have to go up and down the street looking for a buyer. You just tell your stockbroker to sell it and it's done. It's not at all like selling half an egg business.

Today there are 25 million Americans who own stock themselves. Millions of others own the shares of many companies because they own part of the retirement plan of the company they work for. If you become one of the 25 million by buying some stock for yourself, you will learn some things about business you might not otherwise learn. You'll learn to watch for products that your company manufactures. You may find yourself looking through the medicine chest or the pantry to see that your mom is buying the products of *your* company. You may insist on stopping at McDonald's when your family goes out to eat. More important, you'll learn something about the two things that always go together in investing—risk and reward. You'll learn something about the rewards that can come from investing in a good company that does well, but you may learn something about the risks involved in buying the stock of a company that does poorly. We hope you'll make the right choice when you start investing and be encouraged to save and make additional investments as you grow older and are able to invest larger amounts of money.

WHY EVERY KID SHOULD HAVE A JOB, AND WAYS PARENTS CAN HELP

Consider the case of one competitive skier. This young lady is carefully taught everything that is known about racing: how to get a fast start, how to turn, how to get maximum speed on the straight sections of the course. She learns about the gear she will need and obtains the finest in competitive boots, skis, poles, and other equipment. She knows how to file her edges until they are razor-sharp and how to apply exactly the right wax for maximum speed and control under any racing conditions. If, however, she never goes out to practice in advance of the race, what are her chances of winning?

The kid who never gets out and makes some money on his own while he is young is in much the same position. He draws maps to learn geography, works problems to learn math, writes reports to learn composition, and is coached on a variety of other subjects by his teachers and his parents. All this is designed to prepare him for the adult world, just as the skier's training is designed to prepare her to race. But too many youngsters, like the skier, never actually go out and get a job—never practice the real thing in advance.

When you consider how many hours of an adult's life are spent earning a living, it becomes obvious that adults spend more time working than at any other single activity. Getting off to a fast start in the world of working and business can be just as important as a fast start in a race.

A kid who has the kind of job described in The Adventure of Making Money section of this book has many advantages over his nonworking friends. He will learn to sell himself to his customers. This experience will be invaluable when he is an adult attempting to convince an employer that he is the one who should be hired. He will learn the importance of dependability. He won't keep his customers if he doesn't show up when he is expected. And he'll probably have more money to spend than his friends, although this is the least important reason he should work (it will probably seem like the only reason to him).

There are benefits for parents as well. This section discusses those benefits and sets forth a number of steps for the use of parents who want to help their kids get that fast start. It tells why, how, and how much parents should help their kids. It also emphasizes when not to help. It shows parents how they can help their kids develop and use their imaginations—to earn money now and to develop a personal resource that will be of great value to them all their lives.

The lost skill of making money should be reintroduced into the lives of kids. This section can be used by parents to help their kids recapture that skill.

CHAPTER 18

A JOB—IT'S MORE
IMPORTANT THAN THE MONEY

The excitement of making money. It's there whether a kid is 6 or
16! Can you remember the first dime or quarter or dollar you ever
made all on your own? Chances are you were proud and excited
enough to run home and tell your parents about it. It's part of
growing up. A special thrill that is not soon forgotten. Your
parents were probably as excited about it as you were.

And how about your first regular job, your first permanent
source of independent income? That money came with no
strings attached. You didn't have to ask your parents for it. It was
not an allowance. You could spend it wherever you chose. And it
probably felt good.

There was a time in this country when most kids were expected to work. If it wasn't on the family farm, it was in the towns or cities, often doing much the same work as adults. Things have changed. Laws requiring children to stay in school until they are 16, minimum-wage laws, child-labor laws, and even abolishment of the apprentice system all have combined to make it more difficult for young people to find jobs. Because we adults think that kids should be doing something besides just hanging around, we send them to school. In fact, it sometimes seems that their education can go on endlessly, as long as parents can afford to keep paying. In effect, the educational system warehouses young people until the economy is able to accept them into the job market. All this serves to keep them dependent much longer than is necessary and frustrates their need to establish an identity as separate and independent human beings.

None of this is meant to imply that the educational system should be abolished beyond the eighth grade. Instead, the suggestion is that young people be encouraged to work, to go out and find jobs, to get some experience in the world before their education is completed. Kids who work receive some extremely important benefits they can get in no other way.

California's Senator S. I. Hayakawa, an educator before his election to the Senate, made these very appropriate observations:

> What do young people need to enable them to grow up? Most of all they need to experience situations in which they are held accountable for actions and decisions in the real world. They need responsibilities.

> School is not the real world. It is preparation for life, not life itself. The mistake a student makes in arithmetic class is of little moment, but if a bank clerk makes the same mistake, he fouls up a depositor's account. If he is lucky, he is merely reprimanded. He is more likely to be fired.

> Youths in prosperous industrial societies have many privileges, many luxuries, from hi-fi stereos to sports cars. For many young people college serves as a rather expensive play-school for the prolongation of adolescence.

> But all young people, including the serious-minded and studious majority, are in a sense a deprived class. They are deprived by long years of compulsory schooling (the compulsion is both legal and social) of the opportunity to experience adult responsibilities. And because of this deprivation many of them are bored and frustrated

Will sending your kids forth to hustle up a job for themselves end their boredom and frustration? It's not the total answer, but it certainly might help. There are, it turns out, significant benefits for both you and your kids if they're out making some money on

153

their own. For kids, the immediate benefits are clear. They want extra money to buy things that they otherwise might not have. Because what they earn for themselves is not an allowance or money they had to beg for, it comes with no strings attached and they can spend it on whatever they want. A benefit that might come as a surprise to them is the satisfaction that comes from personal accomplishment.

At What Age Should Kids Get Jobs?

Kids should get jobs earning some of their own money when they are young. Before discussing specific ages, however, it must be understood what is meant by "a job." The jobs described in this book actually are independent businesses. The young ladies who knock on your door and say they would like to wash your windows are independent contractors. If you hire them, you are *not* their employer, you are their *customer*. The same is true of mowing lawns, waxing cars, or babysitting. On these jobs there are no age limits, only limits of ability or strength. Some 10-year-olds are as strong and competent as most 14-year-olds.

The age at which an individual kid starts a job depends on a number of factors. These include the maturity of the youngster, the nature of the jobs that are available in your neighborhood, the kind of area in which you live. The business leaders whose childhood stories appear in Chapter 4 all started early. Irv Robbins of Baskin-Robbins started at 6 working in his father's store. Louis Lundborg of Bank of America started selling papers on street corners at 8. Bob McCowan of Ashland Oil was a "top salesman" for the *Ladies' Home Journal* at 10. Auto racing champion Tom Sneva started with his Kool-Aid business at 7.

Over 130 job ideas are described in Chapters 21 through 28, because every neighborhood is different, and every kid is different and has different interests. The scope of the jobs described in these chapters is broad enough to encompass almost any imaginable combination of circumstances.

If, then, your neighbor could use a mother's helper a couple of days a week and your 8-year-old daughter is interested, don't tell her she's too young. How do you know she can't do it until she tries? Kids should be allowed the freedom to try anything within reason and try it whenever *they* think they are ready. It doesn't matter that no profit is made on your daughter's Kool-Aid stand, or that the guppies your 7-year-old son was raising to sell all died. What is important is that they tried something. If it fails, they should be encouraged to try again, or try something else.

154

Why Jobs for Affluent Kids?

If your family's income is limited and your daughter *has* to have a ten-speed bike, getting a job may be her only means of getting that bike. Many families, however, can afford to buy their kids almost all of the things they want. For these families, the question is not how much money is available but how much they should spend on their children. Why should kids in such families work?

Perhaps the question should be: How do you teach your kids self-reliance and responsibility if they get whatever they want without putting out any personal effort? The comment of a teenager from an affluent suburb suggests what continuous taking from your parents does to a sense of responsibility. Catherine, the 17-year-old president of the Student Government Association at her high school, reported, "Some of us are taking a trip to Russia that's costing more than $500 apiece, and I was trying to get some of the kids interested in fund-raising projects. But they don't care because they get the money from their parents anyway."

Saying "no" to some of your children's requests when they know you can afford the money—in fact, know you'll never miss it—is not easy for most parents. But who gets more enjoyment out of the trip to Russia, the kid who earned all or part of the money or the one whose parents simply wrote a check? Which kid takes better care of his bike, the one who earned the money to buy it or the one who got it just because he asked?

In one national survey, nine out of every ten adults polled said they believe that most people spoil children by giving them too many material things. In fact, some 43 percent of parents said they feel they have spoiled their own youngsters. So the advantages we are able to give our children are a mixed blessing. The classic "I worked hard so my children wouldn't have it as tough as I did" sounds fine until you consider that those children may have received everything *but* the chance to succeed at something on their own. They haven't even had a chance to fail at anything other than school.

Clarence B. Randall, former President of Inland Steel, commented on the attitudes of many self-made businessmen in his book *The Folklore of Management*. Noting that many such individuals complain that federal and state inheritance taxes reduce incentive because they make it difficult for a businessman to pass on his wealth to his children, he said, "Those who say it are usually the very men who boast that they themselves started from scratch. They seem to have no confidence in their children, to be dead set on taking away from them the rich experience which they declare has been the source of their own strength."

How Do Kids Feel About Earning Money?

One of the reasons some kids lie around and complain that there's nothing to do is that they're not sure where to start. The next two chapters, plus the eight job idea chapters that follow, are intended to help parents help their kids get that start. All the evidence indicates that kids generally want to earn their own money, and that opinion is not restricted to any particular age group. For example, a national poll showed that 95 percent of the 15- to 21-year-olds interviewed felt that they should earn at least some of their own money.

To compare, let's look at the opinions of a third-grade class, which was asked: "If you want to buy something, is it better to get the money from your parents or earn it yourself?" "Get it from parents" was the response of only 13 percent of the class. The other 87 percent said "It's best to earn it yourself." It turned out that responses from schools in several cities, from kids in third to eighth grade, were almost identical. An overall average of 82 percent said they would prefer to earn the money themselves; 8 percent favored getting it from parents; and the other 10 percent liked the idea of splitting the cost of the item purchased.

It's worth looking at a few of the responses just to get a better idea of how kids view this subject. A few had unusual reasons for earning their own money:

"I'd rather earn my own money because I need something to do after school."

"I have to earn it. My mother wouldn't give me any money if I shot her."

The responses of most kids made it clear that they liked earning their own money because it gave them a feeling of personal accomplishment, or of independence from their parents.

"It is better to earn the money yourself, because you have a better feeling and you care for it more."

"I think it's better to earn it yourself, because then you'll know if you buy something you really earned it and it's truly yours."

"I think it's better to earn your money so then your parents can't tell you what to do."

"I think getting it from your parents is fine, but I'd rather earn it because then it will be MINE!"

"I think you should earn it. You spend it much better if you earn it."

The Benefits for Kids Who Work

What positive results might we expect if our kids get out and earn at least some of what they want on their own? Let's list some of the lessons they can learn, some of the personality traits they are likely to develop, some of the skills they will acquire that will be useful later in life.

1. Once they get a job, they have to show up on time. In order to keep most jobs, they are forced to develop promptness and dependability. The principal skill they will acquire is that of planning their time.

2. They will find that the world is competitive. This will be an important discovery in terms of their future ability to understand the adult world. The degree of competition they encounter will, of course, depend upon the job and their age. There may be no competition to run errands for a neighbor at age 8. There will be plenty of competition for a job at McDonald's. Your hope is that they will acquire the ability to compete effectively in the business and job world.

3. Depending on what approach they use to make their money, they might discover that a lot of money can be made with the right idea. This discovery can have a very positive effect on their attitude and stimulate their creativity as they search for even better job ideas in the future. If they can acquire the ability to apply their imagination to the practical problems they will confront later on, they will have a substantial head start on their contemporaries.

4. They'll find that they must make choices—that they cannot do and have everything all at once. Youngsters typically want to make their own decisions. At least they think they want to until they have to make the difficult ones. Then they probably expect you to make those for them. If you are able to hold back and force them to decide things for themselves, they will develop decisiveness. The ability to choose between alternatives is something that many adults have never quite mastered.

5. With some help from you, they can find that failures along the way are normal, expected events and should be viewed as lessons rather than disasters. If this lesson can be learned and accepted, they will never lack courage to attempt something for fear they will fail, and they will develop the determination to succeed at whatever they try. If, rather than giving up, they acquire the ability to analyze their mistakes, see what went wrong and why, they will be able to avoid those mistakes in the future.

6. A job can expand their horizons. It's very easy for any kid to assume that the whole world is just like the one he knows if he has had no experience outside that world. Many of the jobs kids can do will bring them into contact with a wide range of people, people who live differently from the way they were raised and who have different backgrounds and interests.

Sound like magic? The fact is that these lessons, traits, and skills can and will be learned to varying degrees by almost any youngster who gets a job outside the family environment doing almost anything. Given enough time, almost all young people could learn all these lessons if they did enough different jobs.

The story of one imaginative kid and a business he created for himself illustrates the advantages that can accrue to a kid from having a job, and the lessons that can be learned in the process.

The early experiences of Bobby McCowan, master magazine salesman, were presented in Chapter 4 to illustrate how youngsters learn by doing. In that case, it was McCowan discovering the secret of "selling benefits." Now we'll pick up his business history as he enters the University of Kentucky and he is looking for a way to make some badly needed money.

Bob McCowan's first effort after arriving at college involved a promotion to sell advertising. The ads, he decided, would be printed on dividers for three-ring student notebooks. The project never got off the ground because the market was limited to students and the printing and production costs were too high. The effort, however, led to a related, but different business which proved to be highly successful.

One day, browsing through the printing shop, Bob noticed some large desk blotters lying on the floor. He asked the manager of the shop how much it would cost to print ads on them. The answer—one-fourth of the cost of notebook dividers—meant he had found his new business. "I also learned the importance of low-cost operations in any business," McCowan recalls.

The blotter business was a great success. He sold ads to businesses in the area, had the ads printed on his blotters, and distributed the blotters free, not only to students but all over town. McCowan made $1,000 in each of the next two years on his blotter business. It provided the income he needed at school and paid for his first car.

The lessons a kid can learn from his own business enterprise are well illustrated by Bob McCowan's experiences. Here's how he describes the lessons and the meaning they had for him:

This little project not only was profitable, but provided me with the confidence I needed. I learned to consider the cost of a project as well as how to sell the product, which obviously today are still the most important ingredients in any business, whether it is selling blotters or operating an oil company. The important lesson that came from this project was the value of planning my enterprise and taking advantage of an opportunity that was being overlooked by others. The result was that I made a profit, the printers enjoyed my business, the advertisers benefitted from the ads, and the ultimate consumers were pleased to receive the blotters which were used in dormitories, schoolrooms, hotels, and business offices throughout Lexington."

But My Kid's Situation Is Different . . .

Now, let's suppose that, despite the overwhelming array of evidence offered to support the idea that kids should earn all, or at least part of, their own money, there still lurks in the back of your mind the question of whether or not it applies to *your* kid. After all, each family situation is unique. It may be that you're right. There may be valid reasons your youngsters shouldn't work, at least not just yet. So, let's look at some possible objections you might have and evaluate them.

How About Grades?

Not every kid gets straight As. Some get Cs and worse. Suppose your kid is having trouble with math. Your solution? To tell him to "spend more time studying." In the midst of all this, one of his friends moves away and the friend's paper route is available. Your youngster wants to take it over. Your first response might logically be "Not until your grades are better." Logical — until you consider that most kids can only spend a certain number of hours each day in productive study. Chaining his ankle to the desk in his room may produce limited results.

Actually, that paper route he wants is just school of a different kind. Collecting from customers represents a practical application of math learned in school. It also represents genuine motivation to get the problems right, since doing one wrong can lose you some of the week's profits.

There are many things of value to be learned along the road to adulthood, and the subjects kids study in school are certainly among them. Some kids, however, are more oriented to the real world outside the classroom, and to sacrifice these interests on the altar of straight As can be a tragic error.

Take, for example, the case of a little Japanese boy named Soichero. One of his principal childhood memories is that he was "very poor." He was the first son of a blacksmith, and little

Soichero loved to tinker around in the shop even before he was old enough for school. His father owned a bike shop later on, and Soichero also loved to spend time working there.

Soichero remembers doing poorly in school on exams. He did not enjoy the basic subjects he was required to learn. Then, in the upper grades, courses on batteries and test tubes, scales and machinery began to appear in the curriculum. Suddenly he began to excel in many of his classes.

In 1922, at the age of 16, he left home and went to Tokyo to work in an auto repair shop. Working on cars had been his dream for many years. Today, the boy who liked cars better than spelling can look back with a great deal of satisfaction at the path that led him to found the Honda Motor Company. By almost any standard, Soichero Honda's company is today one of the most successful auto manufacturers in the world.

Honda's story does not make the case that delivering papers is better than studying. Both are important, and there is room for both in the life of any kid. All As are nice but they are no guarantee of later success.

You May Not Feel You Have the Time to Get Involved

Let's get back to the paper route for a minute. There are kids who deliver their papers from the right-hand front window of the family station wagon driven by mom or dad. That's not being involved. That's doing the job for them. You can, however, be involved in a constructive way without a major investment of time. With the help of the following chapters, you can make your ideas and experience available to them in deciding on what they should do. You can provide tips on do's and don'ts along the way and you can supply moral support when they need it, without taking a lot of your time.

You might think they're too young to handle an outside job in a reliable fashion.

Maybe you're right. Then why not start them with some jobs at home. And insist on the same quality and reliability standards you would apply if it was someone else's kid working for you. Once they perform on the home court, they should be ready to go forth on their own. On the other hand, maybe you underestimate their capabilities. Maybe they've grown up a bit while you weren't paying attention. There is only one way to find out. Let them try.

160

Just as an example of what one young kid did and what even your kid might be able to do if necessary, consider the case of poet-composer-singer Rod McKuen. Rod was born in Oakland, California, in 1933. When he was only 11, he left his fatherless home and spent six years going from one job to another throughout California, Nevada, Oregon, and Washington. During his odyssey, he worked as a lumberjack, cowhand, stuntman, and rodeo performer. McKuen returned to Oakland at 17 and got a job as a disc jockey. The reaction of the listeners to his poetry that he read over the air prompted him to study composition so he could the put the words of his poems to music.

You may not have this pattern in mind for the development of your 11-year-old, but McKuen's story demonstrates that kids, at least some kids, have a lot more capability than we often give them credit for having. It's when *they* think they're ready to go to work that counts, not when you think so.

There may not be enough time available for them to hold a job because you need them at home.

If you have one or two youngsters who need supervision after school while you're at work, your 14-year-old's services are really needed. What if, instead of a flat "no job," you sat down with your son and tried to think up some ways he could earn money at home? The last section of this book presents numbers of ideas — like addressing a mailing for a local store to send to their customers, or addressing Christmas cards for one or more neighbors. How about afternoon babysitting for a nearby family that has the same problem you do?

They already have what seems to be a full schedule of activities and are neglecting the assigned hour-a-day piano practice.

You may feel that the piano comes first. Fine. But if they can find time to practice *and* have a job, what's wrong with that? As they grow older, if earning extra money is more important to them than certain other activities, at some point you have to let them make that decision themselves.

Amazing as it may seem, more than a few college students reach graduation having never worked at any job. When they enter the job market, they face employers who almost always favor the individual with some history of work experience, no matter how simple. Having a work history, however, is simply a side benefit. The real benefits are the money and business skills kids will learn, and the values and traits they will develop as they become successful in their business efforts.

Irv Robbins of Baskin-Robbins is one business leader who has strong feelings on the subject of kids getting involved in working and business while they are still young. According to Robbins:

The kid who waits until he gets out of school and announces, "Now I'm going to start thinking of ways to make money on my own," is dead. The learning process has to start earlier than that.

Robbins is not alone. His feeling is shared by Duke Boyd, founder of Hang Ten, the highly successful line of sportswear identified by the two little feet. Boyd says that young people who want to prepare themselves for a rewarding financial future should do several things. One is to get the tools and skills needed for their chosen occupation through school, but even more important, they should be sure to take business courses as well. Many experts in their own fields, according to Boyd, find themselves totally unprepared to properly handle the income they receive from their success. Here's his conclusion:

Success in money must cover all the bases. You must discover how to make it and how to use it. And you should start now. Don't wait until you are out of high school or college to get into business. Learn now through your mistakes and get the jump on success. Business, like the game of chess, is intriguing, challenging, and demanding. It's also a lot of fun, and not limited to adults.

CHAPTER 19

WHEN TO HELP— AND WHEN NOT TO!

"Well, Todd, you said you wanted to get out and earn some money, so I got you a job today. I talked to Bob Smith down at the gas station on my way home, and he says he can use some help afternoons and Saturday."

"But I was thinking about working over at . . ."

"Never mind that," interrupted his dad, "this is a good job, pays pretty well, and it's close to home. Just one thing. You be sure to be on time when Bob needs you. And work hard. Bob's an old friend of mine, and I don't want him to be sorry he took my advice and hired you."

That's one way to help. Here's another.

A young fellow named Roger grew up in Los Angeles in a neighborhood where you needed a bike to get around. It wasn't optional, it was essential. Whenever the subject of a bike had come up in the past, it had always ended with Roger's parents saying, "maybe later on." The subject came up again when he was 10. This time Roger's dad surprised him.

"How much money do you have?" his dad asked.

The answer to that one was easy, "None."

"Then, maybe you'd better go out and earn some," was his father's suggestion.

Within a short time, Roger located an available paper route.

The first delivery, however, was half a mile from his home. The entire route covered about two miles and ended a mile away. That kind of a territory couldn't be covered on foot. So his father suggested a deal. He agreed to pay for half of the bike, and he would lend Roger the other half right away so he could get started. They looked around together and found a good used bike for $35. Roger sanded and painted it, and with a sheepskin seatcover and new grips on the handlebars, he had himself a "new" bike. He had a special place where he kept the money he saved from delivering the papers, and he can still remember how it felt when his savings finally added up to the $17.50 he owed his dad. Now he had a bike all his own. And from that point on he *always* had a job.

If you were a kid, would you rather be in Todd's position or Roger's? Todd is in a tough spot. Maybe the job at the gas station will be a great job for him, even if it's not the one he would have picked. He might enjoy the job and like working for Bob Smith. He might make more money there than somewhere else. But it's also true that he starts with at least one strike against him. *He has to live up to his dad's standards, not his own.* If his dad had sent him down to talk to Mr. Smith and Todd had made his own decision to work there, it would be a lot more comfortable. But what if he doesn't like working at the station? What if he finds something else he really wants to do? It might be pretty difficult to quit.

The way Roger got his bike is a classic example of constructive help. He had the experience of going out and getting a job on his own, the experience of borrowing money and repaying it, and got a bicycle in the process. But it would not have happened without a helping hand from his dad. So there are right ways to help and wrong ways to help.

Why Help at All?

It's not always easy to know when and how to help, and it is sometimes even harder to tell where "helping" stops and "interfering" begins. One solution might be to let the kids do it on their own. Give them no help or support. For many families it would be far easier to just give them some money and be done with it.

But will the kids know the difference between lack of support and lack of interest? There are a number of reasons you should spend some time—devote some energy—to helping your kids make a few bucks, and one of the best of those reasons has nothing to do with money directly. It has to do with how our children fit into our lives and how we fit into theirs in this modern age. Rapid changes have brought about changes in today's families. For example, families once included grandparents, aunts and uncles, and cousins, so there were almost always adults around with whom children could spend time. In contrast, today's family tends to consist of mom, dad, and the kids, or just mom *or* dad and the kids.

To a significant extent, we have withdrawn from our children's lives. This withdrawal doesn't mean we have less affection for them. It is not a planned or welcome event. Evolving patterns in our society have simply caused or encouraged it to happen. Besides parents spending less time with their children, children spend less time with *any* adults. In smaller communities, before the age of technology, kids generally had more contact with all kinds of adults. Once a kid could talk to the butcher while he cut meat. Now the butcher is in a glass cage or out of sight. What substitutes for the adult contact that has disappeared? Perhaps a number of things not to our liking, but two of those substitutes seem clear: kids spend their time with other kids or watching television.

What does all this have to do with kids and money and jobs? Just this. If you're looking for ways to spend more time with your children, and if your kids have indicated an interest in getting a job, working with them to help them figure out what kind of job they should get might accomplish both things at the same time. Also, kids who work come into contact with numbers of adults; they get to deal with adults on almost an adult-to-adult level, instead of just the child-to-adult level they almost inevitably have with parents.

The childhood experience of E. L. McNeely, Chairman of the Wickes Corporation, illustrates the value to a youngster of adult contacts outside the home and immediate surroundings. McNeely's family lived in Hamilton, Missouri, in the 1930s. He earned money as a kid with a variety of different jobs, one of which was rounding up stray cattle for one of his neighbors. Each evening he would get on a quarterhorse and herd all of the neighbor's Hereford calves into the feeding area."This chore took me about an hour, for which I got 25¢," McNeely remembers.

Like many other boys, McNeely had a paper route for several years. One of his customers was the sister of J. C. Penney, founder of the retailing chain. Penney had a close attachment to the town of Hamilton, partly because his sister lived there but also because he had opened one of his first stores in that town and had later purchased land there for the purpose of breeding cattle. When Penney was in town, McNeely was his paper boy. "From that association," says McNeely, "developed a friendship that was maintained for more than thirty-five years, until Mr. Penney's death."

The friendship meant much more to McNeely than simply knowing a pioneer in the business world. Penney represented to him an example of a person who practiced the Golden Rule and lived an exemplary life while being highly successful in business.

McNeely's story illustrates the significance that adult contacts away from home and school can have. Such contacts can be the most important factor in expanding kids' horizons, and their opportunities. Encouraging kids to get a job is a first step to widening their experience.

Here's How You Can Help

The starting point in helping your kids is to make them understand that there are ways they can make money at any age. If you're the one suggesting the job, you may hear "no one wants to hire a 12-year-old" or "I can't get the job I want until I'm 16, and that's another year." But how old do youngsters have to be before they can make some money? A 6-year-old can make money with a lemonade stand if he or she has a good location. A little fellow from Plains, Georgia, started making money for himself when he was only 5. In his first money-making enterprise, Jimmy Carter employed one of the most important principles of making money—taking advantage of what's available to you. His family was in the business of raising peanuts, so Jimmy went into the retail peanut business. During the harvest season he went into the fields and harvested his own miniature crop. After pulling the peanuts from the roots and washing them, he soaked the peanuts overnight. The following morning he boiled them in salt water. Then Jimmy walked several miles into Plains to make his sales. His principal market was the checker players gathered in service stations and in the local mule stables. Not bad for a 5-year-old. And obviously he had some help from his folks.

So age is not a factor. There's something for almost every kid to do. What job can your child do? That's the first decision. Let's suppose you have a 13-year-old daughter who is both bored and penniless. She has decided it would be a good idea for her to figure out some way to make the extra money she needs for herself. Here are some ideas on how *you* can help *her* get started.

First, your 13-year-old gets a pad of paper and a pencil. Now you and she sit down together and she starts listing as many ways to make money, practical or seemingly impractical, as the two of you can think of. Let her do most of the work. If it's her idea that she finally decides to put into practice, she will probably do it with more enthusiasm. Your job is to guide her into as many different subject areas as you can. Don't let her stop when she's listed all the obvious ideas. Keep her going until you're both worn out with it. When the ideas have stopped coming, go through the following checklist. Spend a little time on each item and see what additional ideas you come up with.

Does she have a hobby that might be converted into a money-making idea? Example: She might enjoy raising animals. It might be done for a profit.

Does she have some special skill people might pay for? Example: If she's very good at a foreign language, she might tutor younger children. If she's an excellent swimmer, teaching little kids to swim is a way to have fun earning money.

What things can she do for people that they might not think of themselves? Example: Cleaning the leaves out of rain gutters before the rains start.

What are the things people put off until next year, year after year? Example: Cleaning out the attic.

What are the things adults don't like to do? Example: Washing out the cupboards and installing new shelf paper.

What special opportunities are available to her? Example: You may have several very productive fruit trees in your backyard or a vegetable or flower garden. Selling the excess door to door makes a lot more sense than having the crop rot.

When this process has been completed, your daughter may have arrived at the perfect solution. If not, and you're still looking for additional ideas, she should take a survey. Have her ask all her friends what *they* do to make money. Talk to neighbors. To local businesses. All the new ideas should be added to the list she has already compiled. The final step is to have her go through the job ideas in Chapters 21 through 28. This step should really be the last one. If she looks at all these ideas first, she's not likely to come up with as many of her own, and one of hers might be the best one of all.

Let's see what you've accomplished. You have introduced your daughter to an approach to solving problems, one that she can use in many ways in the future. This time her problem was: What is the best possible way for me to make some money? The steps she took with your assistance were:

1. Brainstorming, getting every possible idea the two of you could think of written down on paper.

2. Using the checklist to come up with additional ideas, such as hobbies that might be profitable.

3. Taking a survey to get even more ideas.

4. Reviewing the job chapters in this book.

All these steps will probably produce several business ideas that make sense. Once your daughter has decided on the job she will do, if she can take it from there and get started that's great. If, like Roger, who needed a loan to get a bicycle, she needs a little help to get launched, fine. Once she's launched make it clear that you are available to give her guidance if she asks for it. For her, one of the biggest advantages of *your* involvement is access to something she doesn't have—experience. She has a lot of lessons to learn along the way, and she'll learn them more easily, with less wasted time and effort and fewer disappointments, if she has a little guidance from you.

Here are some of the problems you can help her overcome. Suppose she is shy and reluctant to knock on a neighbor's door asking for a job. Help her get a friend interested. It's often a lot easier when two kids can do something like this together. Suppose she gets discouraged after having no success the first afternoon. Some kids need a lot of encouragement, especially at the beginning.

Sales ability is a basic and necessary skill for a kid. Kids are not born with it, they learn it by practicing. Let them practice their own sales story on you. You might make some suggestions that will improve it.

Not everyone will hire her or buy her product, but if she is properly prepared, if she knows some people will say no, then she will be able to press on without becoming discouraged. Try to explain to your youngster that the "no" she gets is not directed at her personally. Her prospective customer might not need what she is offering, might have had the job done last week by another kid, might be in a bad mood, or might be unable to afford to hire her. There are plenty of "yes's" out there if she'll just keep at it.

There are lots of ways you can help a kid get off to a good start. Some kids will need no more, but there are also ways you can help after they're started. Doing the job right is even more important than the earlier steps of selecting the job and finding the customer. After all the hard work of getting a customer, it would be a shame to lose him by doing work of poor quality. All customers should be repeat customers, either for the same job or for different jobs in the future.

You can, for instance, help make sure that your kid's job is profitable enough by going through a few simple accounting procedures with him or her. Here's how one parent helped a fledgling catering service stay profitable.

Kim and Suzanne got started doing parties on their own by catering children's birthday parties. They did the whole thing from start to finish. They supplied everything. Every little kid got a "surprise package" with several things inside. They brought balloons and blew them up, made place cards, supplied the paper plates and cups. The mothers could relax and didn't have to worry about any of the details.

Next, they supplied the entertainment. Suzanne played the guitar and Kim had a zither. The two of them performed magic tricks and taught the kids songs and games.

Last but not least, they baked and decorated the cake. The cakes were beautiful, and delicious. Materials to bake and decorate the cake amounted to nearly $1.50. The little "surprise packages" were eight for $1; the balloons and party hats, paper plates, cups, and napkins all amounted to about 30¢ for each child. That meant that a party for ten kids cost them 30¢ each, plus $1.50 for the cake, or $4.50. They charged $10.00 for a party this size and found that almost every mother they asked was delighted at the chance to get out of planning and running the party herself. Kim and Suzanne began to wonder if they were charging enough. They decided to discuss it with Kim's dad.

He began by asking, "How much do you make on one of those parties?"

Kim answered, "Let's see. About $5.50 between the two of us, we charge $10 and it costs us $4.50." She stopped and thought for a moment. "I guess we make nearly $1.50 an hour. That's pretty good for kids our age!" Kim was very proud of her small business.

"Let me show you how to figure out exactly what you and Suzanne are earning an hour," her dad said. Kim followed him into the study where he got a pad of paper. "We'll start at the beginning," he said. "How long does it take you to bake and decorate the cake?"

"Ohh!" groaned Kim to herself, "I never thought of that." She answered, "Probably an hour, if we don't fool around too much."

"And the time you spend shopping for things at the store?" Another half hour. "And don't you plan on getting to the party ahead of the kids?" *Another* half hour.

"Now, that's the time you spend on just one party." Her dad was making some calculations on the pad. "If you have three parties, you only have to go shopping once, and you could bake all three cakes at the same time. That's more efficient. But doing one party at a time, you're spending about four hours apiece. That's a total of eight hours for $5.50, and that's only 68¢ to 69¢ an hour."

Kim stood beside her dad's chair and stared at the figures. She was disappointed to discover how little they were making.

Her dad interrupted her thoughts. "Kim, what does the bakery charge for a decorated birthday cake? Do you know?"

"Around four or five dollars. I know because one of the mothers was complaining about how much she had to pay last time."

"Okay. Your only problem is that the two of you aren't charging enough. Suppose you started by never baking less than three cakes at one time. The ones you don't need, put in the freezer. Do all your shopping for maybe a half-dozen parties, or more, in one trip. Do it this way and you'll spend fewer hours, right?"

"I guess so," Kim agreed, "that might end up being more like three hours apiece instead of four."

Her dad was figuring again. "You say the hats and things cost 30¢ a kid? You could try charging your customers 40¢. That will pay the cost of shopping and so on. And I see no reason for selling cakes for your cost of $1.50. I think you should figure at least $3.50 for them, especially the way you and Suzanne decorate them. You girls do a very professional job. The last thing is the time you actually spend at the party. If you think you should earn $1.50 an hour, then charge $1.50 an hour.

"But how much does that add up to? I mean, if we try and charge too much, no one will want to hire us, will they?"

Her dad smiled. "Who will they hire if they don't hire you two? Are there any other kids around here doing the same thing?"

Kim hadn't thought about that either. She couldn't think of anyone. "I guess we don't have any competition," she admitted.

"I don't think this will be too much more," her dad explained. "If we figure on a party of ten kids at 40¢ each, that's $4. Charge $3.50 for the cake. That makes $7.50. Now charge $1.50 an hour for each of you. If you spend two hours at the party, that's $6. A total of $13.50."

Another way you can help is by encouraging your kids to find out how an expert does the job. Experts make more money. Kids can become experts if they take some preliminary steps. To illustrate let's take the example of Ann, who, after trying a number of different things, decided that washing windows was the way she could make the most money the quickest. Ann planned to go to a particular summer camp and decided she could make a good portion of the money she needed during Easter vacation. She took several steps to get her week's work lined up.

First, she planned ahead. Ann started working on lining up customers three weeks in advance of Easter vacation. By the time vacation came around, she had a full week scheduled.

Second, she advertised her services. In addition to going house to house in the immediate neighborhood, she used posters, which she put up in the windows or on bulletin boards of local businesses.

Third, she was ready before she started. Ann's father helped her contact a professional window-washing firm that did commercial buildings only. The owner was pleased to talk to a youngster who was interested in doing things the right way, and he showed her the tricks that professionals use to get windows sparkling with the least effort.

Finally, she quoted prices in advance. When youngsters are just getting started, they are almost always better off working by the hour. But once they find that they are able to do the job better and faster than most people, they are in a position to quote a price in advance. When they first start quoting prices, they'll make a lot of mistakes. Some of the quotes will be too high, and people will think they are charging too much. Some jobs will take a lot longer than they estimated, and they will end up working for less than they figured. However, the only way they'll learn is by doing it. But charging by the job can really pay off. An "expert" can expect to make at least twice as much per hour for a given job as he would make if he charged by the hour.

If your youngsters are going to learn to be really good at something, perhaps the most important lesson they can learn is to ask for help. They'll find that most adults are both flattered and pleased when a youngster shows an interest in how they make their living. In most cases, the experts will be very happy to help kids get a start doing something on their own. The payoff will be a more sucessful business and more income with less time invested, plus a valuable lesson in business.

Helping your kids out in some of the ways suggested here will be invaluable. Beyond a certain point, however, helping turns into interfering. It's often a fine line, so let's look at some of the guidelines that should be observed, especially by a parent who views a kid's job as a learning experience.

When Not to Help

Most kids first learn to do jobs around home. A 14-year-old, Debbie, became such an expert at washing windows at home that she began doing it for the neighbors to earn money. After several months she had several regular customers. Then one Friday at school she received an unexpected invitation to go away for the weekend with one of her friends. She was so excited that she forgot a special job she was scheduled to do on Saturday for Mrs. Jones. Mrs. Jones did the windows herself before the party she was having Saturday night, and Debbie didn't have that customer any more. In this case, Debbie's parents and the

Joneses were friends. Should her folks intervene on Debbie's behalf, talk to Mrs. Jones and explain what happened? Not if learning responsibility is worthwhile. If Debbie knows that whenever she fails to perform, her parents will bail her out, she is likely to develop an irresponsible attitude toward her job and perhaps toward money as well.

When he was just 6 years old, one little fellow was asked by an elderly neighbor if he could help her with some yardwork. His mother recalls that he was all tired out after the three hours it took to complete the job. Yet, for all that work, the lady paid him only 15¢. When he got home he was in tears. "Didn't you go talk to that woman about taking advantage of your son?" she was asked. "Of course not," was her response. "That was the best 15¢ lesson he'll ever get. You can be sure that from that time on he always knew where he stood in advance."

For kids to learn responsibility, they must—as soon as possible—be allowed to operate on their own. Robin, age 9, lived in a family of four, which included an older sister. She was assigned the task of cleaning the kids' bathroom. Her dad did it with her the first time. This father inspected the job each time for the next few weeks, pointing out spots that were missed and things that needed to be done over. Since then Robin has done a perfect job, and her mother's reaction to having one less bathroom to clean needs no comment.

When kids are just getting started, there are some guidelines that parents should observe. Parents should not require a perfect job. That won't happen. The kids will improve with practice, but they will never learn if too much is expected at the start. Parents should not hover over kids to make sure they don't make a mistake. Parents should let kids fix their own mistakes, do the job again if necessary, but the parents should not redo it themselves. Finally, parents should never give up on a kid and take over doing the job themselves because they are dissatisfied with the results.

Once kids have some job experience at home and are ready to start their own small business, parents should not call their own friends to help their kids line up customers. Suggesting who a kid might call on is constructive help. Parents should not design and produce flyers and posters for kids. Offering suggestions that a poster is too cluttered or does not contain enough information is a proper way to help. Parents should not write a sales presentation for a kid. Listening to what they come up with themselves and making suggestions will result in a more natural sales pitch.

When it comes to doing the job, there is just one rule: don't do it for them. There are obviously many legitimate ways to help, but the sight of a mother driving her kid around the neighborhood while he throws newspapers from the station wagon window is a picture of how not to help.

Perhaps most important, parents should not intervene in order to make sure a child makes no mistakes. Mistakes result in lessons. If things go too smoothly because a parent has "taken over," a kid might not get enough experience to learn much. Of course, you should not stand by and watch them prepare elaborate plans for making money that you know from experience will fail. But if there's a chance it might work, let them give it a try. Don't lose sight of the objective, which is to let them learn, not to make them wealthy their first time out.

The Challenge

The capability of a child to learn is almost unlimited. Psychologist William James once speculated that the average person uses perhaps 10 percent of his potential, and that even the most accomplished members of our society tap only a fraction of their true capabilities. Viewed in this way, it could be said that success is less a function of capability than of how effectively we use what is available. We have little control over the inherent capabilities of our children, but parents can exercise a great deal of influence over the ways kids develop what they have.

Almost all parents want to raise their children in the way that will best prepare them for happy and rewarding lives as adults. Some of what kids need to know will be learned in school. More will be learned from their parents. But you can tell them just so much. The most significant learning will come from the experiences they have as they grow.

That parents can and should help their kids develop an understanding of the world of money and working seems clear. Knowing when to help, when not to help, and some of the ways help can be offered can assist in keeping kids pointed in the right direction.

CHAPTER 20

IF YOU SPOT A TALENT IN YOUR KID, NURTURE IT ALONG!

YOUR IMAGINATION PLUS THEIR IMAGINATION— IT ADDS UP TO $$$

Children have marvelous imaginations, and their natural creativity can be applied to making money. That creativity may go toward discovering a new job, but it can also involve finding the best possible money-making opportunity for one unique youngster, with his or her own interests, living in a particular neighborhood. Finding the best solution for each individual kid requires imagination—yours and theirs.

This chapter's objective is to show how creativity:

Can uncover money-making ideas (jobs) that are just waiting for someone to come along and do them.

Can produce or create new job opportunities that did not previously exist.

Can add some new dimension—a new twist or a better way to do things—to an existing job.

Let's take these thoughts one at a time and look at a few examples. Maybe they'll help you and your youngster come up with something that fits your situation perfectly.

Uncovering Money-Making Ideas

There are actually three sets of opportunities among the money-making ideas that can be uncovered: jobs just waiting to be discovered; things people forget to do for themselves; and things people never quite get around to doing.

The Job Just Waiting to Be Discovered

A young fellow named Mike wanted a new skateboard, and a modest one at that. Only $60. Nowadays, you can spend $200 or more for one of these devices. Times have changed. Some of us parents can recall a vehicle we used to call a "skatecoaster." It consisted of a three-foot piece of two-by-four with half a skate nailed to the front and the other half to the rear. A wooden box was nailed to the front end with a stick across the top for handlebars. That was it, and it cost almost nothing to build.

In any event, Mike's mother pointed out that there was no $60 item available in the family budget. Undaunted, Mike went to the skateboard shop and told them he wanted to buy the skateboard—did they have any jobs? The answer proved to be yes! The store had a large quantity of advertising leaflets they wanted to have passed out. Mike went door to door on his old $10 skateboard, passed out all the leaflets, and earned $35. When the $35 was added to what he had already saved, he had his $60 skateboard.

The job of distributing leaflets for a skateboard shop is not an obvious job like mowing a lawn. There was no "Help Wanted" sign in the window. This job had to be found. Yet, all it took was asking if the shop had any jobs to be done. A lot of kids find it hard to ask, but the ones who learn how to uncover opportunities by asking for them, like Mike did, are way ahead of the game.

Bart Starr, coach of the Green Bay Packers, created a job that was waiting to be discovered, at the age of 14. His father was in the Air Force, and his family lived on the base. Because of their location, many of the base personnel were unable to have papers delivered to them in the usual way. Bart saw this as a money-making opportunity for him. He made arrangements with the newspaper's circulation manager to purchase papers directly from the publisher, and he resold them all over the base. As Starr puts it, "Naturally, the more papers I bought, the more I had to sell."

His paper business became Bart's chief source of income, and when his family moved from the base, he was recommended for a suburban route because of the job he had previously done. It all came about because he looked around, found an opportunity that had been overlooked, and turned it into a job.

The Things People Forget to
Do for Themselves

The number of things some people forget to do for themselves is greater than you would think. A few examples are: cleaning last year's ashes out of the space below the fireplace; scrubbing the bricks on the hearth and around the fireplace; maybe spraying the fireplace screen with a fresh coat of black paint. Almost no one remembers to clean the rain gutters until it's raining, or to clean up the backyard barbeque in time to have it ready for summer. All these people need is a reminder, and some youngster has a job.

The Things People Never Quite Get
Around to Doing

If a kid appears at your door wanting to wash your windows (you've been putting it off for weeks), sharpen the kitchen knives (another job that can wait), or help you organize and conduct a garage sale, he or she just might have a job. Right? And how long has it been since you relined your kitchen shelves and drawers?

Beyond the many tasks that can be put off until later, there's a whole world of things available to a kid who's willing to work hard. This world is made up of things people simply don't like to do—cleaning shower stalls, washing walls or doing floors, even doing laundry.

None of these jobs is new. They are all waiting to be done— by someone. The enterprising kid who is first to ask will probably be the one who gets the job.

Creating New Job Opportunities
Where None Existed Before

Lemonade stands are old hat. Most kids have tried making a buck selling lemonade at some point along the way, usually in their front yard to a few of their friends. They try it one afternoon and that's it. In contrast, two young ladies made selling lemonade a regular and very profitable business. They set up their stand across the street from a Little League field. Whenever a game or practice was in progress, these kids were open for business. They were able to identify a need, a market, and supply it. Another alert youngster's yard backed up to the fairway of a golf course. One day it occurred to him that there was a steady stream of thirsty golfers walking by all day long. He went into the lemonade business over his back fence, and he had a very profitable weekend business for some time after that.

Your family may not live next to a golf course and may not have a Little League Field close by, but the first step is the same. You and your kids have to apply your imaginations in answering the question: *Who* are the customers and *where* are the customers?

They say you can't make a silk purse out of a sow's ear. But Michelle and Chris tried when they were 11 and 8 years old. Their mother worked for a carpeting manufacturer. The yarn for the carpet came to the carpet mill on paper cones. Before Christmas their mother brought a number of the cones home, and the girls sprayed them with paint, gold, green, red, or silver. Then they glued attractive yarn balls and glitter on the cones and went around the neighborhood selling them as Christmas decorations. The price was 50¢ apiece, or 3 for $1. Profit-and-loss records are a little sketchy on this one, but the girls are pretty sure they had $40 left after paying for all the supplies they used.

With enough practice, watching for opportunities can become a very useful habit. Few kids, however, have had as much practice by the age of 12 as Irv Robbins of Baskin-Robbins. By age 12, he had accumulated a lot of experience in the ice cream business. In his twelfth summer Irv went to a camp at Liberty Lake near Spokane, Washington. One of the first things he noticed was that there was no place to buy ice cream in the entire area. Sensing an opportunity, he wrote to his dad back home in Tacoma and requested that he send some ice cream to sell at the camp. Tacoma was 400 miles away, and his Dad suggested that Irv might talk to someone in nearby Spokane. A few days later Irv not only had a company willing to supply him with ice cream but also willing to come out and install an ice cream storage cabinet right at the camp. First, however, Irv needed an initial inventory. He had some money but not enough to buy a cabinet full of ice cream. So he invited several of his friends to share in the profits if they would help finance the first delivery. With that, he was in business.

You're thinking that's pretty aggressive for a little guy. But for him, apparently, it was a very natural response to the situation. Since he had grown up with the ice cream business, it took no effort to figure out that there was none around. The difference between Irv and most 12-year-olds is that he didn't stop there. He recognized the opportunity and moved quickly to capitalize on it. It's a lucky kid who combines the imagination to spot an opportunity with the self-confidence to take advantage of it.

Business at the camp was a fantastic success. After all, kids at summer camp are hungry. He sold ice cream bars just about as fast as he could get them delivered. But that wasn't enough for Irv. He discovered that there was a picnic ground about four miles from his camp, and there were hungry people there, too. Irv had another place to sell ice cream. One of his first customers in his new area was a counselor from a nearby girls' camp. "We should have ice cream, too," was her reaction. Irv countered, "Bring the girls over to our camp, and they can get some there." He says he was never sure if the girls came over for the ice cream or because of the boys, but whatever the reason, sales jumped again. The camp lasted all summer, and Irv went home with a lot of profits.

New job opportunities can be created in unexpected places. Howard K. Smith of ABC News created one that helped pay his way through college. During the college year, in addition to raking leaves and serving as watchman at the gymnasium, Smith "coached laggard football players in history." He discovered a method of teaching the subject that seemed to work much better than that being used by his own teacher. "I chose the ten outstanding events of American history, and forced the men to memorize them by sheer rote," says Smith, describing his technique. "When they had the events down in their minds, I then set to work telling them anecdotes about each event, and the longer-term significance of each one. This process made the history come alive to them, and was highly successful."

Before leaving the subject of ways to create new job opportunities, we must mention one additional set of possibilities. That is swapping services. We heard of a young fellow who wanted to learn how to play the piano. There was a particular teacher he wanted, but he couldn't afford the lessons. One day he simply asked that teacher if he could mow his lawn in exchange for lessons. Last we heard, he was still taking lessons and still mowing the lawn. Opportunities like this may be infrequent, but it's worth keeping an open mind on the subject.

Adding a New Twist—Finding a
Better Way to Do What You're Doing

How many people spend time thinking about the job they do? Thinking about better ways to do it? Thinking about ways to enlarge it, to make it more profitable to them? Here are a few examples that can be used to encourage kids to keep their imaginations sharp once they've landed a job.

Let's suppose Christmas is approaching and you have a youngster who needs to make some money to buy Christmas presents. Since there are normally plenty of babysitting opportunities during the holiday season, she has a number of babysitting assignments lined up. She'll make some money, but not as much as she'd like to. But what if she could do two jobs at once? There *are* people who don't like to address Christmas cards. If her handwriting is decent, she might find several people happy to pay her to do their cards. Now she can address cards after the kids she is babysitting go to bed—and she can end up making twice as much money in the same period of time.

Louis Lundborg of Bank of America added another business to his previously described publishing ventures at the age of 10—raising rabbits. One of the customers for his rabbits was the Cobb Restaurant on 27th Street in Billings, Montana. As Lundborg relates it, "I came close to inventing perpetual motion in my rabbit operation. I would go to the Cobb restaurant and get all of the discarded vegetables—carrot tops, outside leaves of lettuce, and so on—take them back home and feed them to my rabbits. I would then take the rabbits back and sell them to the Cobbs." That's using imagination! And Lundborg had plenty of opportunities to use that imagination as an adult.

The Job Club

We have suggested that a kid take a survey if he's having trouble finding the right thing to do. One answer might be forming a "Job Club." Here, four or five or more kids agree to put their best ideas together in a pool. Each of them agrees to conduct an independent survey of his or her friends, parents, neighbors, relatives, family business acquaintances, and so on. All the ideas are collected, cataloged, and then discussed. One of the objectives while reviewing these job ideas should be to come up with creative and profitable variations on the ideas collected. Some of the jobs would normally be appropriate for one person, but some might require a work crew of two or more (it's easier to go looking for that *first* job with a friend), and the Job Club would provide a ready-made crew.

Take a Fresh Look at the World

Most people, certainly most children, tend to view the world as they have habitually perceived it. Our objective is to encourage *you* to encourage your kids to get "outside" that conventional view of things. The most rewarding ideas seem to be those where someone makes a connection no one else has made, sees an opportunity no one else has recognized. There's a lot of pressure on youngsters to conform to what everyone else is doing—same jeans, same tennis shoes, same parties, same everything. You're on the right track if you get them to see that being unique in at least some areas can really pay off. The implications, in fact, go well beyond the subject of making money. Effective use of their imaginations is one of the most useful tools kids can ever develop.

There are obviously many ways in which kids can use their imaginations to uncover job opportunities, and many ways that parents can encourage the development of this talent. One important test of *your* imagination as a parent is in recognizing talents in your kids that might lead to some future success. Early interests often prove to be very significant in later years.

Racing driver Tom Sneva showed an early interest in the sport at age 10 by organizing neighborhood bike races and "Soap Box Derby" type coaster races. Anyone wishing to participate paid Sneva an entry fee. Starting at age 10, Duke Boyd's main interest in life was surfing. That interest was just as strong in his twenties when he started Hang Ten, making surfing trunks and jackets. Even before he started school, Soichero Honda had shown an interest in mechanics and in cars.

If sheer desire at an early age can foster excellence, then O. J. Simpson stands out as an example. As he puts it, "The only thing I was really interested in as a kid was seeing the San Francisco 49ers play in Kezar Stadium. I did whatever it took to get enough money to see those games." O. J.'s dedication to the sport, even before he was 10 years old, illustrated that a person's imagination will work overtime to come up with ideas if something is wanted badly enough. In addition to washing cars, running errands, and selling tickets, Simpson and some of his friends would go down to a pier on the bay, catch fish, and sell them to workers on construction projects. That money also went to get them into the games. As a college player at the University of Southern California, Simpson won the Heisman Trophy; as a professional, he was named an All-Pro halfback; and in 1978, he joined the 49ers in the town where it all started.

Reggie Jackson's father owned a tailor shop in Philadelphia where Reggie grew up. Sports were one of his principal interests as soon as he was old enough to participate. His dad encouraged his interest in baseball, hoping it might lead to a chance for Reggie to get a college education. Reggie worked hard at the sport, partly because he enjoyed the game but partly because "if I wasn't on the first string baseball team, I had to go home and work." His dad was very interested in his son's progress and would periodically drop by the school to ask the coach, "How's he doing?"

Reggie's dad is an excellent example of a parent who strongly encouraged his kid's early interests. There was work to do in the tailor shop and there were chores to be done at home, but Mr. Jackson gave these a lower priority than encouraging an early talent he felt might amount to something important if properly developed. That bet paid off.

Special interests, then, if encouraged, can lead to significant success later in life. Sometimes, however, it may not be a "special interest" that is demonstrated by a kid. It may simply be a talent for business, an instinct for leadership that shows up early. Eileen Ford of the famous Ford Models, Inc., of New York, was a kid like that. Between ages 8 and 9, Eileen formed a club. She was president, and anyone who wished to join "had to pay me one penny." She changed the name of the club periodically, and, as she puts it, "Every time I changed the club, everyone had to pay me another penny." Eileen also put on theatrical performances in which she was "always the star." The potential for business leadership can obviously show up early.

So, if your daughter loves animals, why not encourage her to earn some money walking dogs, grooming pets, or raising them for sale? You might have a veterinarian in the family some day. If your son likes to draw and make posters, maybe he is a budding commercial artist or architect.

To assist both you and your youngsters in the search for ways they can make money, the following chapters present a wide variety of job ideas that have been collected from many sources. While there are well over a hundred specific jobs described, imaginative use of these ideas to fit each kid's situation can expand the list many-fold. Coming up with one or more "best" ideas for each individual kid is the challenge. With your imagination and theirs both working on it, you're sure to be successful.

THE ADVENTURE OF MAKING MONEY

To Kids:

So you want to earn some money! You've come to the right place. On the following pages you will learn:

How to pick the money-making idea that is best for you.

How to get the customers you need, and get them quickly.

How you can double your hourly income.

When and whom to ask for help.

How to get more jobs with less effort.

Tricks you can use to do a better job and do it faster.

How to decide how much you should charge your customers.

Making money should be fun—it should be an exciting adventure. If you're like most kids, you want to make some money of your own, but you might not be sure where to start. The following eight chapters will show you how to get started.

All the ideas for making money described in these chapters are called "jobs." However, they are not "regular jobs," like working at a gas station or at a theater. They are ways you can make money by starting a business of your own. If you mow lawns for five customers, you're in business for yourself, just like a professional gardener.

Chapter 21, "Starting Your Own Business," tells you how to figure out which are the best opportunities in your area. This is the first step—deciding which job is the best for you.

The next step is to let people know that you are available and interested in working for them. You do this by advertising. This step is where the money-making plans of many kids (and adults) fail. An imaginative approach to advertising is the answer. Examples of advertising and promotional techniques that have been used successfully by kids are included in Chapter 22.

Altogether, in Chapters 23–28 you will find over 125 specific job ideas described. Some need little explanation. Others are described in considerable detail. Chapter 23, "Money in a Hurry," describes jobs that can be done with relatively little advance planning and that require no specialized training or experience. If you are in a hurry to get going, this is a good place to start. Chapter 24, "Jobs in Your Own Neighborhood," lists more than 40 jobs that can be done right on your own street. If you live in the city, Chapter 25, "Apartments and Condominiums are Gold Mines," offers a wide variety of ways city kids can make money. "Summer Can Be Profitable" and "Holiday Profits," Chapters 26 and 27, are ideas for special times of the year, and include many ways to make money when school's out."

"The More, The Better," Chapter 28, is intended to encourage you to use your imagination when looking for things to do. Chances of getting a job doing something are much better if you offer several things at once in a package.

In using the job chapters, one of the most important things to remember is this: even though the jobs are arranged in categories where they seem to fit best, every chapter has ideas that you may be able to use, no matter where you live. Read them all.

Right now there are many people living right in your neighborhood who have jobs that need to be done and no one to do them. Helping you find those people and get those jobs is the objective of these chapters.

To Parents:

Making money should be an exciting adventure for kids. Kids want to make money of their own, and want the challenge of making it on their own. But getting started can sometimes be a big obstacle. Some kids may think they're too young to get a job. And it's true that some "regular" jobs like working at a fast-food restaurant or a theater, cannot be obtained by kids under 16, or sometimes 18. But all the "jobs" listed in this section are things kids can do on their own—they're actually small businesses. More than 130 ideas are listed here, and some can be done by kids as young as 8.

The material in Chapters 21–28 is written to kids so they can understand it and use it on their own. It will show them what they need to know and answer most of their questions. This does not mean you should just hand it to any kid and expect him or her to get busy making money right away. That will no doubt work with some kids. But others will need a helping hand in order to get started.

If your youngster will be looking for his or her first job, the world outside your home can appear very intimidating. Many kids will be reluctant to even get out and look unless they have some moral support. Your judgment about which job ideas are the most practical in your own neighborhood should be very helpful.

Although you will profit from having your kids earn some of their own money, the big gainers will be your kids. They will gain self-reliance, learn responsibility, and learn any number of practical lessons in dealing with the world themselves.

CHAPTER 21

STARTING YOUR OWN BUSINESS

If you do it right, being in business for yourself is the best way of all to make money.

One thing most kids never realize is that when you go out and earn some money on your own, doing the kinds of jobs explained in this chapter, you are doing what many adults would love to be doing themselves—running your own business. If you get a job at the local gas station or bakery, you are an employee and the owner is your employer. This means that your employer decides what you will do, the days and the hours that you will work, and how much you will earn per hour. When you work for yourself, it's a different story. You might start off waxing floors and shampooing carpets but discover along the way that you really prefer doing carpets and that you can earn more money doing them. So you decide to stop waxing floors. It's a choice you can make. It's your own business and you're the boss.

If being in business for yourself is so much more attractive than working for someone else, why don't more adults do it? Mostly because a steady job is safer, it's a more dependable source of income. As a kid, you're in the fortunate position of not having anyone to support, so you can do whatever you choose.

To some extent, the jobs that are best for you depend on your age. If you're only 7 or 8, you can't get a regular job. You must be 14 years old to be hired by some businesses, 16 for others, and 18 for most. But if you're 7, there are several things you *can* do. One thing is collect bottles or aluminum cans, and there are others too. You won't get rich doing them, but you don't need to be rich. You will be earning some of your own money to spend, won't you? That's the point.

If you are old enough to be hired by a gas station, a local theater, or a Kentucky Fried Chicken store, you have to decide whether you're better off in one of these jobs or being your own boss. There are several advantages for you if you decide on your own business. The first has to do with the hours you work. It's up to you to decide whether you prefer working in the afternoon or on weekends. In addition, you are the one who decides how many hours you want to work each week. If you need more money, you can find more customers and work more hours. Once you become an expert at what you're doing (shampooing carpets, for example) you can learn to quote jobs in advance instead of working by the hour and make quite a bit more money.

Another advantage is that you cannot be fired from your business. You may lose one customer by doing a sloppy job, but if you're smart, you won't make the same mistake again. You'll have to replace that customer, but you're still in business. Finally, you'll learn more about business and how it works by running your own than you will working for someone else.

There are, of course, some disadvantages to being in business for yourself. One is that you never *have* to go to work. It's sometimes quite easy to put off doing a job until tomorrow when you're in charge of your own time. Another possible disadvantage is that you may have to work hard to get new customers; you have to keep at it, even when many people tell you they're not interested. In other words, your own business demands more from you than a regular job. Because of all this, you might make less money doing your own thing. But you *might* make a lot more.

Many of the jobs you can do will give you experience in handling competition. You'll learn how to charge for the work you do, how to go out and get customers, and how to keep them once you find them. In the process, you'll learn a lot about how the real world of business works. And you'll make some money of your own.

There is no shortage of jobs for kids! To show you the many ways kids can make money, more than 130 different job ideas are listed in the eight chapters in this section. There are city jobs and country jobs, jobs you can do in the winter or summer. Some of the jobs are simple enough to be done by a 7-year-old. Others are jobs that require the know-how or responsibility of teenagers. *All* of the jobs can be done by either girls or boys. There is something for everyone. So there is no reason for you to say, "There's nothing to do." There's *plenty* to do!

Where Do You Start?

There are three questions you need to answer before you get started:

What do you already know how to do?

What would you really like to do?

What job will people pay you to do?

Let's look at these questions one at a time to see how answering each one of them will help you decide which job fits you the best.

What Do You Already Know How to Do?

If your responsibility at home is mowing the lawn or cleaning and waxing the kitchen floor, these are jobs you don't have to learn. If you've done babysitting for your own family in the past, you have the experience you need in order to get other babysitting jobs. One advantage of a job at which you already have some experience is that you an get off to a fast start.

Another advantage of picking a job at which you have had some experience is that you can often charge more than if you need to do some learning on the job. You will also be more convincing when you look for new customers, because you'll be more confident that you can do the job correctly. You'll be able to discuss specifics of the work when you talk to people, and you can say "experienced" on your flyers and posters.

Here's what you should do. *List* all the jobs at which you have some experience on a note tablet, whether that experience was at home or somewhere else. Then, to see what else you can come up with, answer the next question.

What Would You Really Like to Do?

If you can answer this question honestly, you might turn up some real surprises. Maybe you've made some money at one particular job in the past and see no reason to consider something new. But even if that's true, you have nothing to lose by spending a little time thinking about other possibilities. Look around to see if there's something else you'd rather do. If you are good at guitar, tennis, or swimming, have you ever considered teaching young children how to do those things? Have you ever thought of running your own business, like gardening or raising chickens to sell eggs? Is there anything *special* about your neighborhood? The area in which you live? Ever think of doing anything crazy? Many people have made fortunes on some rather odd ideas. Have you ever heard of *Pet Rocks?*

Write down every idea you can think of, even if it does seem crazy. When you get your list of job ideas together and have added the best ones you can find in the following chapters, it's time to answer the most important question.

What Job Will People Pay You to Do?

This is the key to success. It doesn't matter *what* you can do, or what you would *like* to do, if you can't get any customers interested in paying for your services or products. Until someone will pay you, you don't have a job. The best jobs of all are often things no one else thought of doing. After all, if you're the only one in your neighborhood who's doing the job you do, you'll have no competition, at least for a while. But even if you do come up with what looks like a great new job idea, will anyone pay for it? Even with established jobs like mowing lawns, you can't be sure how many people will hire you until you ask.

Let's suppose you decide that mowing lawns is the thing you want to do, so you get all excited about the idea and go out and buy a power mower and various other tools. Then you find out that no one in the neighborhood will hire you. They may all have regular gardeners, or they may prefer to do their own lawns. It doesn't matter why they won't hire you: it only matters that you've wasted a lot of time, energy, and money because you assumed people would pay you to mow their lawns without really knowing. That's not just disappointing, that's poor business. The problem can be avoided by checking first to see if there is any demand for your money-making idea.

What Things Will People Buy from You?

There are lots of things kids can sell to make money. Some are things you can buy, like Christmas cards. Some are things you can grow, like plants or vegetables. Others are things you can make yourself and sell to people. And the same rules apply here

187

that apply to jobs. Before you get too involved, make sure you know who your customers will be. Growing plants and making macrame plant holders are good examples. Both of them take time and money before you make your first sale. With plants, you must first buy small plants and raise them until they are large enough for you to make a profit. With plant holders, you must first buy the materials and spend time making them.

There are two approaches you can take. The first is to buy a lot of small plants. While the plants are growing larger, make

TIPS

Picking the Right Job

Follow these steps:

1. Get a pencil and notepad.

2. Write down *every* job you can think of yourself, and do it *before* you read all the job ideas in these pages. Write down *every one*, even if it sounds a little crazy.

3. Think about which jobs people put off "until later"—jobs like cleaning the attic—and ones they forget to do, like painting the fence.

4. Now ask your parents for additional ideas. Also ask your brother and sister, your friends, even your neighbors.

5. Next, think about your hobbies. Can any of them be turned into a profitable business? Like jewelry making or sewing.

6. How about special skills? Could you give lessons in swimming or Spanish?

7. Look out the window. Is it snowing? There will be snow shoveling jobs available by tomorrow. Are there ripe plums falling on the ground? Pick and sell them before the rest fall on the ground.

8. Then read the job ideas described here. Add the ones you like to your own list.

9. Go through and pick the jobs that make the most sense to you where you live. Select one, or several, jobs to do.

10. Make sure you know how to do the jobs. If not, find yourself an "expert" annd then pactice at home.

11. Prepare your flyers and posters, or whatever you select from chapter 22.

12. Now go make some money.

several dozen plant hangers. When the plants are large enough, take them around the neighborhood and see if anyone will buy them. A much better way is to first find out how many people might be interested. The way to do this is very simple. Buy a few full-grown plants and make a few plant hangers. Now take these around and see how well they sell. If they sell quickly, you may have found a good way to make money. If they don't, you'll save a lot of time by not getting too involved in something that won't work.

This is the same process a company goes through when it is considering any new product. Before they spend thousands of dollars introducing something new, they want to be very sure it's going to be a winner. By doing this kind of "market testing" with your plants, you will be doing the same thing a large corporation does in planning its business.

Do a Market Survey

There are two ways to identify possible customers. The first is the most obvious—ask them. The second is to advertise and see what kind of response you get.

Asking for Business

Once you've picked your job, it's time to see who's interested. The fastest and most direct way to find out how much business you might get is to go door to door in your neighborhood and ask. When you talk to people, ask them in whatever way seems most comfortable to you. It might go something like this:

"I'm Jan Smith and this is Billie Jones. We live in this neighborhood and we're looking for more customers for our window-washing service. We'll do all your windows—inside and outside—and get them really clean without making any mess. Would you be interested in having us wash your windows?"

In this example you are offering to do just one particular job. Another way to do this is to offer a "package" of jobs to the people you talk to. In this case, you might say:

"I'm Billie Jones and this is Jan Smith. We live in this neighborhood and we're looking for more customers for our window service. We'll wash all of your windows—inside and outside—and if you want us to, we'll clean paint off the glass and remove and scrub screens. We can also wash venetian blinds and replace putty if any of your windows need it. Would you be interested?" Chapter 28 offers a number of ideas for such job packages.

A third possibility is offering to do several things that are not related to one another. After introducing yourself, you might say,

"I have experience babysitting, walking dogs, and doing laundry and housework. Do you need help with any of these things?" Offering more than one thing gives you more than one chance to find out what people need.

After one or two afternoons of this, you will learn several things. First, you'll know whether or not the people in your area are interested in the jobs you are offering to do. If you have offered to do several different jobs and you find that most people are interested in just one of them, you will know where to concentrate your future efforts. In other words, let the customers tell you what *they* want. Don't stick to what *you* want if there is little or no interest.

If you just haven't been able to figure out what you want to do, the following chapters will be sure to help you come up with some ideas. Take some notes as you go along, and add as many of your own ideas as you can. Maybe you can get an idea from a job described here and improve on it yourself.

Everyone in your neighborhood is a potential customer for some job. What you have to do is find out which job, or jobs, they will pay you to do. Once you know that, you should end up with more jobs than you can handle.

Starting your own business is not as simple as answering a Help Wanted ad. To do it right, you must decide what is the best thing for you to do and figure out where you will find customers. Then you have to decide how to let people know you are in business and have a product or service to sell. The best way to tell people is by advertising. The next chapter describes a number of advertising techniques you can use to make your business a success. Once you're successfully making money on your own, chances are good that you'll enjoy being your own boss, and enjoy the feeling that comes from making your own decisions.

TIPS

Competition Is Part of the Game

Competition is when you've been mowing the neighbor's lawn for eighteen months and charging $5 for both front and rear, and you lose the job to a kid who will do it for $4.

Competition, however, works both ways, and you can use it to your own benefit. Suppose you have decided mowing lawns is how you want to earn money, but in your survey of the neighborhood, you discover that all those jobs are already taken. You have two choices — to pick a different job or to figure out a way to get some of the lawn-mowing business for yourself. One way is by offering to do the job for less money. If *you* are the one who cuts the price to $4, will you get all the customers? The answer is no! Some will not switch to you. It might be just because they like the kid who is already doing the job. Others will be very satisfied with the job that's being done. But you will probably find a few customers who are unhappy with the person they are using, and saving a dollar might be enough reason for them to give the business to you. If you pick up three or four customers, you're off to a good start.

But what if some other kid comes along and offers to mow *your* customers' yards for $3? How can you protect yourself against that?

There are three ways that people and businesses compete with each other—price, quality, and service. You already know about price competition. That's how you got your customers. *Quality* refers to how good a job you do. If you do the best job on the street, you'll not only have happy customers who will stay with you, you'll attract new ones who can see that you do good work.

Service really applies more to a business like a retail store than it does to mowing lawns. Friendly sales cclers who are helpful or box boys who carry groceries to the car are "extras" that bring customers back to shop at these stores again. But even in your lawn business, you can be friendly and courteous. Even more important, you can be dependable and always do your job when it's supposed to be done. That's providing good service, too.

You can use *price*—charging less to do a job—to get business, but you must provide quality and service to keep it.

CHAPTER 22

ADVERTISING WILL GET YOU JOBS

In a typical community somewhere in America one Saturday morning, Mrs. Lampert (who is divorced, has one daughter away at college, and works full-time) is complaining over a cup of coffee to Mrs. Jacobs (who has two children under 5 and a husband who travels a great deal): "I'm so mad at the company that sold me the firewood. Considering how much I paid for it, I expected them to stack it in the garage for me. But no, they just dumped it in the driveway, and I have to figure out how to get it into the garage. Do you know anyone I can call to help me put it away?"

"If I did, I'd hire them too," answers Mrs. Jacobs. "Jack's been promising to clean out *our* garage for months. I can hardly get to the washer and dryer to do my laundry because there's so much junk in the way. But he always has something more important to do on the weekends that he's home."

"And by the way," she continued, "now that your Alice has

192

gone off to college, I don't have a babysitter to count on anymore. Does she have any friends near here I could call?"

Meanwhile, two blocks away, Ann and her brother Roger are feeling sorry for themselves. Their mother has just told them that, if they want to go to the rock concert coming to town in two weeks, they'll have to earn the money themselves. They've decided there's no way they'll be able to go, since neither one of them can think of a single way to earn any money in a hurry.

If Mrs. Jacobs and Mrs. Lampert knew Ann and Roger and knew that they were available, they would call them today! But they've never met. What's the answer? Advertising is the answer.

Advertising

It makes no difference how desperately you need to earn some money, how hard you are willing to work, or what jobs you are interested in doing, you won't earn a nickel until you get some customers. The objective of advertising is to reach as many people as possible with a message. If you are selling a service, your message is this: You are interested in working and are available at a reasonable cost to help people when they need to get a job done. If you are selling a product, your message is this: You have desirable items that you are selling at a reasonable price. The more people who get your message, the more business you will get. And the faster you let them know, the sooner you'll earn some money.

Here's what Ann and Roger can do to solve their problem:

They can sit down and figure out what they want to tell people.

They can print or type that information on a sheet of paper and have copies made.

They can distribute the copies to everyone in their neighborhood.

Their flyers might look something like this.

... BABYSITTING
... YARDWORK
... CLEANING
... ODD JOBS
When you need help — call us.
Available most weekdays and on Saturdays.
Dependable — Reasonable Rates
Ann Phillips   **Roger Phillips**
Age 15   **Age 14**
222-1722

If Mrs. Lampert and Mrs. Jacobs had found a copy of this flyer in their mailboxes or at their front doors the previous week, Mrs. Lampert's firewood might already be stacked neatly in her garage, Mrs. Jacobs' garage might already be cleaned up and reorganized, and Mrs. Jacobs might have that new babysitter she was looking for. Ann and Roger would also have solved their problem.

The purpose of advertising is to get two people who need each other together. Remember that if you are delivering your message in person. When you go door to door handing out your flyers and someone answers the door, you don't have to be apologetic. You are not looking for charity or asking people to give you a job because they feel sorry for you. You're looking for someone who *needs* you. You are willing to do what they need in exchange for money. So look them straight in the eye, tell them what you are available to do or ask them what they need, and do it with enthusiasm.

There are many ways you can get your message out to people, and the rest of this chapter describes some of them.

Flyers

A flyer is the simplest advertising you can use. Take a sheet of plain white paper, 8 1/2 x 11 inches, type or print your message on it, and make copies to distribute. Copies can be made on an office copying machine or by a printer. The printer should charge you less than $10, perhaps as little as $5 or $6, for 200 copies. Here's an example of a flyer you might distribute in the spring to line up summer house-sitting jobs:

HOUSE SITTING   **HOUSE SITTING**

THIS SUMMER YOU GO _____**I'LL STAY**

AND

_____ **water your yard**
_____ **mow the lawn**
_____ **keep the weeds pulled**
_____ **take in papers and mail**
_____ **feed and care for pets**
_____ **water houseplants**
_____ **keep your house or apartment
looking "lived-in"**

Call soon — certain weeks still available.
Reasonable rates   **References**

CALL: Gordon Jones 828-8911

Posters

A poster can be something special and attractive that you do on colored paper or cardboard. You can add some artwork as long as it doesn't make your poster appear cluttered. Put the posters up in places where a lot of people will see them. Laundromats, churches, supermarkets, and other kinds of businesses have bulletin boards for this purpose. If you have a friend who works in a store, or if you know the owner, see if you can put one in the window. If you live in an apartment, put one up in the laundry room and anyplace else posters are permitted. You can also put up your flyers instead of making special posters, but it's probably better to use both.

Business Cards

The advantage of having a business card is that it makes you look like a professional. The other advantage is that most people keep the business card you give them, which means they will have your name and phone number if they need you. Cards can be passed out in all the same ways you would pass out a flyer.

TIPS

What About Experience?

Most people prefer to hire someone who has experience at a particular job. That's understandable. If they are paying for something, they want it to be done right. But if you're looking for your first job, you have no experience. And if no one will hire someone without experience, you'll never get any, will you?

Fortunately, there is a way to get experience before you start out. That's by doing the job right at home. The obvious place to learn to mow a lawn is in your own front yard. Your mother will be delighted to have you practice waxing floors in her kitchen. So practice at home first, especially on more complicated jobs. For example, if waxing cars sounds like a good way to make money, try it on your Dad's car first. If you make a mess of it, you'll have to do it over, but that's better than making a mess of your neighbor's car. And don't forget to check with an "expert."

You have one big advantage when you're young. Most people don't expect too much experience from a kid. So don't worry too much about experience. Do the best job you can, and you'll be an expert before you know it.

They can be left in mailboxes or under windshield wipers or distributed door to door. You can pass them out in front of your local supermarket or shopping center. The disadvantage of cards is their cost. Printing 500 cards will cost you from $15 to $25, so if you decide to use cards, shop around for the best rate in your area. Here's a sample of a card you might use.

```
RESPONSIBLE SITTERS

"We're in the Neighborhood"

Kary Jones              Sally Jacob
Age 14                  Age 14
724-5086                722-0648

            * Also Available *

            For Ironing, Light

        Housework, and Errands
```

Business cards or flyers can be used along with a poster on bulletin boards. Make up an envelope that will hold ten or fifteen of your cards and fix it so the ends of the cards can be seen. Print TAKE ONE on the envelope and tack it up below your poster. Or staple several of your flyers together so the top one can be torn off and write TAKE ONE on each copy.

Another trick you can use is to post a flyer with tabs that can be torn off by people who are interested. If a lot of single people live in your apartment building and there is a laundry room, post a flyer like the following one. Cut along the dotted lines at the bottom so that the little pieces of paper with your name and phone number can be torn off easily. When all the tabs are torn off, put up another one just like it.

	LAUNDRY 328-1010 Kathy
Find yourself wearing the same underwear two days in a row?	
Your LAUNDRY problem is solved!	LAUNDRY 328-1010 Kathy
— Pick-up and delivery at your apartment — Shirts and blouses on hangers	
— Clothes folded neatly	LAUNDRY 328-1010 Kathy
I am experienced from doing my dad's laundry. I will furnish supplies if you furnish money for the machines. I charge $1.50 for each load. I am 11 years old.	
Call Kathy 328-1010	LAUNDRY 328-1010 Kathy

Whether you use cards or a flyer with tabs, the whole idea is to make it convenient and easy for people to take your name and phone number with them if they are interested. You can do the same thing any place you put up a poster.

If a simple poster plus flyers get you a lot of calls, you've selected the right job. If no one calls you, however, that means one of two things—either you have picked the wrong job or you'll have to go door to door to get the business.

Personal Calls

Going door to door is the best way to get business. If you have a flyer or card to leave with people so they can call you later, if they need you for anything in the future. People are more likely to hire you if they have talked to you and know what you look like. Be sure to be enthusiastic and let people know you're interested in doing a good job.

Classified Advertising — Newspapers

In some cities and towns, newspapers set aside a section in their classified advertising pages for kids to use without charge. One paper calls it the "Kids Free Classified." Here are some samples of actual ads placed by kids at no cost to them.

Student hauling. 2 seniors have truck. Reasonable rates. Tom, age 17, 325-5245.

Odd jobs, painting, yardwork, gardening, windows, watering, light handyman. Atherton-Menlo Park, Dave, age 15, 325-6442.

Will do house or babysitting. Lindwnwood area. Responsible. Sheryl, age 14, 322-9390.

English riding lessons. Equitation, horsemanship & ring etiquette. Will travel to instruct. Nancy, age 16, 967-7337.

Birthday Parties? Victor the Magician amazes and entertains all! 5 years experience. Victor, age 17, 493-7083.

Experienced person will exercise horse, clean paddock for reasonable price. John, age 14, 854-3664.

Experienced dog walker. Reliable. West Menlo only. $1 an hour, all summer. Robin, age 9½, 327-8122

Need work done? Gardening, interior painting, pulling weeds? Dan, age 15, 255-7893; Jon, age 14, 996-1973.

Los Altos (Rancho, Blossom) babysitting, watering plants, pet care, fruit picking. Reliable. Joyce, age 13, 967-0103.

Magic Mike Magic Shows for birthday parties. Six years experience in magic. Mike, age 12, 493-7637.

Three boys will help with dinner parties. Dishes, serving, etc. Rinconada area. Kevin, John, Peter, age 13, 326-1163.

Call me for pet walking, vacuuming, dusting, housekeeping, mother's helper, pet feeding, doing dishes. Bonnie Jeanne, age 9, 941-9053.

All day babysitting, Available all summer except July 15-31. I enjoy young children. Dan, age 15½, 257-6504.

VW Owners!! Let me fine tune your engine!! Guaranteed work! Lowest prices!! Kevin, age 17, 961-2804.

Do you need a mother's helper to clean, babysit in Green Gables area? Kirsten, age 13, 321-5422.

Can do any bike repair that can be handled on the spot. Leon, age 10, 494-6196.

Gunn student will tutor math $2/hour. Also experienced babysitter $1/hour. Dave, age 15, 493-6657.

Tennis lessons cheap. Varsity player, private court, ball machine. $3.50 beginners/advanced. Roy, age 18½, 941-2796.

Student with fluent knowledge of Spanish and some Portuguese looking for job. Dave, age 16, 941-9740.

Responsible high school student will tend your toddler, make your house spotless. Debbie, age 14, 965-2254.

Keep your eyes open for other ways to find jobs. In one town a referral service was organized by people interested in helping kids find summer work. They called it RENT-A-KID. Any kid who was interested could register with RENT-A-KID and tell them what kinds of jobs they were available to do. RENT-A-KID advertised that they had young people interested in working, and when people called them, they called the kids. Check to see if anything like this exists where you live.

There are other places to look. If you know the mailman or milkman, ask him for ideas. Don't forget to ask your parents if they think any of their friends would be interested. If you have a paper route already but want to earn more money, talk to all of your customers about extra jobs next time you collect. If you have a friend with a paper route, ask him for ideas. Maybe if you offer to fold his papers, you can include a flyer like the following one that he will deliver for you.

GET A NEW LOOK AT THE WORLD!

Let me do your windows
— wash inside and out
— clean screens
— louvre windows

Call Frank Gregory   384-9735

Or one like this:

TIRED OF LOOKING AT DIRTY WALLS?

We specialize in:

• Kitchen walls and ceilings
• Greasy hoods and ventilators
• Bathrooms

Why paint? We'll make it like NEW!
Call

Mary Zapata   Julie Dandridge
742-6020

The first job you do for anyone is the most important one. Stacking firewood is a once-a-year job, but if Mrs. Lampert likes you, she'll have you back to do other things. If Mrs. Jacobs likes the job you do on her garage, she'll tell Mrs. Austin about you if the subject comes up. And when you're through with the firewood and the garage, be sure to ask if there's anything else that needs to be done.

Advertising is the way General Motors sells Chevrolets, General Mills sells Wheaties, and Mattel sells toys. It's the way the people at Disney get you into the theater to see their films and the way McDonald's sells hamburgers. If it works for them, it can work for you.

Set up a "Job Club"

Kids set up clubs for a million different reasons. Why not one for jobs? Why not a club just for the purpose of helping its members make money?

Here's how it works. From all your friends, select several who, like you, are interested in making money. Hold a meeting and think up all the money-making ideas you can. Write them all down. Then have each member ask everyone he or she can think of—parents, brothers and sisters, neighbors, friends—for additional ideas. At the next meeting, add the new ideas to your list.

But why go through all this? After all, if there are 120 jobs listed in this book, why look for more? There's a very good reason. That reason is that, in many parts of the country, there are things kids can do to earn money that are special to that area alone. Those jobs do not appear in these pages. They are jobs that people who live anywhere else have probably never heard of. One of them might, however, be the very best thing for you and your friends to do to earn money.

So try the "Job Club" idea. You have nothing to lose but a little time. The Job Club also provides you with enough other kids to put together work crews for those jobs where two or more kids are needed.

CHAPTER 23

MONEY IN A HURRY

Many jobs must be planned far in advance. If you want to be a counselor at a summer camp, you usually have to apply for the job many months ahead, often as early as the previous fall. Even getting a paper route often means waiting in line until a spot is available near where you live. A party-catering service can be quite profitable once you get it going, but it takes time to learn how to do this kind of job properly. It also takes time to line up enough steady customers to make it worthwhile.

But what if you need some money right now? What job will you choose that doesn't require a lot of advance planning? What's the best way to get off to a fast start? For most jobs that can be done in a hurry, you should look for the following five things:

1. *The job requires no complicated training and experience.* It should be a relatively simple job you already know how to do, or something you can learn very quickly.

2. *The job needs to be done right now.* You won't decide to make money shoveling snow in the summer or raking leaves

in the spring, but there are dirty kitchen walls and dirty cars in most areas all year. Taking care of children and polishing floors also represent jobs that are always available.

3. *There are plenty of customers available.* Pick a job that a lot of people in your neighborhood need to have done. If there are many families with young children living near you, babysitting may be the best place to start. But if most of the people in your neighborhood are retired, you can run errands or shop for those who find it difficult to get out.

4. *Little or no cash investment is needed.* If you live in Florida and you and a friend decide to offer a swimming-pool cleaning service, you may need $100 or more worth of equipment and chemicals just to start. Better try something else until you get the money together. On the other hand, you can probably get into the window-washing business for $10 or less, and babysitting requires no advance cash on your part.

5. *You can charge enough to make it worth doing.* If there are posters all over your neighborhood offering babysitting at 50¢ an hour and you don't think that's enough, try something else. If you offer to do something people want that no one else is doing, you can obviously get a better price. Maybe you should think of washing kitchen walls. It's a hard job, but it's worth more and you'll probably have a lot less competition.

To decide the best way to get going in a hurry, find out what other kids in your area have done. Check with your older brother or sister or other kids on your block. Ask your parents what they did when they were kids. Better still, ask your parents what kinds of jobs they would pay some kid to do for them. Maybe they'll be your first customer and you'll get some experience right at home.

The rest of this chapter contains a list of jobs that can be done by young people in most parts of the country, can be done almost any time, and can be done in a hurry.

Babysitting

Babysitting is one of the best possible ways to make money. It is a job that is easy to do, requires very little training, and can be done close to home. It's available the year round and is needed by everyone with small children. Watching young children is usually a job done in the evening when the parents want to go out to a friend's, a movie, or dinner. You may be busy until your little customers' bedtime, but bedtime is early for small children and the rest of the evening is yours. What other job will pay you for doing your homework, reading a book, or watching television?

Babysitting is not just a job for girls. Many boys who have

figured this out are able to make a great deal of money watching people's children. Some parents may even prefer hiring a boy.

For all these reasons, babysitting is an especially good job, and because it is such a good job, there is usually plenty of competition. There are, however, several ways you can beat the competition and probably end up with more babysitting jobs than you can handle.

The first step is to advertise, to let people know you are available. If you live in an apartment, make posters and put them up in the laundry rooms or recreation rooms of your own apartment complex and of the other apartment buildings close to your home. If you live in a suburban area, make some leaflets and pass them out in your neighborhood, especially to the homes where you know there are small children. Ask your parents to tell their friends who have children that you are interested in doing some babysitting.

The thing to remember is this: On any given evening, there are many frustrated parents who can't find a babysitter and many frustrated kids who need to earn some money—all sitting home because they don't know each other. The more people who know you are available, the more work you'll get.

There are two steps in making money. The first step is getting the job. The second step is keeping it. The way to turn your first babysitting customer into a permanent customer is to be the best babysitter those parents ever hired. Being good with kids obviously helps. If the kids want you back, chances are the parents will call you the next time they need someone. Playing games with the children, reading them stories, or arriving with a couple of balloons in your pocket—all these will help ensure that the kids want you back. Use your own imagination.

The parents will also appreciate coming home to a place that is neat and clean. Pick up the kids' toys after they go to bed. If the dinner dishes are still on the table, put them in the dishwasher and straighten up the kitchen. The parents might even pay you for doing some of those extras, but even if they don't, you are almost sure to be the first one they call the next time they need someone.

How much should you charge? There's no simple answer since it depends on your age, your experience, and where you live. You can ask around to find out what the going rate is in your neighborhood. You might charge a little less when you're getting started to help you get customers quickly.

Mother's Helper

This job might also be called "father's helper" or maybe "parents' helper." It's different from babysitting because you are not alone with the kids. You're helping the parents by watching their children at times when the parents are home but are either too busy to do it themselves or just looking for some peace and quiet. It's also different because customers for this job may not know they need you until you explain to them what you can do for them. This is a job for which advertising might pay off with a lot of business.

You might be hired to help the parents in the evening when they are entertaining guests and do not want the children underfoot. Or they might want you to be there all day Saturday because they are going to be very busy preparing to entertain guests that evening.

Although some parents might want you one day a week or just for special occasions, others might want you to work every day. The most likely time parents would like to have a helper on a regular basis is around dinner time. In a typical family, that's the time mom is trying to fix dinner, the baby is crying, the young children and the dog are pestering for something to eat, the family room is a mess, and dad (or mom if she's the one who works) is about to arrive home from work hoping for a few minutes of peace and quiet. Most parents never realize how nice it would be to have someone come in and help out for a couple of hours during this hectic time of the day. You could offer to feed and care for the baby, entertain small children, or help straighten up the house. You might even help with dinner.

You should charge at least as much for being a helper as you do for babysitting—and probably a little more. Look for customers the same way you would look for babysitting jobs.

Lawn Mowing

This job may be so obvious that it is often overlooked. It's one of the most dependable and consistent ways for kids to make money. In some areas of the country, lawns require mowing and attention the year round. Mowing lawns has a big advantage over many jobs, because once you get a customer, it's usually a job you can count on doing every week. In other words, you can count on a steady income; you know in advance how much money you will earn next week, and next month. Mowing, edging, raking, and sweeping are the principal things that must be done on a weekly basis.

Some people will want to pay you by the hour to do yard work for them. Others may prefer to pay you a certain amount for the whole job. If you're working by the hour, $2 to $3 per hour might be typical for your area. However, if you are a fast worker, you are better off getting a certain amount of money for each job. A large lawn might take one of your friends two hours to do. If he earns

$5, he's getting $2.50 an hour. But if you can do the same lawn in only an hour and a half, you're earning $3.33 an hour. If you have your own power mower and work fast enough to do the job in an hour, you'll make $5 an hour.

If you do a top-quality job, the yard you take care of is the best advertising you can get. Your customer's neighbors will see you mowing the lawn, and if the yard always looks great when you're finished, it should be easy to get them as customers. One or more of them might even stop by while you're working and ask if you'd like to do their yard as well.

When you're getting started, your best potential customers are those who have their own lawn mowers and yard tools. If all of your customers have a power mower, there's no need for you to consider getting one. If not, you may want to buy your own power mower at some point, along with other tools that let you do the job better and faster.

Pulling Weeds

Pulling weeds sounds like hard work, and it is. That's why you might be able to make some fast money offering to do the job. The older you get, the more your back hurts after a morning of pulling weeds, so many adults would prefer giving the job to a kid. Just get on your bike and ride around the neighborhood. Every yard with a lot of weeds in it is a potential customer.

Most weeds cannot be mowed because they'll just grow back unless the roots are pulled up as well. From your point of view, the nice thing about weeds is that they grow everywhere. There are weeds to be pulled out of the lawn, out of flower beds, out of parkways between the sidewalk and the street—everywhere. You'll probably work by the hour, since it's difficult to predict how long it will take on any particular job. Charge at least as much as lawn mowing is worth in your area. Do a good job and it's likely to lead to more jobs for that same customer.

Car Washing

As long as it's not raining or snowing, you can make money all year and in any part of the country by washing cars. You can do it alone, but it's easier and more fun if two or more of you work together. You can wash the cars where you live or take your equipment to the customer's home or apartment building and do the job there. If you're going to wash the cars where you live, the owners can deliver them, or, if one of you has a driver's license, you can go pick them up.

There are several ways you can line up customers. In the suburbs you can go from house to house, in an apartment from door to door, telling people about your service or leaving flyers. In apartments you can also leave flyers under windshield wipers of the cars in the parking area. In any neighborhood you can leave your notices on cars parked at the supermarket, the train station, or any place people leave their cars. Gas stations that do not offer car-washing service are good places to put posters.

Since finding customers is probably the most difficult part of the job, keeping them after you get them is very important. The best way to keep customers is to do a better job on their car than anyone else does. That means doing more than just getting the outside clean and shiny. It means scrubbing the whitewalls and cleaning the wheel covers, vacuuming the inside of the car, emptying all the ashtrays, getting all the dust out of the inside with a damp cloth, washing the inside of the windows, and vacuuming the trunk. You should probably charge about the same as the local car wash charges.

Why should people have you wash their car instead of going to the car wash? If you do all the things listed in the previous paragraph, you're doing a better job than the car wash. That's the most important reason. Convenience is the other reason. If you're willing to pick someone's car up when they're not using it, wash it, and return it in perfect condition, almost anyone would agree that's better than waiting in line at the car wash. And if pick-up and delivery plus a super job is worth $3, you and a friend could each make $15 every Saturday morning by doing ten cars you had lined up in advance. If you need to make more than that, find more customers and wash more cars every week.

Painting House Numbers on Curbs

Some house numbers just cannot be seen from the street. These houses could profit by having their numbers painted on the curb in front of the house. What you need for this job is a few supplies in advance: two cans of spray paint—one black and one white—and stencils for the numbers. Be sure to buy paint that is both fast-drying and weather-resistant. After you have your materials together, go door to door and offer to do it for every home that seems to need better identification. The job is probably worth $1.50 to $2.50, so if you pick a street where every house needs it, you might make $15 to $30 with just a few hours' work.

Probably the best way to do the job itself is to paint a white rectangle on the curb that is about 4 inches high and 8 to 10 inches long, depending on how many numbers there are in the address. This rectangle can be spray-painted using a stencil cut out of cardboard. After the white paint has dried somewhat, spray the numbers with black paint. If some of the houses on the street already have numbers painted on their curbs, make yours look as much like the others as possible. One nice thing about this job is that you can do it anywhere—you're not restricted to just your own street. Your customers are anywhere you are willing to walk or ride your bike.

Mailboxes and House Numbers

In many areas, mailboxes are not attached to houses but are placed alongside the street, and homeowners may prefer to have their house numbers painted on the mailbox. On mailboxes where the numbers need to be repainted, offer to do it. But if all the paint on the mailbox is weathered and peeling, this presents you with another job opportunity. Offer to clean up the mailbox, repaint it, and then paint new house numbers. The job should be worth $3 or $4 if you do both.

Some homeowners might like to have numbers on the house itself. They may want them painted on, or they may prefer the metal numbers you buy at a hardware store. Be sure to have both stencils and metal numbers with you. Then you'll be prepared to do either one. In some cases you might be hired to both put metal numbers on the house and paint house numbers on the curb.

Washing Windows

No matter where you live, everyone has windows and they all get dirty. But don't most people wash their own windows? The answer is no. It's one of those jobs people can put off, almost indefinitely. Washing all the windows in a small apartment can be a pretty big job. Washing all the windows in a large home can take most of the day. Remember that one of the secrets of picking a job where you can make lots of money is to find something that people would like to have done but don't want to spend the time on themselves. Washing windows is a perfect example of this kind of job.

What does it take to get into the window business? You'll need a ladder, a pail, a squeegee, paper towels, and a good cleaning agent. Washing windows is trickier than mowing lawns, and if you do it wrong, it'll take twice as long and you'll leave streaked windows behind you. How will you know how to do it right? Find an expert, perhaps the local janitorial supply house or a janitorial service. One way or another, find out how to do it right before you start.

Washing windows is a good job for a crew of two kids. One can work on the inside, one outside. And one of the best ways to get customers is just to go house to house, carrying your ladder, your bucket, and the rest of your equipment.

You should probably charge around $2.50 an hour to start. As you get better, raise your price to $3 an hour or more. Pay careful attention to how long it takes you to do certain types of jobs. After a while, you should get to the point where you can estimate in advance how many hours it will take to do the job. Then you can start making more money per hour by quoting people a figure to do their whole house or apartment; instead of making $2.50 to $3 an hour, you can make $4 or $5 an hour if you're willing to work hard.

Cleaning Venetian Blinds

Although fewer people have Venetian blinds today, people who do have them seldom clean them often enough. See if you can add them onto the job when you are washing windows or doing any other job for a homeowner. The reason many people put off cleaning the blinds themselves is that they have to be taken down, laid out in the yard, and washed with detergent. Wash the blinds with a sponge and the fabric straps with a small bristle brush. Rinse them off with a hose and hang them up wherever you can until they dry.

TIPS

What if the Job You Try Is a Failure?

No problem—unless you don't learn anything in the process. It's better to risk failing at something than never to try anything. Many people, however, are actually afraid to try things for fear they won't work out. People who feel that way miss most of the adventure in life. And business can be an exciting adventure, even if you have to try several things before you have your own first big success. There are dozens of stories about famous men and women who failed many times before reaching the top. Remember that failing at something does not make *you* a failure; it only means you tried something that didn't work. So if you're worried about failure—*FORGET IT!* The only way to avoid risk is never to try anything.

Window Screens

Sometimes when you can't see through a window, it's because of dirty screens, not dirty glass. Over time, window screens corrode and get clogged with dust and dirt. The best way to get them clean is to take them down, lay them in the driveway, and scrub them on both sides with a stiff bristle brush and a cleanser like ammonia or detergent. Rinse them with a hose, and, if necessary, do them again, scrubbing in both directions. Properly cleaned, most screens can be made to look shiny and new, and your customers are certain to be pleased with their new view of the world. In most areas, $2.50 to $3 an hour would be a reasonable charge.

Leaflet Distribution

Distributing leaflets is a job that may or may not be available, but you can find out very quickly by visiting your local stores and businesses. Ask them if they have any advertising material they would like to have distributed. You can't tell in advance who might be interested in hiring you, so ask as many as you can find. The best prospects would include new businesses that have just opened in the area. It might be an auto repair shop that wants you to put a leaflet under the windshield wipers of automobiles.

When you visit a small business, don't explain what you want to the first person you see. Ask to see the owner or manager. There are two good reasons for doing this. The first is that the person in charge is the only one who can hire you. The second is that even if the owner has no leaflets for you to distribute, he might be interested in hiring you to do something else. For you, that should be just fine. You don't care about leaflets in particular. All you care about is earning some money. You might even ask if there's anything else you can do to earn some money. After all, you have absolutely nothing to lose.

Knife Sharpening

Most people's kitchen knives seem to be dull most of the time. It's probably because sharpening knives is an easy job to keep putting off until later. In addition, some people may not know how to sharpen their knives properly. To do this job, you'll need a knife sharpener. To decide how much to charge, sharpen all your mother's knives and see how long it takes you. Then charge enough to make it worth your while. For example, if it takes you thirty minutes to do all the knives for one customer, $1.50 to $2 would probably be a reasonable charge. That's $3 to $4 an hour

208

for the time you're working. Apartment buildings are ideal for this kind of job, since there are many potential customers close together.

Washing Walls

Of all the jobs people put off because they are hard and messy, washing walls—especially in kitchens—is near the top of the list. Because of this, finding homes or apartments with dirty kitchen walls is no problem. One of the things that makes it tough is that, in most cases, you can't wash kitchen walls without washing the ceiling. And after you finish all that, the floor's going to need cleaning too. You really should have a crew of two to tackle this job.

Some of the especially tough spots are the greasy ventilators or hoods over the stove and the walls behind the stove and refrigerator. The cabinets get greasy, too. Use a sponge mop to do the ceiling, and be certain to cover everything that might be damaged by the cleaner.

Unless some magic new cleaner has appeared just recently, the best one is probably still TSP (tri-sodium phosphate). You can buy it at hardware or paint stores. It's an inexpensive white powder you mix with water, and it probably does the job better than anything else around. For this kind of work you should get at least $3.50 an hour for each of you. After you get some experience, you can start quoting a price for the whole job.

Kitchen Cabinets and Drawers

If you want to find out how people might like the idea of having you take everything out of all the kitchen cabinets and drawers, wash them, reline both shelves and drawers with fresh shelf paper, and then put everything back neatly organized, ask your mother how she'd like someone to do it for her. Her reaction should give you an idea of how big a money maker this job can be. Cooking grease collects inside cabinets. Shelf paper tears. Food gets spilled into drawers. Anyone with a kitchen—housewives, working women, and bachelors—is a potential customer. And you're not likely to run into much competition on this job.

Cleaning Showers

Cleaning tile showers is another one of those jobs people hate to do themselves. In many cases this will be a job you can add onto other things you are doing for a customer, but in some cases a shower is a big enough job to do by itself. Getting the tile—and especially the grout (the cement) between the tiles—clean requires cleanser, a stiff bristle brush, and a lot of energy. A complete job would include removing the shower head and cleaning out the filter, as well as cleaning out the drain.

Envelope Stuffing and Addressing

Many businesses have special or monthly mailings that their regular employees do not have time to handle. In some cases they want the envelopes addressed by hand. In other cases, typing is preferred. The envelopes must then be stuffed with whatever is to be mailed. If you have decent handwriting, can type, or both, you might be able to handle the whole thing yourself. Visit or call the businesses in your neighborhood to find out what opportunities exist. You might also watch your parents' mail for a while to see which local companies do a lot of mailing. These might be your best prospects. Watch for companies that have a lot of special sales promotions, new stores about to open, or businesses moving to a new location.

Delivery Boy or Girl

There are businesses that provide pick-up and delivery service for their customers. Some deliveries require a car; among these are dry cleaners and laundries. Others, however, can be done with a bicycle. For example, you can get dozens of prescriptions in a backpack, so the local drugstore would be a good place to start looking for a delivery job. Any business that delivers something to people at home might provide you with a job, but there are also businesses that deliver to other businesses. Your local auto parts store may deliver parts to repair shops. If this kind of work appeals to you, don't spend too much time guessing who might need you. Try them all.

Basements and Attics

Cleaning out the basement or the attic is another job most people plan to get at "next month." You and a friend can help them get it done this coming weekend. Then you'll have some money, and those people can stop worrying about their messy basement. Wear your old clothes, because attics and basements collect dirt as well as junk. You'll spend your time moving things, cleaning up, organizing what's to be kept, and carrying out junk. The homeowner will have to decide what to keep and what to throw away. It's hard work and worth at least $2.50 an hour.

House Washing — Including Mobile Homes

If you live in or near a mobile-home park, washing mobile homes might provide you with a permanent source of income. It's a job for at least two kids who have ladders and a hose, long-handled brushes, and a strong cleaning agent (TSP or some other). Mobile homes get dirty, just like cars, but you can't take a mobile home to a car wash. How frequently they need to be washed depends on where you live and the time of year. Vary what you charge depending on the size of each mobile home.

Washing mobile homes makes sense, but how about regular houses? The fact is that a good washing will make a huge improvement in the appearance of most homes, as long as the house has a decent coat of paint. A crew of at least two is required for this job. You'll need the same long-handled brushes, ladder, hose, and cleaning agent. Again, TSP is probably the best. Spray each area to get it wet, scrub it with the brush and cleanser, then rinse it with the hose. Be sure to start at the top and work your way down to the ground. You'll be amazed at how much dirt comes off and how much better the house looks when you're finished. When you've finished half the first wall, have the owners come out and see the difference. They'll be amazed, too. Once you get some experience, this kind of job is perfect for quoting a price in advance.

Handyman

No matter where you live, there are people around you who have difficulty doing certain things for themselves. Many people do not know how to replace the plug on the end of a lamp cord. Some have trouble removing ceiling fixtures to change burned-out light bulbs. Others feel completely helpless if the toilet or sink gets stopped up. Many elderly people are physically unable to do these things for themselves. If you use posters and flyers to let people in your neighborhood know you are available to do the things they can't do, you might get a lot of business in a hurry. It's difficult to say what you should charge. Quote a price that seems fair for you and your customer.

Which Job is the Best?

That depends partly on you. If you're 9 years old, you probably won't be washing houses. If you're 17, you might not care to be a mother's helper in the afternoon. Where you live also makes a difference. If you live downtown in a major city, mowing lawns and pulling weeds might not be available to you. On the other hand, if you live in the country, there may be no small businesses close enough to your home to provide you with a job addressing and stuffing envelopes.

Most of the jobs in this chapter, however, are generally available year round in almost all areas. They are offered as suggestions, as a place to start if you want to make some money in a reasonably short period of time. However, the best idea for *you* to make some money quickly may be one of the jobs described in the following chapters.

TIPS

Selling — It's Both Necessary and Fun

No matter how you plan to make money, you have to sell something to someone! There's no other way. It might be a product, like Christmas cards or hand-tooled leather belts. It's more likely to be a service, like walking dogs, shining shoes, or raking leaves. But whether it's a service or a product, it must be sold.

The advertising materials you use must also *sell*. Otherwise, no one will notice them. What would you think if you saw a large poster in a store printed with tiny letters? It's much better to use a smaller poster with big, bold letters. After all, your posters and flyers represent you. They let you "talk to people" without meeting them. You want the posters to invite people to buy what you are selling.

The best way to sell things to people is in person. People are more likely to hire someone they have met. If you knock on the door of a neighbor you don't know, does it matter how you look and what you say? You bet! You're in business, and you're there to sell them something, so act businesslike. You should look neat. That doesn't mean dressed up. It means your jeans should be clean, not covered with mud or grease. You should have a cheerful and confident attitude. that means you should act friendly and give people the impression that you know exactly what you are doing. You should look people in the eye when you talk to them. People do not like to talk to someone who stares at the ground. You can't sell anything to the doormat, so look where you can sell something — at your customer.

Before you start out, ask yourself the question, "Why should someone be willing to buy what I'm selling?" If you can't answer the question, don't start until you can. That's what sales is all about — telling people why they should buy from *you*. Know what you are going to say in advance and practice it before you start. Think about the questions people might ask you and try to be prepared to answer them.

Everyone has to sell something at one point or another. Your parents had to sell themselves to their present employers in order to get their jobs. No one came knocking on their door wanting to hire them. You're doing exactly the same thing. Fortunately, selling is probably the most exciting part of any business. When someone says, "Sure, you can wash my windows. Be here Saturday morning at 9 o'clock," that's exciting! If you are prepared in advance and know exactly what you're doing, selling can be a lot of fun.

CHAPTER 24

JOBS IN YOUR OWN NEIGHBORHOOD

The very best job you can possibly get might be waiting for you right on your own street or in your own apartment building and you don't even know about it. This chapter will show you many ways to make money close to home. Some of the jobs are every-day things people need to have done. Some of them are a bit unusual but might be perfect for you.

When you have a choice, working close to home is best. To illustrate, suppose you have two customers who hire you to do yard work for them each Saturday. One is three houses down the street. The other takes you half an hour to get to on your bike. Each job takes two hours and pays you $5 a week. It's easy to see that you're earning $2.50 an hour on both jobs, except that getting to and from one of the jobs takes an extra hour. When you add that hour to the two hours the job takes, you find you're actually spending three hours, which means you're earning only $1.67 an hour.

Another advantage of having customers who are close to home is that you are immediately available if a regular customer should need some help on a different project. In other words, there's a better chance to get extra jobs and earn extra money.

There might be times, however, when you come up with a super job that's not close to where you live. Take it—at least until you find another just as good that's close. Your neighborhood is just the best place to start looking.

This chapter contains more than forty ideas for you to consider. Some are more appropriate if you live in a rural area where you have some space to work with; some will work better in the city; some are best in the suburbs. All of them will let you experience the challenge and excitement of making money on your own.

Cleaning Rain Gutters

In many areas of the country, the rain gutters on most houses fill up with dirt and leaves. But a lot of people never think of cleaning them out until they see them overflowing in the first heavy rain. If you go door to door and remind people that this is a job that should be done, you could have a customer at almost every house in your neighborhood. You'll need a ladder, a bucket, and some small hand tools to get inside the gutters and clean them out. After you've removed the dirt and leaves, rinse the gutters out with a hose to get them clean and to make sure all the downspouts are working properly. This job is ideal for a couple of older kids, and it is probably better to charge by the hour since the time it takes to do the job will be different at each house.

Herb Gardens

There are a number of fresh herbs that you can easily grow in trays and sell in your neighborhood. Most cooks prefer to use fresh herbs when they are available, and the herb garden you provide them will grow right on the windowsill in their kitchen. You can grow them from seeds in trays that are a convenient size. Some popular herbs are parsley, chives, basil, and oregano. Ask your mother if she has any other suggestions. Four to six weeks after you plant them, they should be ready to sell, and you should get $2 to $3 a tray. Check with your local nursery for tips on the best way to raise them.

Cleaning Barbeques

The time to clean barbeques is when the weather is warming up in the spring. Many people cook on a dirty barbeque all summer because they never get around to cleaning it. Bring your own brushes and cleaning compound, and don't make a mess in the yard. You'll probably charge $2 to $5, or more, depending on the type and size of the barbeque.

Paper Route

A paper route falls somewhere between working for someone else and working for yourself. It provides a steady and dependable source of income but often requires that you apply well in advance and wait until a route is available in your neighborhood. Once you get the job, you may find that it provides all the money you need. But if it doesn't, you can use it to get other jobs. Remember that on a paper route you're going to see your customers once each month when you collect. This gives you a chance to ask them all if they have any other jobs you can do for them. If you've been doing a good, dependable job delivering their papers, chances are you'll end up with as many extra jobs as you want.

Raking Leaves

You can't do this job all year round, but when the leaves start coming down in the fall, offering to rake leaves can make you some quick money and give you a chance to let people know you are available and reliable to do other jobs for them.

Gardening Service

You'll probably start your gardening business by mowing and edging lawns. There are, however, some real advantages if you learn how to do other things as well. One advantage is that you don't need as many customers, since you'll spend quite a bit more time with each one you have. Gardening can include trimming hedges, pulling weeds, applying fertilizer, spraying for insects and other pests, raking leaves, and watering. In the fall there are trees and shrubs that should be pruned. In the spring you can plant flowers. You'll want to learn how to take care of the things that grow well and are popular in your area.

Mowing lawns is simple, but you can't offer a complete gardening service without knowing what you're doing. You'll need an expert to tell you what to do. Your local nurseryman is the person to talk to. He'll be happy to help you, since you'll be buying supplies from him, including seeds, fertilizer, insect sprays, and plants. He can tell you which flowers and plants grow best where you live; when to prune trees and plants and how to do it; which fertilizers to use and when to apply them to keep the yard looking at its best. You'll probably start off working by the hour. Once you become an "expert," it's best to charge a certain amount per month for all gardening services, with your customers paying for plants and special supplies. As your business develops, you will probably want to buy your own power mower and other gardening equipment.

Making Fireplace Logs from Newspapers

It's actually possible to make a fairly good fireplace log from newspapers. You start with something around which you can wrap the newspapers, like the handle of a shovel or broom. Soak the newspapers in water containing detergent (it makes the paper stick together when it dries), wrap the wet newspapers around the broom handle, and let them dry. What you can charge will depend on where you live and the size of the logs you make. You might get 25¢ to 75¢ each, especially in areas where wood is hard to get and very expensive. Finding enough newspapers will be no problem. People are happy to get rid of them. This job allows you to accomplish three things: you are converting trash into something useful; you are providing people with something they want and are willing to pay for; you are making yourself some money.

Vacation Area Cabin and Rental Service

If you live in or near a vacation or recreational area, you can arrange to do a number of services for the owner of a mountain cabin, especially during the ski or snow season. Before the owner or renters arrive for the weekend, you can turn on the water and heat. After they've left to return home, you can clean up the cabin, turn off the water, drain the pipes so they won't freeze, and make sure that all lights and appliances are turned off. Unless you've used a cabin in the wintertime, it may be hard for you to appreciate how welcome this service would be. Anyone arriving at a cabin late Friday night—often after a long, tiring drive—and finding it warm and ready for occupancy would consider it a real luxury. It would also be a luxury for the tenants to be able to leave knowing everything would be taken care of. People will be willing to pay for such luxury.

Your first step in getting this service going is to locate the owners of a number of cabins in your area. Find the names through local records, realtors, or by going door to door during weekends when the cabins are in use. Owners who rent their cabins to other people for weekend use should be especially interested in this service, since renters cannot always be depended upon to leave things in good order.

The same or similar services can be offered to anyone who owns property for his own use or for rental at the beach, in the woods, at lakes, or in the mountains. It's hard to suggest how much you should charge. Make it reasonable enough to get the business and high enough to be profitable for you. A certain amount for each weekend would probably be the best policy.

Beyond the weekly service just described, you might be able to make a great deal of money getting places ready for the season—in the fall for mountain cabins, in the spring for beach cottages. Many owners would appreciate having a complete housecleaning job done at that time. This might include washing windows, scrubbing and waxing floors, cleaning the stove and oven, cleaning out the refrigerator, washing cupboards and drawers and replacing shelf paper, and vacuuming rugs and furniture. It might also include some outside jobs, such as stacking firewood, doing whatever yard work needs to be done, possibly even doing some painting. Some owners rent their cabins through local realtors or rental services who are responsible for taking care of all these things. Working through them would be one way to get this kind of business going in a hurry.

Growing Plants for Sale

Here's another job, like growing and selling herb gardens, that takes a little money to get started but takes very little of your time. House plants are very popular today in homes and offices. Raising and selling plants is a way you can make money all year round. People add plants to those they already have and replace plants that have died. When you're at a nursery, you'll notice that plants come in different sizes. The small size may be $1, the next size $4, and the largest size $10. All the $1 plant needs to become a $10 plant is water, a little fertilizer, and some time. You buy a selection of several varieties of the smallest plants, take care of them until they're larger, and sell them house to house. How much you sell them for depends on how long you want to let them grow.

If there are a number of small businesses in your area, consider supplying them with plants as well. The businesses might even turn out to be your best customers. Go back every few weeks and buy a new supply of small plants, so you'll always have a supply of more mature plants ready for sale.

Raising Vegetables to Sell

If you have a large yard or some space anywhere to raise a garden, raising certain vegetables can be quite profitable. Certain types of vegetables will produce a fairly large crop in a small space. Examples are tomatoes, zucchini, or string beans. Tomatoes are one of the best crops if they will grow in your area, since the ones you grow in your yard will be of much better quality than those available in the stores. If you're not sure which are the best plants for your climate and soil and which should produce the best crops, ask at the nursery.

If you live on a farm, consider what one midwestern farmer did every year to help his two daughters earn money. When he planted his field corn, he planted two long rows of sweet corn at the edge of the field. For him the cost of two extra rows of corn was fairly small. For the girls, it was one of the ways they made quite a bit of money every summer. Early each summer before the crop was ready to be picked, the girls went to houses all over the small town where they lived and took advance orders for their corn. Each year they had all, or almost all, of the corn sold before it was ready to be picked. Whether it's corn or something else, if your family has a farm, doing something like this can be a good money-making venture.

Running Errands

Running errands might not sound like a way to make much money, and if you just do an occasional errand for someone, it won't be. But under the right circumstances, and with good advertising, you might find yourself with more requests than you have time for.

Who are your potential customers? The largest and most obvious group are the elderly. Some are no longer able to drive, and others find it difficult to get out for physical reasons. Younger people might need you, too, since they are often too busy or don't want to take the time to run errands.

What are the things people need to have you do? Grocery shopping, picking up and delivering laundry or dry cleaning, picking up and returning library books, mailing letters—these are a few examples. People might need your services for a variety of different reasons. Some may leave for work before the laundry opens and get home after it closes. Others may simply be unable to carry a large bag of groceries. It's difficult to say what you should charge for your services. As with many other jobs, it should be a reasonable charge to your customer but enough to make it worthwhile for you.

Moving Services For Homeowners

Watch for FOR SALE signs in your neighborhood. Also keep your ears open in case you hear of someone who is about to move. The list of things you can do for people who are selling their homes and moving is almost endless. A house that is on the market must look good to potential buyers. Start with the yard. Getting it in really top shape takes time, and people about to

TIPS

How Much Should You Charge?

If you're 15, charge more than if you are 10. If you're experienced at a particular job and a fast worker, charge more than if you're trying something for the first time. Find out what the going rate for the same job is in your neighborhood. If other kids are charging $2 an hour for a particular task, you won't get much business if you're asking $3. On the other hand, a job worth $2 an hour in one neighborhood might be worth $3 an hour in a different one. To summarize:

You charge more if you're older.

You charge more if you are experienced.

You charge more in areas where wages and prices are higher.

If you have a lot of competition from other kids wanting to do the same jobs in your neighborhood, you may have to charge less than "going rate" to get started. If people are paying $1.75 an hour for babysitting, you'll get more babysitting jobs in a hurry if you offer to do it for $1.50 an hour. After all, ten customers at $1.50 an hour are better than one customer at $1.75 an hour. The same thing is true is you are selling things that people can buy in the stores. In this case you should probably always charge a little less, whether it's lemons or peaches from the trees in your yard or a macrame plant holder you made yourself. It gives people one more reason to buy from *you*!

move don't have much time. You can mow, trim hedges, pull all the weeds and get it looking great. The house itself may need some work. Walls may need to be painted or washed, windows may need to be cleaned, or floors may need to be waxed. When moving day finally comes, packing is a big job that you could help with. If it's a local move, the customers may need you to help load the truck and unload it at the new residence. That's a big job and might take a couple of days. If the people move before they sell the house, the cleaning will probably have to be done after they leave, and that's a job very few people will want to go back and do. So just make yourself available for whatever people need, and you might have half a dozen jobs.

Magazine and Book Delivery

In certain parts of the country, a number of magazines, such as *Time, Newsweek, Good Housekeeping,* and *Reader's Digest,* have started having their magazines delivered by private companies instead of by the post office, since it appears to be cheaper and faster. It's possible that many, and perhaps all, magazines will be delivered this way in the future. If so, there will be many delivery jobs available for those who apply early. Book publishers and distributors may eventually handle distribution this way as well. If you're interested, try writing to the publishers of one of the magazines mentioned, tell them you're interested, and ask if and when this job will be available in your area.

One other delivery job available once a year is delivering telephone directories. Contact your local telephone company office well in advance to apply for this once-a-year job.

Pet Grooming

Pet grooming is a year-round job you can offer in any area where there are a lot of pets, especially dogs. You can offer a fairly simple service, such as shampooing, brushing, and combing. You don't need much equipment for this: just shampoo (check with your local veterinarian to see what kind to use), a large tub, brushes, and a hose. A shampoo is probably worth $2.50 to $4, but check around to see what professional groomers charge and charge a little less.

If you really want to get into the business, you should start by getting a book on the subject and finding yourself an expert to talk to. A complete service might include clipping, shampooing, and nail trimming. For this you can charge quite a bit more. Price your services according to those in the area.

Pet I.D. Tags

If there are a lot of pets in your area, contact their owners by going door to door and offer to make identification tags for the pets' collars. For about $20 you can buy a stamping machine to make the tags. For about $12, you can buy 100 round brass tags, 1 1/4 inches in diameter. You can carry your stamping machine and tags from door to door and make the tags right on the spot, with the name of the pet, the address, and phone number. If you charge $2 for each tag, fifteen tags will pay for your stamping machine and first 100 tags. By the time you've used up your 100 tags, you will have collected $200. That's a profit of $170 after paying for your initial supply. You can do this job anywhere there are people with pets, so you're not restricted to your own immediate neighborhood.

Raising Pets for Sale

Some small animals that are quite easy to raise make excellent pets for children. Among these are hamsters, white mice, guinea pigs, and gerbils. Make sure that you get a good quality male and female when you get started, but if you're unsure of the care and feeding of these animals, don't try to figure it out yourself. Buy a good book on the subject or get one from the library. Ask for tips from your local pet store. Check prices at the pet store, so you'll know what to charge. You probably won't get rich at this job, but if you like animals, this is a way to make some money doing something you really enjoy.

Bird Feeders and Other Pet Items

If you live in an area where there are many different types of birds (especially hummingbirds) and you like to make things, try making and selling bird feeders. It's a good idea to sell these items door to door, but instead of selling just one thing, try to think of something else you can make and sell. Are there lots of pets in your neighborhood? Some people might be interested in a "Doggie Doorbell," which is simply a small bell on a macrame hanger to hang on the doorknob. It lets a dog tell people when it wants to get out instead of scratching the paint off the door. Can you think of anything else? Take it along and offer it at the same time.

Fishing Bait

If you live in the right area, digging or collecting clams or mussels can be quite profitable. They can be sold directly to fishermen or to bait stores. With the right facilities, such as a stream or pond, you can raise minnows for sale. Fishermen sometimes need additional fishing items once they get to their destinations. So if you're selling them bait, you might also be able to sell them hooks, sinkers, leaders, and so on.

Smoking Fish

If you live in areas where sport fishing is popular, you can set up a service to smoke the fishermen's catch. Favorites to smoke are salmon, tuna, and albacore, but there are many other varieties that can be smoked. The basic equipment is a large steel drum and a pipe like a chimneypipe to bring the heat and smoke from a small fire. You'll need to talk to someone who has experience in smoking fish to make sure you set up your equipment just right. Advertise by putting posters in sporting goods stores, on docks, in boat rental offices. Tell the boat skippers and everyone else in the area that you are available for this job. Charge by the pound or take one-fourth to one-third of the catch in exchange.

Ducks and Wild Game

Many people love to hunt duck, pheasant, and other wild game and also enjoy eating them. What they don't like to do is clean and dress what they shoot. If a lot of hunters live in your area, offer to do this chore by putting posters in game clubs, sporting goods stores, or at military stations. Once you get a few customers, they'll tell their friends, and during hunting season this could be a very profitable business. What you charge will depend on your local area and the type of game.

Producing and Selling Eggs

You can get into the egg business in rural areas, or in any area where you have room and are permitted to raise chickens. Once you get this business started, it will provide you with a steady, dependable source of income. Everyone likes to buy fresh eggs, and lining up enough customers to buy all the eggs you can produce each week should be no problem at all. How much you make will depend on how many chickens you have space and time to raise. You should have no trouble charging the same prices people would pay in the stores, since your eggs are fresher. It takes some time and a little money to get started, but once your hens start laying, it's a very profitable business.

Storm Windows

If you live where people use storm windows on their homes, you can offer to put them up at the beginning of winter. This job could be added to a "package" of services you might offer for people's windows; the package would include removing the storm windows in the spring and replacing them with screens.

Storm Clean-up

A big storm can leave a lot of broken branches, leaves, and other debris in people's yards. You have to move fast as soon as the weather clears to land these jobs, but if you do, you might be busy for several days. The first storm of the season can also call attention to things that need to be done: rain gutters that may be plugged, storm windows not yet installed, patio furniture that needs to be moved and put in the garage. The main point is to take advantage of what's happening around you. A heat wave, a wind storm, or a heavy snow all can create opportunities for you to make some extra money.

Snow Shoveling

Shoveling snow is a job people cannot put off until later. Until the driveway is shoveled, the car stays in the garage. Walks, sidewalks, and driveways of both homes and local businesses must be cleared. Many people are too busy to do this job for themselves, and some, such as senior citizens, are unable to do it. Some people might be interested in hiring you for the season. It's hard work, so $2 to $3 an hour should be a reasonable charge.

Raising Bees

Raising bees for the honey they produce is a fascinating way to make money, although you probably will only be able to do it if you live in a rural area. It's not a quick-money job, since you can't hurry the bees. However, bees require almost no attention while they are making their honey, so it takes very little of your time. A good source of information on how to raise bees is your State Department of Agriculture or the U.S. Department of Agriculture. You can write for information.

Raising Livestock

Kids on farms and in rural areas who belong to the 4H Club have been raising animals profitably for many years. Check with the 4H Club in your area. Raising such animals as cattle, sheep, and pigs can be rewarding and profitable.

Raising Rabbits

You don't have to live on a farm to raise rabbits, since they require relatively little space. Rabbits are easy to raise. They mature in very little time and don't require much care, so this job could be done as a sideline. It would be a good idea to line up customers in advance by going door to door in your neighborhood. Since the principal use for rabbits is food, you will need to know how to slaughter and skin them and dress the meat. The hides can be put on wire stretchers to dry and can be sold as well.

Raising Worms

Earthworms are actually very easy to raise. Several thousand can be raised in a box only 2 feet square containing soil 8 to 10 inches deep. Manure and peat moss can be added to the soil along with vegetable trimmings. Start with some worms from your local bait store or sporting goods store. They'll lay hundreds of eggs, which produce full-grown worms in approximately three months. You can sell directly to fishermen, or to sporting goods or bait stores. If you end up with more customers than you have worms, simply add another one or two boxes or tubs, and you'll double or triple your worm supply. The key is obviously having a place to sell them.

Shampooing Carpets

A lot of money can be made by shampooing carpets. By lining up customers in advance, you should be able to work as many hours a week as you choose. Getting customers to let you clean their carpets is easier than getting customers for most other things, because few people are willing to do the job themselves. It's no job for amateurs, so practice at home before you go out on your first job. You can rent the equipment and buy the cleaning solution at hardware stores and supermarkets. It's a good job for two kids to do together, since you'll be moving furniture.

Find out what professionals in your area charge and then charge somewhat less. If professionals are charging 10¢ per square foot and you charge 7¢, let's see what you could make in one day. A living room or family room that is 20 by 20 is 400 square feet. If you and a friend worked fast, you would be able to do three jobs this size in a day. That's 1,200 square feet at 7¢ a foot, or $84 for your work. Renting the machine and buying the shampoo should cost no more than $20. That leaves $64, or $32 for each of you for the day. If you and your friend did this every Saturday, each of you would be earning more than $130 per month.

Once you get your business going, it would probably be smart to buy your own equipment. It's more convenient if you don't have to pick up and return the machine each time, and after five or six jobs (as long as it takes to pay for the machine), your profit will increase since you no longer have to pay the rental charges.

Upholstery Cleaning

Special equipment can be rented or purchased for cleaning upholstery in a professional manner. Instructions and the necessary cleaning fluids can be obtained where you rent the equipment. Start by practicing on some old furniture—and practice until you know what you're doing. (On your first few jobs it would be a good idea to decline jobs where the furniture has very expensive coverings.) Price your services by finding out what professional firms charge in your area and, as in shampooing carpets, charge somewhat less. Upholstery cleaners usually charge by the piece—so much for a large couch, so much for a small one, so much for an overstuffed chair, and so on. If you are a fast worker, you can expect to make $50 or more for each full day you work.

Shampooing carpets and cleaning upholstery are both jobs that most people are not willing to do for themselves. If you and a friend were to become expert at both these jobs, you could offer both services at the same time by going door to door in your neighborhood. Posters and flyers are also good ways to advertise this type of business.

Neighborhood Newspaper

Publishing a small neighborhood newspaper is a way to make a little money and have a lot of fun at the same time. You might specialize in news of what's going on in your neighborhood and have your friends and neighbors contribute articles and stories, or you might specialize in classified advertising, printing ads for people who want to sell things or ads for kids who are interested in doing certain kinds of jobs. If adults looking for kids to work also put ads in your paper, it would serve a very useful purpose. This could be a fun project for several kids to work on together.

Tutoring

Many youngsters who are having problems in school need special help. You can earn money helping them get caught up if you know a subject well and think you would enjoy teaching it. Younger children most often have trouble with reading and math. For junior-high and high school students, it might be a foreign language, chemistry, or physics. Tutoring can be a year-round job, since many students need help during the school year and some need help over the summer. To get customers, you could advertise in a local community newspaper or use posters, but the best way is probably to talk to school officials, including counselors and the instructors who teach your subject. Find out from them about the usual charges for this service.

Teaching Gymnastics

These days youngsters often take gymnastics training at a very early age. If gymnastics is something you are good at and you think you understand it well enough to explain it to others, try teaching a class for young children. Posters and handbills for your immediate area would probably be the best way to start. With as few as five kids signing up for your class, it would be worth your while; even with a charge as low as $1.50 per class, you would be earning $7.50 an hour. You might get quite good at it and enjoy it enough to consider teaching gymnastics on a more advanced level. When your students have learned the basics, you can graduate them to a regular gymnastics school in your area.

Birthday Cake Service

Here's an interesting idea that you can use to make some money if you live in a college town. You can bake and deliver birthday cakes to students who are away from home. The most difficult part of the job is obtaining the names and addresses of parents so they can be contacted and told of your service. You might be able to obtain the names from the school registrar. Other sources might be campus clubs or fraternities and sororities. The cost of ingredients plus a profit of $2.50 to $4 for your efforts would seem a fair amount to charge.

Some small businesses make a practice of ordering cakes on employees' birthdays. To obtain this business, you only have to talk to one person—the owner or manager. That person can provide the names of employees and the dates the cakes should be delivered. Just make sure you have a "birthday cake" calendar so you don't forget anyone's birthday.

Companion to Senior Citizens

There are many things elderly people cannot do very well for themselves. They might be interested in having you read newspapers or books to them. Many have difficulty writing and might want you to write letters for them. You might do some minor mending, like sewing on buttons; make simple repairs to appliances; and replace light bulbs—all the little things that are difficult for old people to do for themselves. Some of your customers may not be able to pay you much, but for those who can, $1.50 an hour seems like a reasonable price.

Typing

If you can type at a reasonable speed with good accuracy, you can charge for typing services. Besides making some money, you'll also be able to practice your typing and improve your skills while you're getting paid. Whether you're a boy or a girl, typing is a valuable skill to have in college and later on in business. Your customers might include college students who need to have papers typed (because they didn't learn how to type themselves) and local businesses. One jewelry store, for example, keeps records of wedding anniversaries of members of the surrounding community and sends out letters of congratulation on these dates. Many professional people who have regular clients send greetings to those clients on special days, such as their birthdays. They also send other special mailings to their clientele from time to time. Work out what you will charge based on local rates in your area.

Cleaning Swimming Pools

If there are a number of swimming pools in your area, pool cleaning can be a really good job. All these swimming pools are now being taken care of by either a professional service or the pools' owners. All of them are potential customers for you. It's ideal if you have a pool in your own yard and have learned to take care of it. You already know how to test the water with a test kit, when to add chemicals and how much to add, how to clean or backwash the filter, and do all the other things required to keep a pool sparkling and clean.

Your best bet is to charge quite a bit less than a regular pool service. Many of the pool owners in your neighborhood who previously thought pool service was too expensive may now hire you because you're cheaper. Some people using a professional service may also give you a try because you're less expensive. You won't have any pool equipment of your own when you're starting, so you will have to make arrangements only with pool owners who have their own cleaning equipment. Suppose you had four pool customers and charged them only $25 a month for two visits a week. You could take care of your pool business on Wednesday afternoon and Saturday morning and have an income of $100 a month.

Photography

Photography is listed as a job idea mostly to remind you that hobbies can be profitable. If one of your hobbies is photography, you might make enough money taking pictures to pay for all your film. You might start by taking pictures at birthday parties or other special events. Charge for the film, the processing, and $3 or $4 extra for your time. As you get better, move up to larger events.

Recycling Cans, Bottles, and Paper

Any kid can collect these items, no matter what his or her age. It's something that can be done over a fairly long period of time; especially with aluminum cans, you can just keep on collecting until you have enough to make a trip to the collection center financially worthwhile. Good places to collect cans and bottles are parks and playgrounds, and cleaning up after a large party can bring a good haul. Don't forget that every can you pick up on a beach means less litter and a cleaner beach for people to use. This type of project is really ideal as a group or club project where the objective is to raise money to finance some special event.

Pick the Thing That Fits

Raising worms might be the last thing in the world you would ever consider doing. Many kids, however, might see this as a great way to earn a little extra money with very little work. The dream job is one where you are doing something that's fun and getting paid a fortune for doing it. Unfortunately, such jobs are pretty hard to find. Sometimes making the most money involves the most work. The important thing to remember is that there are people who live in your block who have jobs they will hire you to do. You don't have to go across town. You should be able to make as much money as you need right in your own neighborhood.

Double Your Income by Becoming an Expert

There are some obvious ways to take advantage of special skills. One of those ways is to teach something, like guitar. When you teach anything, you have the advantage of being able to charge by the lesson rather than by the hour. Some people might object to paying you $3 an hour when they will happily pay you $5 for a one-hour lesson. In many cases people would rather pay by the job than by the hour, and because of this you have the opportunity to double your income. If you learn how to do a certain job expertly, you can tell in advance how long it will take you and you can quote a price for the whole job that actually gives you a very high hourly income.

Some things are easy to quote (to quote means to give a price in advance). Waxing a car is one example. Mowing lawns is another. Some things are a bit more difficult but still fairly easy, like scrubbing and waxing floors, shampooing a carpet, or running an errand. Some things, however, are not easy at all. One example would be washing windows. It takes quite a bit of experience to be able to look at a house and estimate how long it would take to do all the windows, inside and out. Finally, there are some things you cannot quote in advance. Helping anyone do a job like cleaning out a garage is an example. You can't tell how long it will take because you can't know in advance what you will be asked to do. Here you must work by the hour.

Here's how to become an expert:

Ask a *real* expert (probably an adult) for advice.

Find out what tricks can make the job easier and faster and at the same time provide the best results for your customer. Example: one professional window-washer advises that you use a brush with long bristles to wash glass. He puts approximately one thimbleful of pure ammonia (no soap) into a bucketful of water—nothing else! He then wipes the glass clean with a rubber squeegee, not paper towels and not rags. Rags or towels are used to wipe the blade of the squeegee clean as you work and to wipe away any water that runs down from the glass.

Once you learn the tricks, work by the hour until you are experienced and can do the job fast. As you do each job, pay careful attention to the amount of time each type takes to do.

Then start quoting a price in advance for the whole job. If you were earning $2.50 an hour before, you should now end up making $4 to $5 an hour for doing the same job.

Advertise your services by using the most "professional"-looking flyers and cards possible. You're running your own business now, so what you use to get business should look businesslike. Spending a few dollars on your advertising program will pay off in big dollars for you later on.

CHAPTER 25

APARTMENTS AND CONDOMINIUMS ARE GOLD MINES

Living in the city gives you some real advantages. It doesn't matter whether you decide to make your money by washing windows, raising and selling herb gardens, waxing floors, or framing pictures, one big advantage you have as a city dweller is lots of potential customers. If you like to make things, like macrame plant holders, for example, you may have several hundred potential customers within a couple of blocks of where you live. If you lived in the suburbs or country, you might have to go miles to talk to that many people.

It is true that in the city there are probably no lawns to mow, and little, if any, room to raise animals. However, there are more ways for you to make money than you will ever get around to trying, and a number of them are described here to help you get started.

If you have worked to earn your own money in the past, you probably have already learned that a lot of people you want as customers are going to tell you "no." But if you are about to make your first attempt at selling something or looking for work, there are a couple of things you should know before you start.

One is that not everyone you ask is going to want you to do the job. Let's suppose the job you select is waxing and polishing floors. Some people will refuse your services because they would rather do it themselves than spend the money. Some may not be able to afford it. There might be some people who actually like to wax floors. Some families will have kids your age who are already doing the job. Some will have carpeting in their kitchens and baths. There are probably other reasons, but the thing for you to remember is that when someone tells you "not interested," *don't* take it personally. It has nothing to do with you. Sometimes people will say no just because they're in a bad mood. Again, it has nothing to do with *you*. The thing for you to concentrate on is how many people might say "yes." Let's suppose one person out of every five says yes. That doesn't sound too bad, does it? Maybe not, until you realize that in order to get one "yes," you have to get four "no's." If you get discouraged after the first four people say no, you will never get to the yes.

The jobs in this chapter are all things you can do right where you live. Several of them describe things you can make at home and sell to your neighbors. However, the jobs listed here are by no means the only ways you can earn money in an apartment or condominium. You can do many of the jobs listed in Chapters 23, 24, and 26 – 28. The job ideas that follow are just the ones that seem especially well suited to the kid who lives in the city.

Dog Walking

People who live in apartments or condominiums usually have no yard in which a dog can run and get some exercise. Their dogs must be taken out and walked, usually twice a day. Many dog owners who live in apartments work long hours and do not have time to walk their dogs themselves. Others get home late and would rather not walk their dogs after dark. You can arrange to do it for them. How much you charge will depend on where you live. In some cities you might get $2 an hour or more, so find out what's being paid in your area before you get started. Walking dogs is a way for you to get some exercise and be paid for it. Try arranging to take out a couple of dogs at the same time. Then go out and jog. If you're charging $1.50 an hour for each dog, you'll be earning $3 a day just for staying in shape.

Pet Sitting

A flyer delivered door to door and a couple of posters might be enough to get you started in the pet sitting business. Pet owners often have difficulty finding someone reliable when they go away for a weekend or longer. The pet doesn't have to be a dog or a cat—fish, turtles, hamsters, and parakeets also need to eat. Dogs, of course, need to be walked each day. In most cases the animal will stay at its own home and you will go there once or twice a day to feed it. You might, however, keep small animals like hamsters or mice in your own home while their owners are away. Charge 50¢ to $1 per visit and extra for walking the dog. If you are old enough to read this, you're old enough to make money taking care of pets.

Laundry Service

Finding time to do the laundry is difficult for many people, especially single people who live in apartments or condominiums. One problem is that the machines are often busy during the evenings and on weekends when all the working people are trying to do their laundry at the same time. You can provide an extremely welcome service by picking up laundry in the evening, doing it the next afternoon when the machines are not busy, and delivering it that evening. The customer provides money for the washer and dryer, but it will probably be easier for you to provide the detergent and fabric softener yourself. A charge of $1.25 for each load plus 15¢ more for detergent and fabric softener will probably be reasonable in most areas. You will return the laundry with permanent press shirts or blouses on hangers that the customer provides and the rest of the laundry neatly folded.

As long as you do the job right, the customers you get should be permanent customers, people you do laundry for each week. This means that you have a steady and predictable source of income. With only six customers, assuming each has two loads a week, you will make $15 a week, or $60 a month for two afternoons' work. Do three customers one day and the other three later in the week.

Ironing

Ironing can be done at your customer's home or apartment or in your own home. If you're fast, charge $2 to $2.50 an hour. If you're not, charge less.

Shining Shoes

Many bachelors would consider it a real luxury if some youngster provided them with a pick-up and delivery shoe-shining service. A good shine is probably worth 50¢ a pair, but check the prices in the area where you live. Maybe you should charge more. What you want are customers who will have you shine their shoes on a regular basis, say, once a week. If you get enough customers, it could become a steady job. If you're doing laundry for people, you might offer to shine their shoes as well.

Framing Pictures

Getting a picture framed at a shop can be very expensive, so this is a very good way to make money if you are willing to take the time to learn how to do it correctly. You can learn how from the owners of a shop that sells framing supplies. They'll be happy to show you the right way, since you'll probably be buying your supplies from them. They can also tell you how much to charge. Many people have one or more photographs, paintings, or posters that they have been wanting to get framed. All you have to do is let them know you are available.

Aquarium Service

In recent years tropical fish have become very popular. Many people end up owning fish without understanding that to keep the fish healthy, an aquarium must be completely cleaned out every few months. Some fish owners know this but would rather not do it themselves. You can find out how to do the job properly from your local tropical fish store. Find out how much the store charges to do this kind of work and charge a bit less. Many parents who get fish for small children should be very happy to have you do this job for them on a regular basis.

Changing Filters for
Heating/Air-Conditioning Systems

When filters get dirty and clogged, a central heating or air-conditioning system does not work as well as it should. Dirty filters waste energy and, as a result, the system is more expensive to operate. Condominiums usually have their own systems, but many apartments also have their own. You might line up thirty or more tenants in one or two apartment buildings or in one area of condominiums who would be very happy to have you take care of this chore for them whenever necessary. If you charged $1.50 plus the cost of the filters, you'd make $45 on thirty customers, and you'd make it in just a few hours. You have to find out from an expert how often the filter should be changed. You won't be doing it every week, or even every month, but it is another $45 for you every time it's needed.

Child Care

You might be able to start a pretty nice business by watching several small children on Saturday mornings. For many working people, Saturday is the day they get most of their errands done. Let your neighbors know that you are available to care for and entertain their small children from 8 A.M. to 1 P.M. each Saturday. A charge of $3 per child is only 60¢ an hour—less than a babysitter would cost. If you take care of five little kids, you are earning $3 an hour, or $15 each Saturday morning. Take them to the park, read them stories, do whatever it takes to keep them entertained and out of mischief and make yourself $60 a month.

Apartment Sitting

There's more to looking after a vacationer's apartment than just feeding the fish. For example, it's very important to pick up the newspaper every day. Newspapers piling up in front of an apartment door are an invitation to burglars. If apartment windows are visible from the street, it's usually a good idea to turn on a different light each day to make it look as if someone is home. Mail needs to be picked up, and house plants require watering. Finally, there may be one or more pets to care for. People should be happy to pay you $1 a day for taking care of newspapers and mail, changing the lights, and watering the house plants once each week. If there are pets to care for, charge $1.25 to $1.50 a day. Most people should consider that a pretty good price for knowing that someone is looking after their place while they're gone. (See the chapter on "Job Packaging" for ideas on how to make additional money from house- or apartment-sitting jobs.)

House Cleaning

Many of the jobs discussed in earlier chapters involve certain types of housecleaning. But here we're talking about a job you do for people on a regular basis, probably weekly. The people most likely to be interested in hiring you are single men and women, or families with two working parents. The job will usually involve cleaning up the kitchen: washing and putting away any dishes in the sink or dishwasher, washing all kitchen counters, and sweeping and damp-mopping the kitchen floor. Cleaning bathroom tubs and showers, as well as counters and floors, is often part of the job, as are vacuuming and dusting. But some people may want you to do additional things, such as watering plants or changing the bed linens.

Depending on your age, experience, and how fast you work, you'll probably get $1.50 to $3 an hour. But some people might want to pay you by the job. As an example, one 15-year-old was offered $10 a week by a bachelor to do certain things each week. After she had done the job three or four times, she found that when she worked hard, she could complete it in two hours. For her, that worked out to $5 an hour. The nicest thing about this kind of job is that you do it every week. Three jobs like this and you could make $30 a week by working three afternoons. That's $120 a month that you can depend on in advance.

Apartment Clean-up Service

When people rent apartments, they usually have to make a cleaning deposit in advance. When they move, if they leave the apartment clean, the cleaning deposit is returned. However, mov-

TIPS

Should Your Parents Help You?

Sure! They can help you with job ideas, offer suggestions on which job might be best in your neighborhood, and help you avoid many mistakes.

But "helping" you does not mean doing it for you! They can make suggestions, but you are the one who should decide what to do and how to do it, and you must do the job *on your own*. Conning your mother into driving you around on your paper route because it's "too cold outside," because you're "too tired," or because you didn't wake up in time puts her in the position of doing a large part of *your* job. If your parents have to remind you, push you, or help you, you're not ready to do something on your own.

ing is one of the most difficult and busy times in a person's life, and many people do not have time to go back and clean up after they leave. This is a good job for a work crew; you can set it up with several friends. You can all pass out flyers letting people know you are available. Each of you can also watch for people in your neighborhood who are moving. This service is often worth $35 to $50 to someone who has made a cleaning deposit of $100 or more.

Moving Services/Local

For busy people, senior citizens, or anyone who is unable to move heavy things, you can provide assistance in several different ways. From time to time, people need to have things moved from their apartment to their storage area, or the reverse. If you or one of your friends has a driver's license, you can offer to move heavy things to and from outside storage facilities such as mini-warehouses. Taking television sets to the repair shop is another way you can help. Since it often costs an extra $10 to $15 when the repairman makes a house call, many people would be happy to pay you $5 to take the set to the shop and bring it back for them. These are only a few of the many ways you can help people who need to get things moved.

Making Jewelry

Jewelry-making courses are offered in many places today, including schools and community centers. Most people think of jewelry making as a hobby, and they do not expect it to be profitable. But once you become experienced enough to make good-quality jewelry, this hobby might make you quite a bit of money. All of the materials you normally need are available in craft or hobby shops, and if you are able to collect shells or stones you can polish—either near your home or when you're on vacation—that's even better. If you decide to make jewelry for the purpose of earning money, you have to think about where you will sell what you make. If you live near the seacoast and use seashells in your jewelry, there are always gift shops in resort areas that might be interested in buying your necklaces, bracelets, pendants, or pins. It might cost you $2.50 to make a necklace you could sell to a gift shop for $6.50, which they will then sell to a tourist for $12. If people buy the jewelry you make, you'll have a profitable hobby that you can do right at home whenever you want to.

Sewing

A lot of people — men and women — don't know how to sew, even when it comes to something as simple as sewing on a button or adjusting a hem. Since it's a nuisance for these people to take small jobs out to a tailor, they would most likely welcome anyone who would pick up and deliver. Such a service should end up with plenty of business. Doing hems probably offers the best potential for business. Hemlines go up and they come back down, and lots of women either don't have time or don't know how to alter the skirts themselves. You'd be smart and get more business if you charged less than the local tailoring shop. Have your mother help you figure out what to charge for various items. Once you get good at the job, you might get business referred to you by local clothing stores that do not do alterations themselves. To get this kind of business, you'll have to prove that you do high-quality work.

Plant Holders

Decorating a home or apartment with attractive plants adds beauty to the surroundings. One of the best ways to do this is with hanging plants, supported by interesting macrame plant holders. Macrame is a technique for knotting twines or yarns into intricate and attractive patterns. If you've never tried macrame, it's fun and can be learned very quickly. The plant holders can be dressed up with wood or glass beads to make them even more attractive. Making macrame plant holders is a perfect job to combine with the job of raising and selling plants. Why do one without the other? If you offer both to everyone, some customers may want just plants, others just plant holders, but many may want both. Look around the stores to see what you should charge. Charge a little less than the stores do, and you should have plenty of business.

Placemats and Other Things
You Can Make

There are many things you can make at home and sell at a profit. Placemats are one of those things. Napkins to match the placemats are another. Hand-painted porcelain knobs for cupboards and drawers might be another. Making things is fun, but if you also want to make money, you have to think about who your customers will be. Will you sell what you make door to door, set up a stand and become a sidewalk vendor, or sell to a novelty or gift shop? Many people start off selling what they make door to door but later find a shop that is willing to buy their products for later sale to the shop's customers.

Your imagination is the only limit to the number of special items you can make for sale to others. One 11-year-old girl made a good business of buying the plain white ceramic knobs used on dresser drawers or cupboard doors and painting a red and black ladybug on each one. She sold these through a gift store, and it was a very successful business for her.

For information on a variety of different crafts in which you might be interested, write to: American Handicrafts Company, #3 Tandy Center, Fort Worth, Texas 96101.

Leather Goods

Making hand-tooled belts, purses, wallets, and other leather items can be both fun and a potential money maker. Write to: Tandy Leather Company, Tandy Center, Fort Worth, Texas 96101, for information that will help you decide whether or not you are interested in this hobby for profit.

Fly Tying

If you have a good eye, a steady hand, and some patience, tying flies is another of those hobbies that can also be a money-making business. You can learn how to tie flies by reading a book, but finding an expert who ties his own is probably a much better way to learn. Your best markets for selling the flies you make are sporting goods stores or bait shops. If you live in an area where there's a lot of fishing done, you might sell directly to fishermen.

Teaching Dancing

If you have studied ballet for several years, why not try teaching what you've learned to other kids? Chances are that the customers for this kind of activity will be younger girls. Advertise your services in the area and see what kind of response you get. If you get a class of ten girls and charge them each $2 for a two-hour lesson, you'll make $10 per lesson. Earning $5 an hour isn't bad, especially if you're doing something you enjoy. It might be pointed out that teaching anything is excellent experience for many things you will do later in life. Giving other people explanations and instruction in a way they can understand is a real accomplishment and requires practice. Teaching something like dancing would be excellent experience and help you get future jobs doing things like directing playground activities, being a camp counselor, teaching school, or being a business executive and supervising other people's activities.

Don't restrict yourself to ballet. If you're the best disco dancer in your neighborhood, you can teach that to kids of all ages and make some money while you're having fun.

Teaching Guitar

Depending on your experience both playing and teaching the guitar, you might charge anywhere from $2.50 to $5 per lesson. There are two requirements. The first is obvious: you have to be able to play the guitar and understand it. The second is less obvious but just as important: you have to be able to explain the techniques so your students understand them.

Pasting Premium Stamps

Premium stamps—Green stamps, Blue Chip stamps, and others—are offered with purchases by stores in many areas of the country. Some people collect them for long periods of time and just toss them in a drawer; they find it hard to get around to putting the stamps in the stamp books. You might advertise this service or just keep the idea in mind while you are babysitting or housecleaning. You might come across someone who has a drawerful of stamps; then you can offer to paste them in the books for payment of one book out of every four or five. In other words, if you paste stamps in five books, your customer gets four and you keep one. It's just like earning money, and you can do it while you're watching television or babysitting.

Recipe Service

Some cooks have "recipe files" that consist of a drawerful of old envelopes with recipes written on the back, clippings from magazines and newspapers, and other miscellaneous slips of paper. You can offer to convert this mess to a well-organized recipe file, for a fee. You make the file by taking all the recipes that are written on pieces of paper and printing or typing them on 4-by-6 cards. You can tape recipes clipped from magazines onto the cards. Then arrange the file by food categories: file all of the sauces together, the meat dishes, casseroles, salads, desserts, and so on. Look at the contents page in cookbooks if you need help in deciding on categories. Put the cards in a small metal filing box, and your customer is suddenly a well-organized chef. The job is probably worth $2 to $2.50 an hour.

Continental Breakfast

This job is a bit complicated, but if you live in or near an apartment building where most of the occupants are singles, it could be a money-maker. What you will do is serve a breakfast consisting of doughnuts and Danish rolls, orange juice, and coffee to your customers. There are two ways this breakfast can be served. You can deliver to your customers individually, door to door, or you can set up a buffet in the recreation room or some convenient central place, such as the pool area. To get customers for this service, put a handbill on every door or mailbox in the building telling that you are planning to offer this service and see what kind of response you get. If a lot of people are interested, you're in business. If they're not, do something else. What you charge will depend on what you provide and how much it costs you.

Telephone Services

There are people in this world who have trouble waking up in the morning. If you don't mind getting up in the morning yourself, you might offer a wake-up service. If you can find ten hard-to-wake-up people who think your call would help them get going in the morning and you charge them as little as 20¢ a day, that would amount to $1 a week per customer, or $10 a week. You could probably do it in fifteen minutes each morning. That's not a bad way to start your own day, is it? There are also people who habitually forget special dates like birthdays and anniversaries and who might pay to be reminded ahead of time by phone. Set out posters and distribute handbills to see whether you can get enough customers to make the job worthwhile.

Jobs in the City

If you live in the city and didn't find a job in this chapter that appeals to you, don't give up. almost a hundred other jobs are described in the other chapters in this section. You're sure to find at least one that fits your situation and personality.

The Right Attitude Is Good Business

Can you remember the last time you bought something at a store and the sales clerk acted as if she thought she was doing *you* a favor? Or she acted as if she thought you weren't worth the time it took to wait on you? Or she was in a bad mood, and it showed?

Next time, did you go to a different store?

Your customers are no different! People will always choose a kid (or an adult) who is cheerful over one who is grumpy. Everyone prefers to hire a kid who says "What else can I do to help?" instead of the one who just stands around waiting to be told. Most important, if you want your customers to keep asking you back, *act as if you are interested in the job!* If you give the impression that you are bored, or not interested, most people will find someone else—fast!

The best guarantee that you will *never* lose a customer (and probably the best way to attract new ones) is to do something extra, something you haven't been asked to do, something you're not being paid for. It might be cleaning up the dishes on a babysitting job or sweeping out the garage after you've stacked someone's firewood. It could be running an errand for a customer who is too busy or can't get out to do it himself. The few minutes you spend at something like this will be well worth it later on!

CHAPTER 26

SUMMER CAN BE PROFITABLE

Summer, for a few kids, is all planned in advance. They spend the time at summer camp, on visits to relatives, or on family vacations—and suddenly it's September and time to go back to school. Other kids seem to feel that from June to September there's absolutely nothing to do. For most kids, however, part of the summer is busy and part of it is a bore.

Summer does not have to be a bore. There's plenty to do if you'll just give it a little thought. One thing about summer is that it provides plenty of time to make money.

Summer is only three months long. If you wait until school is out before you start looking around for something to do, many jobs will already be filled. The job of counselor at a summer camp is a super way to make money. You have to work, but in many camps it's like a paid vacation. Because jobs like this are so popular, they are hard to get. You might have to apply in October or even earlier for a job during the following summer. Jobs at amusement parks, in resort areas, at the beach, in the mountains, or in other recreational areas are jobs you must apply for well in advance. The same thing applies to jobs in our national parks, as a lifeguard or a playground supervisor.

The point is, plan ahead for your summer and think about what you will do. If you plan to do gardening, don't wait until June to line up your customers. Start in March before anyone else asks them. House- or apartment-sitting is a very good way to make money during the summer, but most people will give the job to the first person who offers to do it. That means you should line up your summer house-sitting jobs in the spring.

Although this chapter describes some jobs that might be especially good for you to do in the summer, many of them can be done all year round.

Berry Picking

Picking berries, of course, can only be done in the summer, and you have to live near an area where blackberries, raspberries, blueberries, or other varieties grow wild. With a few friends you can make a day of it and have a picnic lunch for a break. Try not to eat all the best ones you pick, so you'll have some left to sell door to door. Charge what the local stores are charging or a little bit less. You should have no trouble selling all you can gather.

Bicycle Repairs

Some people know how to fix mechanical things like bicycles, but a lot of people do not. If you are able to repair anything that goes wrong with your own bike, you might assume everyone else can do it too. You're wrong! Many kids your own age cannot fix their own bikes. Many fathers are not much help either, and a lot of young children who own bikes are not old enough to attempt their own repairs. As a result, a lot of broken bicycles are sitting around on patios or in storage rooms and garages waiting for someone to take them to the bicycle shop.

You can become a traveling bicycle repair shop, and if you do the work for a reasonable price, you could end up with a very profitable business. A big plus for your business is the fact that you save people the trouble of getting the bike to the shop and back again. Don't advertise yourself for this job unless you really know what it takes to make a bike run properly. Find out what the local shops charge for repairs and, if you want to keep busy, charge a little less. If you know what you're doing and work fast, you can probably make $4 or $5 an hour, or even more, while charging less than a regular repair shop would charge. It's really a question of having enough customers. Use all of the tricks you find in chapter 22.

Car Polishing and Waxing

Unless you are already experienced at this job, you need to talk to an expert. Find a place near you that does polishing and waxing and talk to one of the people who actually does the work. Tell him you would like to know how to do the job right—which wax or polish to use and how much you should charge. Chances are he'll be happy to tell you what you need to know. Now go practice on your family car. You might even consider offering a half-price job to a couple of your neighbors for some more practice.

Charges are different in different parts of the country, so check local prices. A small car might be worth $7.50, a large one $15 for one coat. Ask your expert how to vary your charges depending on the condition of the paint. For example, if the paint is in top condition, you can simply wash and wax the car. But if the paint surface is getting a little dull or has road tar on it that won't wash off, your expert might tell you to use a polish on the car before you wax it. Finally, a badly oxidized paint job, one where the paint no longer has any shine, may require buffing. Any of these special steps means you should charge more for the job. This can be a very profitable business. If you do three cars a week at an average price of $10, that's $120 per month. If you need to earn more, find more customers.

Cars—Engine Cleaning

Engines need cleaning, too, and people who like to keep their cars looking nice would rather not have a dirty and greasy engine under the hood. You can buy a can of degreaser at your local auto supply store for around $2. The job itself is quite simple, once you have seen it done. You spray the degreaser on the engine and everywhere else inside the engine compartment that is greasy. Let it sit for a few minutes and then wash it thoroughly with water. If you have a driver's license and there is a do-it-yourself auto wash near your home, that's the best place to do this kind of job. One caution: when you wash off the engine, you must be very careful to have the carburetor and distributor covered with plastic so they do not get wet. The distributor, especially, must stay absolutely dry or the car will not start when you're through. Charge $7 to $10 for the job—more if the engine is especially dirty and it takes more than one can of degreaser.

Name Signs for Homes or Cabins

Some people like to have their names on signs in front of their homes. If you enjoy woodworking, you can make signs like this by woodburning or carving the names. If you're good at metalwork, you can make the signs of wrought iron. You will probably need a small shop in your garage to do this work.

Decorative Arrangements

You can put together unusual and attractive arrangements of various types of dried plants for people to use in decorating their homes. Cattails and wheat are often used for these arrangements, but in most areas of the country there are a variety of plants,

TIPS

Take Your Business to the Customers

There is one auto mechanic who runs a very successful and unique kind of repair business. Each morning he sets up shop in the parking lot of a large Lockheed plant and fixes the cars of employees. He is always booked up well in advance because his customers can park their cars in the morning and the work is all done by quitting time at 5 P.M. That's much more convenient for his customers than having to figure out how to get their cars to a shop.

You should look for opportunities to do the same thing, even though most of your job possibilities will be at your customers' homes. For example, picking up and delivering laundry or a car to be washed or bikes that need repair is a real convenience to your customers. But you can also consider doing any of these things, and many more, right at your customers' homes. Take what you need with you to fix the bike or wash the car, and see how many people might like to have you do their laundry in their own washer and dryer then put it all away when it's done.

Make things as *easy* for your customers as possible. They'll pay for it.

some of them weeds, that you might never notice growing in a field but that are very attractive when dried and arranged in a vase. Look at the prices of similar arrangements in gift shops to help you decide how much to charge.

Desk Blotters

Making and selling desk blotters is actually a business of selling advertising to local stores and businesses. The ads you sell will be printed on a standard 20-by-24-inch desk blotter, and the blotters will be distributed to people for their use, free of charge. The ideal place to do this is where a lot of people are living in a fairly small area. It could be a small town or an area around a college, university, or military station.

Who will buy your ads and why will they buy them? If the local Chinese restaurant specializes in food-to-go and you pass out 500 to 1,000 blotters for people to put on top of their desks, the restaurant has its phone number in front of all those people for a whole year. In a small town every business would be a potential advertiser. Near a college or military station, some of the businesses that might be interested in buying one of your ads are: tuxedo rentals, tutors, restaurants, clothing stores, bakeries, laundries, plumbers, auto supplies, auto dealers, and television and stereo stores.

The first step in this business is to get a quote from a local printer about the costs of printing and figure out how much to charge. Make sure the printer can help you set up the ads properly. If you can easily give away a thousand blotters, you can charge more for the ads than if you're only giving away 500, because twice as many people will see the ad. The printer can probably help you decide on how much to charge per ad or will refer you to someone who can tell you. A 20-x-24-inch blotter has 480 square inches. If you reserve 80 inches for a date calendar and a calendar of local events, you have 400 square inches to sell. If you sell these at $3 per square inch, your total advertising receipts will be $1,200. If blotters and printing cost you $200, that leaves a profit of $1,000. (Your costs will vary and you should get quotes from more than one printer, if possible.) Your minimum ad should probably be 2 by 2 inches, for which you will charge $12 to $16. If the size of the average ad you sell is 2 by 4 inches, the charge will be $24 to $32 per ad and you will need to sell fifty ads.

You obviously have to start well in advance. It takes time to sell the advertising. Don't commit yourself to print the blotters untii you've sold enough advertising to make sure it will be profitable to you.

Door-to-Door Sales

There are two secrets to success at this job. The first is having something to sell that you believe in, that you think is a good product; the product should be available at the right price and should be something people are willing to buy. The second secret is your own personal sales ability. You have to be enthusiastic and cheerful and willing to knock on a lot of doors. With the right combination of these things, door-to-door selling can be very profitable for you.

Several different items can be sold door to door. For cars, you can sell highway flares, portable fire extinguishers, scrapers to remove snow and ice from windshields. Personal items include greeting cards, Christmas cards, gummed labels imprinted with the customer's name and address, doormats, or other housewares. Selling magazine subscriptions is another way to make money, and older kids can sell Fuller brushes and cosmetics. Finally, don't forget the other items mentioned throughout the chapters, items that you can make and sell yourself, such as leather goods, placemats, or jewelry.

Cleaning Driveways

The oil that drips from cars can turn an otherwise attractive driveway into a mess. Garage floors get dirty as well. With some bristle scrub brushes, cleaning compound, and a lot of rags or paper towels, you can offer a very welcome service to people who might never get around to doing it themselves. Charge by the hour or the job, depending on how big the mess is that you have to clean up.

Showing Films

Interested in movies? Here's another way to make some money and have fun during the summer. If you own, or know someone who owns, a 16-mm projector and have a library in your neighborhood that lets you check out films overnight with no charge, you can make a lot of money at this. However, even if you have to rent a projector for $12 to $15 a day, you can still make money showing films to the youngsters in your neighborhood. Charge 75¢ to $1.50 per showing, depending on your costs. You might provide free popcorn and cokes. On the other hand, you might charge 15¢ or 25¢ for popcorn or soft drinks. If you get a good audience for the first one or two films you show, you might decide to set up a regular schedule and show a film at the same time each week. As more kids hear about it, your audience could grow until, by the end of summer, you may be running with a full house. Make sure you plan in advance and do a lot of promotion in your immediate neighborhood before showing your first film. But don't stop there; if you decide to show films all summer, advertise every week. The only other thing you need is a good place to show the films. It's obviously best if you can locate a place that will not charge you any rental. That might be in your local community center, the recreation room of your own apartment building, or the basement of your own home or that of a friend.

Magic and Puppet Shows

If you can learn to do enough magic tricks to put on a show, the next thing to do is find an audience. Why not get paid for doing your tricks? It's possible to put on a local magic or puppet show and charge kids 25¢ or 50¢ to come and watch. A more reliable way to make money, and more of it, is to offer your services for entertainment at events like birthday parties. As you become more and more experienced, you can get jobs at adult events as well as at children's parties. What you charge will depend on your experience and the kinds of jobs that are available. But charging as little as $10 for a half-hour show at a birthday party is pretty good pay for getting some real experience and doing something you enjoy.

Repairing and Painting Fences

Some jobs are easier to find than others. Fences that need repair or painting are a good example of jobs that are easy to find. You can see them from the street, at least the fences in the front. All fences need periodic repairs, and painted fences need to be repainted more often than most things. You can locate possible customers just by riding around the neighborhood on your bike. Knock on the door and offer to do whatever appears to be needed. If you charge by the hour for the repair work you do, the owner will supply all needed materials, including paint. If you're fast, you can make more money per hour by quoting what you will charge for the whole job in advance. Be sure to include paint and material costs in your bid.

Fireplace Service

The time to get ready for winter is during the summer, and you can make money getting people's fireplaces in shape for the coming winter season. What can you do for a fireplace? Let's start with the ashes. Most fireplaces have a trap door so that ashes can be dumped into the space below the fireplace. The ashes that collect can be removed through another door below the fireplace, either outside the house or under the house. Very few people ever think to empty these ashes until the space gets so full that no more will go through the trap door.

There are many other tasks to be done involving the fireplace. Inside the house, there are often smoke stains on the bricks around the fireplace and on the mantel above the fireplace. Brick hearths get dirty after a year of use. Your service, then, will consist of emptying all the ashes, scrubbing the bricks around the fireplace and on the hearth until they are clean, cleaning the fireplace tools and polishing the handles, cleaning and polishing the andirons, or cleaning the grate inside the fireplace. Fireplace screens need periodic repainting with black paint. Special black paint in aerosol cans can be purchased from stores that sell fireplace equipment. You can offer to do all these jobs at the same time, as a package. You might be able to earn good money at this job, especially if you live in one of those neighborhoods where almost every home has a fireplace. Going door to door in just a few blocks of homes might provide you with enough business to keep you busy for several weeks. You might end up charging $10 per job and could easily do five jobs each week in your spare time. That will give you $200 a month.

Selling Fruit

One of the problems with fruit trees you have growing in your own yard is that all the fruit usually gets ripe at the same time. Your mother may can some of what you cannot eat, but why not make money selling the rest of it door to door? When you sell fruit from your own trees, don't try to get the same price as the supermarket. Charge a little less. It gives people another reason to buy from you.

You can also keep your eyes open for neighbors who have a number of fruit trees. You might offer to pick the fruit for a certain amount per hour, or you might suggest that you pick the fruit, sell it door to door, and split the money with them. A fair split might be one-third of the money for your neighbor and two-thirds for you if you do both the picking and the selling yourself.

One additional idea that might make you some money is learning how to dry fruit. Certain fruits, such as apricots or figs, can be dried if you have enough room, but you'll need specialized instructions on how to do the drying.

Cleaning Garages

Summer is a good time for people to get rid of all the junk that they accumulated in the garage over the winter. Helping people clean out that junk is a good job for a couple of kids, since it's usually a lot of work and there are often some heavy things to be moved. Some people will want everything carried outside, the floor swept and scrubbed, the junk thrown away, and everything that's to be kept put back neatly. A couple of kids and a homeowner can spend most of a day just getting a garage in shape. Looking for dirty or messy garages can be like looking for fences that need repair, since garage doors are often open on the weekends and you can ride around on your bike and see who needs your help. Otherwise, going door to door is your best bet. Once the garage is clean, you might suggest a garage sale to get rid of the junk.

Garage Sales

Almost everyone has drawers, cupboards, and closets full of things they would just as soon get rid of, but organizing and running a garage sale takes time and effort. You can offer to do it for people, advertising with posters or handbills. All your customers have to do is decide what they want to get rid of and how much they think they can get for each item. After you have some experience with several garage sales, you can even help them decide on the price for each thing to be sold. You set up the tables and organize the things to be sold, put out signs to tell people about the sale, and run the sale. Your pay is 20 to 25 percent of all the money taken in. This is a good job to do with a friend. It can be fun. You can spend a Saturday morning or afternoon making some money and getting some sales experience at the same time.

Golf Balls

There are a few places on most golf courses where many golfers hit balls over the fence and lose them. A lot of kids make extra money finding the balls and selling them. There are two places golf balls can be sold, as long as they are still in good condition. The first is to golfers who are playing on the course. The second is to the pro shop. You'll probably get more money from the golfers themselves. In either case, you will sell the balls for less than they cost in the pro shop, depending on the condition of each ball. If they are in top condition, three for $1 or 50¢ each is about right. For others you'll get $1 for four or five balls.

House Sitting

House sitting is one of the best jobs you'll ever find for the summer. It doesn't take much time, so you are free to do other things during vacation. It's help that people need, and if you start early enough to line up a number of customers, you can make quite a bit of money in one summer. There are a number of reasons people need someone to house sit while they are away on vacation. Most important is to make the house look lived-in in order to discourage burglars. Yards and houseplants need watering. If there are pets, they need to be fed. Here are the things you should offer to do for people to make the house look lived-in while they are gone.

1. Pick up newspapers, mail, packages, and handbills and put them inside the house.

2. Open and close drapes or window shades, and change them from one day to the next.

3. Turn the lights on in the evening and have a different light on each night, a hall light one night, a bathroom light the next, and so on. Use a light timer to turn lights on and off automatically if one is available. If you supply light timers yourself, it's another reason for people to hire you instead of some other kid.

Most people will have other things they want you to do, such as watering house plants on a regular schedule, watering the yard, and maybe mowing the lawn. Unless the homeowners do it themselves, you should tell each of the immediate neighbors how long the people will be gone, that you are looking after the place, and that they should report anything suspicious to the police.

How much will you charge for all this? For the basic job of taking in the mail and papers, changing drapes and lights, and watering the house plants once a week, charge $1 to $1.50 a day. If there are pets to feed, charge an extra 25¢ a day. If there is yard care, charge what you would normally charge for doing that kind of work. What you can earn for a typical house-sitting job for people on a two-week vacation comes to something like this: Basic charge of $1.25 per day plus an extra 25¢ a day for feeding either a dog or a cat—$1.50 per day times fourteen days = $21; mowing a lawn twice at $3 per week = $6; watering the yard twice a week for $1.50 each time is another $6. Total for the job—$33. If you have as few as ten customers during the summer, you'll make $330. Start advertising or go house to house early, when people are planning their vacations. If you're the first one there, you'll probably get the work.

Lemonade

It may sound a little corny, but it doesn't have to be a lemonade stand in your driveway; it doesn't even have to be lemonade. One youngster whose yard backed up to the edge of a busy golf course made a great deal of money one summer selling lemonade over the fence to thirsty golfers. Two young ladies had a very nice business once every week setting up a refreshment stand at the Little League park near their home. With the permission of the job superintendent, you might make a lot of money offering lemonade and soft drinks to workers on a construction site. With jobs like this, you have to look for special opportunities.

Painting

Painting houses or barns might be a little ambitious for you, but garages, tool sheds, porches, shutters, storm windows, fences, and patio furniture all need repainting from time to time. These are jobs kids can do if they have any painting experience at all. Before you start, find yourself an expert to make sure you know what you're doing, and do yourself a favor by buying good-quality rollers, brushes, and paint—they make the job a lot easier. Charge by the hour until you have some experience. Once you've learned how to estimate the time each job will take, charge by the job.

Patio Furniture

Most patio furniture needs to be cleaned up for summer use, and it should be done in the early summer, maybe as soon as the weather warms up before school is out. You can scrub and clean patio umbrellas and canvas or plastic chairs and lounges, and you can polish chrome or aluminum. Wooden patio furniture often needs refinishing. Charge by the hour, and while you're at it, offer to clean up barbeques and do anything else that might be required to get the patio or yard in shape for summer use.

Record or Book Swap

The simplest way to handle this business is to start with some cash and offer to buy paperback books or records that your friends no longer want, then resell them at a higher price. You might pay 10¢ a book and sell them for 20¢ each, pay 50¢ for albums and sell them for 75¢ or $1 each. If you have a garage or other suitable place available to you, another way of arranging the swap would be for your friends to bring their records and books and leave them for sale to other kids. Give them 75 percent of the money that you receive from the sales and you keep the other 25 percent. Be sure to keep good records so everyone gets what is coming to him or her.

Collect Seashells for Sale

If you live or take your vacation near the ocean, see if you can put together a nice collection of seashells. The right kinds of shells are very popular for aquariums, terrariums, or as decorative items for display on shelves. You might decide to use some of the small shells in making your own jewelry. Collecting seashells is another example of taking advantage of what is available to you, of keeping your eyes open for ways to make money that other people overlook.

Teaching Swimming

To teach swimming, you'll need to pass the Red Cross course for instructors and be certified. But once you've qualified, it's a great way to make money for the summer doing something you enjoy. Regular summer jobs are available from the YMCA or recreation departments, but you can also give private lessons to small groups of children at a public or private pool. You'll have to start lining up pupils well in advance if you expect to make money in the summer.

Teaching Tennis

In order to make money teaching tennis, it's obvious that you must be a good tennis player. But that's not enough. You must also be able to explain the game to people who do not understand it as well as you. If you qualify, this is a job you can do while you're in high school, in college, and later on as an adult, and you can make good money at it.

Tool Sharpening

Many tools used by homeowners never get sharpened, but even tools like shovels and hoes work much better if they are sharpened from time to time. Hedge clippers, pruning shears, and lawn mowers also need attention. With special instruction, you can learn how to sharpen saws. While you're at it, offer to sharpen the scissors and even the kitchen knives. You can do this all year round, but early summer or even in the spring before the gardening season really gets started is probably the best time.

Find yourself an expert at a hardware store or garden shop to answer any questions and to give you ideas on how much to charge.

Traveling Companion

Many families who take young children with them on vacation like to take an older youngster along to help out with the kids. It's normally a summer job but can also be available during Christmas and spring vacations. For you it's often a chance to take an expense-paid vacation in exchange for babysitting. If you have additional responsibilities, which might include doing housework, cooking, or washing dishes, these should be discussed and clearly understood in advance. If you're going to be busy working most of the time, you should get paid $25 to $50 a week, depending on your duties. You might advertise for this kind of work, but the best possibilities are probably people you and your parents already know, especially families for whom you have done some babysitting in the past. Start looking around in the spring when people are planning their vacations. Don't wait until summer.

Summer Jobs, Winter Jobs

Some of the jobs in this chapter are *really* summer jobs, and it's difficult or impossible to do them at any other time of year. Many of the jobs, however, *can* be done at other times. On the other hand, if you are interested only in summer jobs, don't ignore the other chapters. They are filled with ideas for jobs that can be done in the summertime.

Start early! Many of the best summer jobs will not be available if you wait until June to look for them. For some jobs, you have to start planning in the spring, or even earlier.

TIPS

Asking for Help

You'll probably never become an expert at any job unless you learn how to ask for help. What better person to ask than someone who has already become an expert at what you're interested in doing. Experts can tell you things you will never find in a book, and probably things your parents don't know either. Does your mother clean her kitchen walls with a cleanser she bought at the supermarket? If so, she's using the wrong thing. She could use tri-sodium phosphate (TSP), which can be purchased at a hardware store and probably do a much better job in half the time or less. What's the best wax for floors? How do you clean oil off concrete?

A store that sells janitorial supplies can give you the answers to these and many other questions. Why should they bother? Because you're probably going to be one of their customers and buy your supplies from them.

In addition, you will find that most adults are both flattered and pleased when a youngster shows some interest in how they make their living. Most people are very happy to help a kid get a start doing something on his own. Don't forget that, once upon a time, all adults were kids themselves, so don't be afraid to ask them for help. Ask your nurseryman for advice on plants and gardening, the hardware store for tips on how to sharpen knives and tools. A little advice can start you off earning a lot more money with a lot less frustration.

CHAPTER 27

HOLIDAY PROFITS

The holiday season at year-end offers some special money-making opportunities for kids. If you're old enough and apply early, many stores hire extra salespeople in December and the post office hires temporary workers to help with the Christmas mail. But there are many other ways you can make money at this time of year, and if you need money for Christmas, this chapter will give you many ideas you can use.

Here's something to keep in mind, whether you're thinking of making money at Christmas or in the summer, in the city or in the country. What *you* need to earn is not important to other people. The important thing to you is what *other* people need. The way you make money is by giving other people something they want. All the job ideas in these chapters are here for just one reason—in hopes that you will find one or more ways to provide other people with a product or service that they want and will pay for. All successful businesses do this. The most successful companies are the ones that do it best. So once you figure out how much you need to make, forget yourself and start thinking about your customers, or the people you hope will become your customers. Give them what *they* want, and you'll get what *you* want.

Here are some ways you might provide people with what they want around the holdiays.

Selling Candles

Candles are very popular sellers around the holidays. You can contact a company that makes candles, buy the candles from that company at wholesale prices, and sell them at the retail price door to door, or you can make your own candles. Many people enjoy candle making as an interesting hobby. If you make your own candles, remember you can also give them as gifts.

Addressing Christmas Cards

Finding time to address Christmas cards is a big problem for many people. If you have attractive handwriting, this job can be started as early as November and you can do it at your own convenience in your own home. All you need from your customers is their list of names and addresses and the envelopes and stamps. If you charge 4¢ or 5¢ for each envelope you stamp and address, that means a neighbor with a Christmas card list of 200 names can get the whole thing ready to mail by spending only $8 to $10. If you are able to do at least 100 an hour, you'll be making $4 or $5 an hour. It's a good deal for both of you. Many people have their names printed on the cards they buy, but if not, make sure your customer signs the cards in advance.

Friends and neighbors will be your usual customers, but local businesses also send Christmas cards. Check with owners and managers around October to see if they do plan to send cards. If your customer's Christmas card list is a mess—names and addresses written on scraps of paper and the backs of envelopes—charge more than the usual 4¢ or 5¢, because it will take you quite a bit longer. While you're at it, ask if she would like to have you reorganize the list, perhaps prepare a card file with all the names and addresses typed on 3-by-5 cards. You might create a new job for yourself here.

Selling Christmas Cards

Even selling Christmas cards, you have to get started well ahead of time—probably around September. Selling Christmas cards is a very good way to make money if you will just do three things. First, start early. Second, talk to a lot of people. Third, make sure the cards you decide to sell are of good quality and attractive. There are many mail-order companies that have Christmas cards available for you to sell. In many, perhaps most, cases your customers will select the card they want from a sample book that the card company sends to you. You will order your customers' names printed on the cards they select, and the company will send the cards to you for delivery to them. Selecting a company that offers attractive cards at a reasonable price is the most important thing for you to do. There's a lot of junk available, and it will be very discouraging for you if you exert a lot of effort trying to sell cards that no one will buy.

Christmas Tree Service

Senior citizens and others who have difficulty getting out or people who are very busy might hire you to select and purchase a Christmas tree, deliver it, and set it up for them. Some, especially the elderly, may want you to decorate the tree for them as well. Your final step could be removing and putting away the decorations and disposing of the tree. You'll probably have to charge by the hour, since the time you spend will depend on how far you have to go to get the tree, how large it is, and how your customers want to have their tree decorated.

Decorating Homes for Christmas

You could offer to put Christmas decorations in and on apartments as well as homes. Homeowners often like to have elaborate decorations at Christmas time, including lights on trees and the outside of the house, a wreath on the front door, and other special items. You'll have to charge by the hour since each job will be different.

You might consider making Christmas decorations for sale. Hand-made ornaments made from flour and salt and hand painted can be very attractive. Many people like to put cranberry and popcorn chains on a tree but don't make them themselves because it takes too much time. Any of these things are additional ways you can make money around Christmas.

Block Decorations

In many areas of the country all the residents on one street, or even those of a small neighborhood, put up the same type of outdoor Christmas decorations. If people in your neighborhood do this every year, there are always a number of them who would be happy to have someone else do the job for them. This can give you dozens of possible customers in a very small area. What you charge will depend on how complicated the job is; you should be able to do it quite rapidly, however, since every job will be exactly the same. Another money-making possibility is to sell the idea on your own street. If you can come up with an idea that is fairly simple, easy to put up, and not too expensive, you might try convincing everyone on your block to let you put up identical decorations. You might be able to create your own job. A charge of $10 or $15 per house can amount to quite a bit of money for you and a couple of friends if there are thirty houses on your street.

Decorations for Businesses

Many small businesses decorate their shops or stores for the holidays, and many others would probably like to do so if they could find the time. You might offer to provide and decorate a Christmas tree of whatever size they want, get them a Christmas wreath and some candles, and decorate or paint the front windows. Part of your arrangement will be that you'll also remove all the decorations when the holidays are over. Don't wait until December to offer this service—offer it early.

Children's Party Helper

Helping organize and conduct children's parties is really a year-round job, but it is listed in this chapter because there are so many parties around the holidays. Here are some of the things you can do for a busy parent: help plan the overall party; purchase refreshments and supplies; decorate; organize games or arrange for entertainment; help serve; clean up. If you're good with a camera, you might even take pictures. What you charge will depend on how many of these things you do and how large the party is. During the year, birthday parties will probably provide most of your business. Use posters and leaflets to let everyone in your area know you are available for this service.

Gift Wrapping and Mailing

Wrapping gifts can be very time consuming, and many people would be happy to have some help. Some people prefer to select their own wrapping paper, but you should have it available in case they do not have any. It would be a good idea for you to collect boxes during the year for customers who have none. Find out what the stores in your area charge for gift wrapping. You can make a lot of money if you charge about half that, as long as you do a really professional job. The advantage to your customers is that they can get gifts wrapped for less money without standing in line at the store and without spending a great deal of precious holiday time doing it themselves.

Mailing packages is another service you can provide. Many people find it extremely difficult to get to the post office to do this for themselves. You must know how to properly wrap and address packages and must have transportation available unless the post office is very close. A charge of 50¢ to $1.50 per package is quite reasonable for this service, but you can make quite a bit of money if you take ten or fifteen packages to the post office each trip. Check with your local post office in advance to find out about special wrapping requirements.

Mistletoe Sales

Many people like to have mistletoe at Christmas, and you can charge 25¢ to 50¢ for a small plastic bag of it. You can buy it for resale, but it's obviously much more profitable if you get your own mistletoe free. It grows on trees in most areas, so go out and find your own. Do it early, around the first of December. Be the first kid in your neighborhood to offer it for sale. That way you'll get most of the customers. You can also sell your mistletoe in shopping centers or in front of the local grocery store. All you need is a card table, a chair, and a sign.

Christmas Wreaths

Another job for an "early-bird" is selling Christmas wreaths, since most people like to have a wreath on the front door, whether they live in an apartment or a house. You can buy wreaths for resale or make your own. Take your orders around Thanksgiving time by taking a sample wreath around from door to door. Don't forget local businesses. They are potential customers as well. You'll make more money and have more fun if you make your own. You can buy undecorated evergreen wreaths, and the ribbons, berries, pinecones, and wires to attach them, from nurseries or from shops that specialize in selling decorations. If you can collect your own pinecones and other decorations, that's even better. A wreath that costs you $2 to make should sell for between $5 and $7.50; one you spend $5 on should sell for $12 to $15. Don't forget to start early and take orders in advance.

Pinecones for Decorations or Burning

If you live near the mountains or a forested area where there are large numbers of pinecones, you can collect them and sell them for a number of uses. People will buy them for decorations at Christmas time. They will also buy chemically treated pinecones to burn in the fire. Soak pinecones in chemically treated water, let them dry, and they will burn in a variety of beautiful colors. Table salt burns yellow; borax makes a bright green flame; copper sulphate burns blue; calcium chloride, orange; strontium nitrate, red; and lithium chloride, purple. Check the stores to see how much they charge for fireplace pinecones, then charge a little less.

Silver Polishing

Around the holidays many people entertain and they want their silver to be shiny and beautiful. You can offer a silver-polishing service. Doing this job usually involves more than just polishing knives, forks, and spoons. Other items to be polished include salt and pepper shakers, sugar and cream servers, coffee services, serving trays, serving dishes, candlesticks, and so on. Charge by the hour, depending on your age and experience. Start before Thanksgiving to let people know you are available and interested in doing this job. It's possible that no one in your immediate neighborhood has silver that needs polishing. In this case, try to locate an area where the residents do a lot of entertaining.

Party Set-Up

What do people need when they are planning a party? It depends on the size of the party and the type of party it will be, but there are many possible ways for you to earn money helping people get ready. Here are a few of them: clean the house; clean the yard; put up any decorations the hosts require; set up tables and chairs; help prepare hors d'oeuvres; assist in cooking; and run errands—pick up supplies such as ice, candles, paper plates, rented equipment. From this list you can see that preparations for a large party could keep you busy for several afternoons plus a Saturday. If you are dependable and easy to work with, this is the kind of job that can get you referrals; that is, people who are pleased with your work will tell their friends about you. You should probably get $2 to $3 an hour.

Parties — Serving

Not everyone will need assistance in getting ready for a party, but some people may need help during the party itself. This help could include setting tables, helping in the kitchen, serving guests, picking up dishes, and just being available to do whatever needs to be done. You should probably get $2 to $3 an hour, depending on your age and the responsibilities you are given.

Party Clean-Up

There are probably a lot of people who would give more parties if they didn't have to clean up afterwards. Think of how welcome you might be if you were willing to come to someone's house early on the morning following a party and do any or all of the following jobs: wash the dishes and glasses; empty and wash the ashtrays; sweep or mop the kitchen floor; vacuum the rooms that were used and generally straighten the place up. The hosts might even want you to feed their young children breakfast so they can sleep in.

Each of the three party jobs described can be a job all by itself, but it should be obvious to you that you'll make more money if you do all three — help in getting ready for the party, assist during the party, and clean up afterwards. A good-sized party could involve ten or fifteen hours on your part, and at $2.50 an hour that would amount to $25 to $37.50.

Special Parties

If you and one or two friends have good imaginations and are good at decorating, can do some entertaining, and are willing to work hard, why not set up your own party business? There are many mothers (and some fathers too) who would be happy to give you the entire responsibility for putting on a party for their kids. Think of the fun you could have coming up with new and scary ideas for Halloween parties; the entertainment could be taking the kids out to "trick or treat." For a Christmas party, you might do a skit with one of you playing Santa Claus. There are interesting possibilities the year round, including Easter and the Fourth of July.

Kids' parties are not the only possibility, however. You could do the planning, decorating, and clean-up for a New Year party. Many people, especially single people, hesitate to give such parties because there is so much work involved. You could be the answer.

Holiday Profits

The best way for you to earn money for Christmas or anything else might not be mentioned here. The best job idea is often the one no one has thought of yet. People have special needs around the holidays, and those needs give you a chance to earn some extra money. As always, doing the best job you can is important. You might do a job like putting up Christmas decorations, which only comes along once a year, but if you're cheerful and show that you're interested in doing a good job, you'll probably have a chance to do other jobs for the same person in the future. It might be walking a dog, mowing a lawn, or painting a fence. If you're interested in making additional money, be sure to let people know. Just remember that everyone you do a job for can be a customer in the future.

CHAPTER 28

THE MORE, THE BETTER

Packaging—what is it? It is often smart business to take several different but related things and put them together in a way that encourages people to buy. When all the pieces are combined, it is called a "package."

Packaging is very common in the travel business. An example would be round-trip airfare plus six days and five nights in Hawaii, including two meals a day plus golf or tennis, all for a certain amount per person. That's a travel or vacation package. Retail stores offer complete stereo systems at special prices when you buy a certain package of equipment. Automobile dealers offer special packages of optional equipment on new cars.

So packages are an everyday part of our lives, and people are used to buying them. Let's see how you can use this idea to make money.

Let's assume that, after going through all the job ideas in these chapters, you decided that cleaning fireplaces and getting them ready for winter was the thing that would work best in your neighborhood. You also decided to use several of the advertising ideas from Chapter 22, and you made several posters and put them up around the neighborhood. You also made up leaflets showing exactly what you would do and your price. Then you went all around your neighborhood, knocked on the door of every home that had a fireplace, and left one of your leaflets whenever someone was not home. You spent four or five hours looking for customers, got five jobs at $10 per job, finished the jobs, and made yourself $50. Since you have done all the nearby fireplace jobs, you now need a new idea to make money in your neighborhood. So you decide on cleaning out rain gutters.

Let's stop here and look at what's happening. If you go through the same steps with the rain-gutter job that you did with the fireplaces, you'll make up new posters, put together a new leaflet, and then go door to door to all of the same houses you covered before. You're spending too much time looking for jobs. If you had decided to look for both jobs before you started, you could have "packaged" the two ideas, included them both on your posters and leaflets, and made only one trip around the neighborhood instead of two. Not only that, you could have stopped at *every* house on the street instead of just the ones with fireplaces, since every house has rain gutters and they probably all need cleaning.

If going after two jobs is better than going after one, how about three? The answer is—the more the better, as long as all the jobs are related. With fireplace and rain-gutter cleaning, both jobs are related to getting a home ready for the coming winter. Suppose you told people you were interested in helping them "winterize" their homes? What else could you offer to do? In some areas of the country there are storm windows to be installed, patio furniture to be put away in a garage or a basement, firewood to be stacked, and furnace filters to be changed. Make up your own list, based on what people do to get ready for winter where you live. Then offer your "home winterizing" service and include all the jobs you come up with. List them all on your posters and leaflets and talk about them all when you go from house to house. If you're offering to do five jobs, your chances of getting a job at each house are probably five times as good as they would be if you offered to do just one. And many of the home-owners will probably want you to do more than one job for them.

The advantages of offering a package should be obvious. After all, the first rule for finding a job is to pick something people need and will pay you to do. If they're not interested in fireplaces but are interested in having you stack firewood, you've gotten what you went out for—a job. With any customer, getting them to give you that first job is always the toughest. Once they get to know you and find that you are a dependable worker, there's an excellent chance they will have you back to do other work that is needed.

There is another advantage to offering a package of jobs. Doing two or three chores at one home, working five hours in one place, is much better than working one hour in five different places because you don't waste any time going from job to job.

Here are some fairly obvious packages of jobs that you can put together profitably.

Automotive Care

How about putting together all the jobs that have something to do with cars? The following is an example of what you could put on posters and leaflets to advertise a job that might give you and a friend a permanent source of future income.

KEEP YOUR CAR LOOKING NEW!!

Enjoy driving a clean and sparkling car?
Let us keep it that way with
"Personalized Car Care"

Every week we will

- wash the exterior and tires
- clean and vacuum the interior and trunk
- check tires, batteries, oil

Every four months we will polish and wax your car.

Twice a year we will clean your engine.

All this for as little as $12 a month,
depending on the size of your car.
Pick-up and delivery can be arranged.

Call Frank Lemmon — 329-7771
or Judy Pierce — 866-2200

This is only a sample of the things you can do for someone's car. Exactly what you do depends on where you live. In some areas, waxing twice a year might be all that is needed. In other areas it might be appropriate to do the job every three months.

As you can see, putting together this kind of package involves more than just getting a job; actually, you're running a small business. Here's how you can figure out what to charge, based on prices where you live. For a medium-size car you might charge $2 for each wash job (includes exterior, interior, and checking tires and oil). For fifty-two weeks, that's $104 a year. Two engine cleanings a year at $10 each is $20. Three wax jobs at $15 each is $45. That all adds up to $169 a year; divided by twelve months, it is $14.08 a month. If these prices seem reasonable to both you and your customers, the monthly charge would be $14. Here's what it would all mean to you. If you had ten customers, that would give you a monthly income of $140, or $1,680 a year. In order to make more than this, you must either get more customers or charge more money for the job. But if you charge more, it might be hard to get customers at all. That's something you have to figure out yourself.

Annual Clean-up/Garage Sale

One of the benefits of moving to a new home is the opportunity to get rid of all the junk that's been collected. Until they do move, most people just keep on collecting the junk. You can help them get rid of it. Let's suppose you start with the garage. Everything comes out — the junk in one pile, things to sell in a second pile, things to put back in a third. Now scrub the garage. Then put back everything that goes back and set up the clean garage for a garage sale. Next, clean out the closets, drawers, and cupboards in the house. While they're empty, wash them and put in new shelf paper if needed. Next comes the attic and the basement. Clean them both, throwing out the junk, neatly storing the things to be saved, and putting the things to be sold in the garage. Now it's time for the garage sale. You can handle the advertising and run the sale for 20 to 25 percent of the total received. Finally, as long as you've done all this, see if your customer will also hire you to shampoo the carpets, wax the floors, and wash the windows. The result for your customer — a sparkling clean house with a lot of new storage space created. What do *you* have? A pocket full of money.

Gardening and Yard Care

You can convert lawn mowing into a year-round job. In the spring there are flowers to be planted and fertilizer to be put on the lawn. Getting ready for summer can also include cleaning the barbecue and patio furniture and maybe washing the windows. In the summer there's more fertilizing to be done for both lawns and plants, weeds to be pulled, and shrubs to be trimmed. In the fall, you'll rake leaves and, if appropriate, plant winter flowers. In some areas you might transfer flowers and plants to pots to be brought inside for the winter. You could offer to "winterize" the house, as described earlier in this chapter. In the winter, trees and shrubs need pruning and you might shovel snow. And if there's a swimming pool in the backyard, why not offer to maintain it as long as you're going to be around every week?

Parties

This package was suggested in Chapter 27 but is repeated here to emphasize the idea that you should offer everything to your potential customers at the same time. In the case of parties, the package includes helping to get it organized, addressing and mailing invitations, shopping, helping set up and decorate, assisting in serving and possibly cooking, and, finally, cleaning everything up when the party is over. The more things you are willing to do for people, the more reasons you give them to hire you.

Christmas Help

You can help people by getting their Christmas cards addressed early (you might even sell them the cards). Next is the Christmas tree: you can buy it, decorate it, and, when Christmas is over, remove the decorations and dispose of the tree. You can also offer to do additional decorating inside the house and outside, especially hanging lights on eaves and trees in the front yard. Wrapping and mailing gifts, polishing silver, and assisting with holiday entertaining complete the package. All of these tasks take time in what, for many people, is the busiest time of year. Many people will jump at the chance to have you take the responsibility for some, or even all, of these jobs and leave their time free for Christmas shopping and other activities.

If you think about it, you can see that almost *any* job probably has one or more other things that could be added to it. You should think up your own "packages." You can use the ideas mentioned here, but you should be able to come up with many different ones yourself. And don't forget, no matter what job you are doing for someone, always look for additional things you can add to that job.

Fishing Items

You may have decided to raise worms and dig clams for sale to fishermen. If you have room, why not raise frogs or minnows as well? In some areas, hand-tied flies and salmon eggs are also used for bait, and if you have them available you'll make more sales. If you have found a boat-launching area or a pier where there are a lot of fishermen and you are having success selling bait, why not have a supply of lines, weights, leaders, and hooks available as well? You might even offer to clean fish when the boats come in.

Services for Local Business

You might start off delivering leaflets for a small business in your area and end up addressing and stuffing envelopes for a special mailing. Once a business has become your customer for one service, it may be interested in hiring you for something else. You might provide a janitorial service; wash the windows once a week; provide part-time help for special events such as sales; decorate the windows at Christmas or Halloween. Take a look around. You might be surprised at how many small businesses there are near your home. Talk to them and see what they need.

Job Enlargement

Enlarging a job means making it bigger than it was when you started. It's a way to turn a single job into a whole package of jobs. It's something you should always be watching for the chance to do. To illustrate, let's assume you have lined up a number of house-sitting jobs for the summer. After you have made all the arrangements for taking care of things while the people are gone, ask if they would like to have any of the following things done during their absence: carpets shampooed; floors scrubbed and waxed; windows washed. Look through all these chapters and see what might be appropriate. It's obvious that you should not offer to do a job unless you know how. The idea of coming home to a shiny and newly cleaned apartment or home might appeal to many of your house-sitting customers. In the process, you've picked up a half dozen new jobs.

Some Final Thoughts

There are jobs described in the preceding pages that can be done by little kids or big kids, in the city or the country, in winter or summer. Most of them should work for you as they are described, but if you can think of ways to change or improve them in any way that makes them easier or more profitable for you, do it. Use your imagination. See if you can come up with new ways to do the jobs that are mentioned—or even better, come up with some fresh job ideas of your own.

Keep in mind that many jobs are more easily done by two or more people. It's more fun having one or two friends to work with who are also interested in making some money. Shampooing carpets is much easier if there are two people to move heavy furniture. Cleaning garages, basements, and attics can also require moving things too heavy for one person.

Fund-raising projects for clubs or charities can also be fun with a group. Washing cars is one of the favorites; collecting aluminum cans, bottles, and paper is another. You and your club can go through all of these job ideas and see which ones appeal to you for a project. Then go out and do it—make some money and have fun in the process.

Using your imagination is so important to your future success at making money that it needs to be mentioned again. No list of jobs anyone can give you is a substitute for using your own head. Just look around you. How many things can you do in a backyard? How many jobs are there to be done in someone's kitchen? How many ways can you make money doing special projects for the owner of the local shoe store? How many ways are there to make money that relate to caring for, entertaining, or teaching small children? What can you add to a car-care package? What are the things that people need at Christmas?

Every neighborhood is different. What works in Miami may not work in Buffalo because the weather is different and the people are different. Every kid is different too. What interests you will bore a lot of other kids. You might want to be outside cleaning swimming pools, mowing lawns, or washing cars. Other kids might prefer tutoring math or reading to the elderly. You have to decide what will work best for you where you are. Do that, and you'll find that making money can be an exciting adventure.

Good luck!

TAKE YOUR KID TO WORK

There was a time when kids had a much better understanding of the adult world of work. In many cases, kids themselves worked at adult jobs. At least they saw adults at work every day in the neighborhood. That has changed. At the same time that child labor laws were changing and people were moving to suburbs, business was becoming far more complex. There are now so many highly specialized jobs that the differences between one job and the next are often blurred and hard to explain, expecially to kids. Dad or Mom goes to "the office." In addition, most parents' jobs are located outside their immediate neighborhoods, so those jobs seem remote to youngsters.

The result? Many kids today have little or no idea what it is that their parents do to earn a living.

Have you ever asked one of your children's friends where his parents work and received "I don't know" for an answer? How accurately do you think your own kids would answer the same question if they were asked about you? Even if they could name the firm you work for, could they explain what you do there?

Why not take your kids to work? Give them a chance to learn something about you and the adult world of work at the same time. It's just one more way to involve them in the real world, which is often such a mystery to kids.

One central theme of this book is to encourage actual involvement by kids in a wide range of activities involving money. For example, we have urged parents to let kids start making their own spending decisions at an early age and to require them to begin assuming responsibilities early, too. We have pointed out the importance of including them in family financial discussions and have strongly recommended that kids work to earn some of their own money. Taking your kid to work is simply an extension of the same approach—teaching kids by getting them involved. When your kids spend a day, or part of a day, with you at your job, they will learn a lot more than they can in one day at school.

The approach this book takes toward solving family money problems also focuses on practice rather than on theory. The ideas and techniques presented have been used successfully by many parents in dealing with situations like those described. The same is true for the job ideas offered for kids to use; the jobs have all been done successfully in the past by other kids.

Our overall objective has been to present a set of working guidelines that parents can use in the many areas of raising kids that involve money. We kept in mind both the short- and long-term goals parents have in these areas.

In the short run, if families adopt systematic approaches to money subjects, then confusion and uncertainty can be eliminated. If kids can learn responsibility while they are young, many parental frustrations will disappear. The objective: elimination of hassles and conflicts over money, so that the family home is a happier place for everyone.

The long run objective is to produce young adults who are both prepared and eager to accept the responsibilities and challenges of adulthood.

It all starts with you, the parents. No one else can do the job of preparing your kids for their futures as well as you. The kid with the right outlook will have the best chance for success. To give kids that outlook, you must replace their youthful dependence with self-reliance. Instead of attempting to provide for all their future money needs, you should help them understand the challenge of making money on their own. Giving them a healthy and positive attitude toward money will prove to be a far greater and more permanent gift than giving them money itself.

JOB INDEX

GENERAL INDEX

278